Home Addition & Renovation

PROJECT COSTS

RSMeans

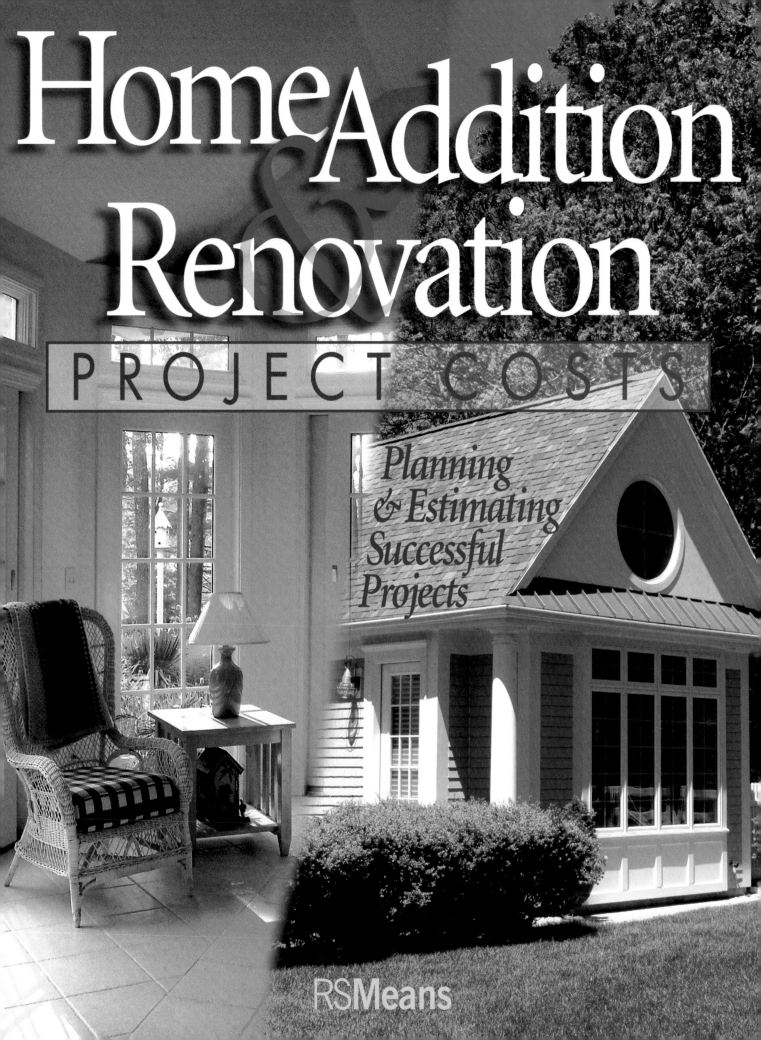

Home Addition & Renovation

PROJECT COSTS

Planning & Estimating Successful Projects

RSMeans

 Reed Construction Data.

Copyright © 2005
Reed Construction Data, Inc.
Construction Publishers & Consultants
63 Smiths Lane
Kingston, MA 02364-0800
781-422-5000
www.rsmeans.com
RS**Means** is a product line of Reed Construction Data.

Managing Editor: Mary Greene. Editors: Robert Mewis and Andrea Sillah.
Contributing Editor: Timothy Jumper. Editorial Assistant: Jessica Deady.
Production Manager: Michael Kokernak. Composition: Jonathan Forgit.
Proofreader: Wayne Anderson. Book and cover design: Norman R. Forgit.
Contributing Photographers: Norman R. Forgit, Jessica Deady, Jonathan Forgit, Andrea Sillah.
Illustrations: Roger Jadown.

Printed in the United States of America

10 9 8 7 6 5 4 3 2 1

Library of Congress Cataloging in Publication Data

ISBN 0-87629-812-9

Table of Contents

Acknowledgments

The editors would like to thank *Professional Remodeler Magazine* for allowing us to reprint two articles as case studies for this book. The builders were Basements and Beyond in Denver, Colorado, and Riggs Design & Construction in Kirkwood, Missouri.

Thanks also to Nick Brewer of Brewer Loft Conversions for permission to include a photo taken by Ray Kitching of Forest Graphics, www.forestgraphics.co.uk

We would like to acknowledge Jill and Dan Haley, Deirdre Larnis, Steven Davis, and all the other homeowners who generously allowed us to photograph their homes.

And finally, our thanks to Howard Chandler, Executive Officer of the Builders Association of Greater Boston, a chapter of the National Association of Home Builders (NAHB), for his review and insights on sections of this book.

Introduction

Room additions and interior renovations can be good solutions to homeowners' needs – and good business for remodeling contractors. These projects can range from small and simple, like a new front entry or interior door opening – to large and complex, such as a major addition with HVAC, electrical, and plumbing elements.

Sizeable remodeling projects require preparation on many fronts – from zoning requirements, to a thoughtful design that blends well with the existing house and meets the owner's needs, to the contractual agreement, to an accurate estimate that ensures a profit – and much more.

How This Book Will Help You

Part One – Planning & Estimating

This section gives you several tools to assess the job, win the owner's approval, and get the project started on the right footing. It begins with pointers on developing the plans and specific ideas for designing additions and interior remodeling. Topics include siting the addition, assembling design input from various sources, and using non-traditional materials – from time-savers like SIPs and prefabricated trusses, to synthetic low-maintenance materials, to green building products.

A major part of this section is "Estimating Project Costs" – step-by-step guidelines from construction cost experts. This information will help you conduct the all-important site visit and evaluate existing conditions – then produce an accurate, complete estimate.

You'll also find pointers for your contractual agreement with the owner, a chart listing typical steps in a remodeling project, and guidance for smooth relations with both your local building department and your homeowner clients.

Parts Two & Three – The Model Projects & Estimates

These are the main sections of the book and contain 35 popular remodeling projects, each with a detailed estimate. The "model" for each project is based on a typical floor plan and uses materials available at most home centers. Each estimate includes:

- All materials needed for the project, with unit and total costs
- Labor-hours to install each item (and demolish/remove items, as needed)
- Subcontractor costs for certain trades and services
- An allocation for overhead and profit
- Total contractor cost

The model projects also include "Alternates (Installed Costs)" – unit costs for different material installations that let you adjust the estimate to your project's particular features.

Use these estimates as checklists to make sure:

- You've included everything if you're planning a similar job
- Your own bid estimate is in the right range for typical contractor costs

You can also use the estimates for preliminary planning discussions with homeowners who are trying to get a "ballpark" idea of what their project would cost.

The project estimate costs can be adjusted to pricing conditions in your specific area using the **Location Factors** at the back of the book. These easy-to-apply factors are given for more than 900 individual areas in the U.S. and Canada, organized by state and defined by zip codes.

The projects in Part Two are all additions – from porches, greenhouses, and sunrooms to many different sizes and configurations of one- and two-story room additions. There are also garages, a carport, and a poolside cabana.

The projects in Part Three cover interior remodeling. They're all focused on what homeowners want more of – actual living space and/or an up-to-date, open feel in their living areas. Several projects are conversions of basements, attics, and porches. Others open up existing living space by taking out walls, creating a cathedral ceiling, or adding dormers or a loft. Both Parts Two and Three have introductions with specific tips on planning these types of projects.

Part Four – Case Studies of Actual Remodeling Projects

Here you'll find three summaries of successful addition/remodeling projects, complete with before and after photos. All of them presented design challenges, and two of the projects experienced major changes after the work was under way. The first case study is an addition combined with a kitchen remodel. The second is a garage conversion to a family room and new kitchen. The third project is an inspired transformation of a cramped, uninviting basement to a guest bedroom, bath, and media room. These studies are great examples of the flexibility and design skills of successful remodeling contractors, and good reminders of what to watch out for.

Estimating Forms

In the back of the book, you'll find takeoff forms that you can use as a checklist when creating your estimate. Photocopy them or use the electronic version, which you can download from **http://www.rsmeans.com/ supplement/67349.asp**

Safety Tips & Resources

The Safety Tips section is a good review of safe practices on the job site – not only for you and your crew, but to protect your clients and minimize insurance/liability problems.

The Resources provide contact information and websites for a wide range of useful information – from professional associations to product manufacturers and more.

Part One

Planning & Estimating the Project

Design Considerations

Developing the Plans

Every successful addition or renovation project begins with a well-thought-out design. Some homeowners will contract an architect to produce a set of plans before they hire a contractor, while others will rely on their builder to design the project. Experienced contractors can, in most instances, come up with workable solutions and suggestions for layout, structural issues, and finishes, and can produce working drawings and specifications. In some cases, the building department will require a set of plans stamped by an architect or engineer in order to obtain permits.

Skill with computerized drawing packages is definitely an asset for builders and remodelers, but the ability to visualize and sketch on paper can be equally important for meetings with homeowners and clarifying construction details for your crew. Many homeowners have trouble imagining a finished space.

Complex projects may require not only an architect or engineer's stamp, but extensive design experience – and familiarity with the details (performance/durability, maintenance, warranties, costs) of a wide range of the latest materials, products, and appliances. When necessary, you'll want to recommend that your client obtain professional design services.

If you're drawing up your own plans, don't rush them. You'll need to take the time to think through the project step-by-step. When you're building it on paper first, you can correct mistakes easily and

cheaply – unlike on the job site, where they'll cost you time, money, and may strain relations with your client and subcontractors.

Designing Additions

The first step is an on-site walk-through with the client, with any sketches they have available and your own notebook, measuring tape, and camera in hand. Whether you'll be preparing the design yourself or reviewing the architect's plans, you'll need accurate measurements to be sure the proposed addition will conform to all zoning requirements (e.g., setback and height restrictions), environmental standards (such as wetlands issues), and, if applicable, historic district restrictions on design, materials, and colors. (If the home has been listed as a historic landmark property, you may have to present the proposed alteration plan to a local landmark board that may be part of the planning department.)

If you'll be designing the addition, listen carefully to the owner's desires for the space they want to remodel or add to, but also consider other options (location, configuration) that they may not have considered. You may also need to offer your client guidance in terms of the addition's size and features, and corresponding return on investment. For example, a small, 10' x 12' addition is more expensive per square foot than a larger one, and minimizing the space may not be a prudent way to keep costs down. If there is room on the site, the extra cost of a larger space may not be as high as they think. And they may be far more

satisfied with a larger addition and the extra features it can offer (e.g., new bath, closets, kitchen pantry, eating area, etc.).

The approval processes vary greatly for special exemptions involving any of these issues, but sign-off is generally required to obtain a building permit. In some cases, you, the architect or an engineer, and possibly one of your subcontractors may need to attend meetings. Keep in mind that committees and meeting dates – and possible delays – will affect your project schedule.

You'll also need to find out if there are any covenants or restrictions on the property's deed that will impact the project design. You may need to have a surveyor provide an accurate plot plan.

Blending New Elements with the Existing Home

An addition or enclosure that is poorly designed, out of proportion, or awkwardly situated will clash with the main house and call attention to itself in a way that is unflattering to both the homeowner and the builder. All new elements, from exterior siding and trim to doors, windows, and roofing, should match or blend with those of the main house. This is not difficult on relatively new houses since the materials, models, sizes, styles, shapes, and colors of most of these elements are still readily available.

Older homes, especially antiques, can be more of a challenge. For example, an addition on the side of a Federal-style five-bay house might have white clapboards and oversize (1 x 8) cornerboards to match the rest of the home. But the brick-mold casing that comes standard on new windows doesn't come close to matching the wide, deep, trimmed casings of the original windows just a few feet away. The solution: order the windows without casings, remove the sills, and custom-mill sills and casings out of two layers of glued-up 5/4 mahogany decking and 1-3/4" band molding, with lead flashing for the drip cap.

Fortunately, books, magazines, and web sites dedicated to period houses offer a wealth of information on materials, techniques, and services. Among these are *The Old House Journal, Old House Interiors, Victorian Homes, Traditional Home, American Bungalow,* and *Early American Life. (See the Resources at the back of this book for web site information.)*

Siting Additions

If possible, an addition should ideally be sited so that it takes advantage of natural elements – sunlight, shade, and views – and enhances the intended use of the space. For example:

- Large or multiple south-facing windows will add warmth and reduce heating expenses in a cold climate.

- A tree-shaded roof and walls with windows oriented toward prevailing winds can keep interiors cool in a warm climate.

- North light through windows and/or skylights is preferred for an artist's studio or workshop.

- A bedroom or bath located on the house side farthest from a street or neighboring yard will provide both quiet and privacy.

Exceeding Code Requirements

Building codes are designed to ensure construction of a safe and stable structure. Many contractors prefer to build beyond code, exceeding minimal standards to produce rock-solid, optimally insulated houses – framing

walls with 2 x 6s instead of 2 x 4s, placing 2 x 10 joists 16" O.C. instead of 24", using 3/4" tongue-and-groove plywood for a sub-floor instead of 5/8" CDX, or using shrink- and twist-proof engineered wood I-beam joists instead of "2-by" lumber. The client must, of course, understand and appreciate the long-term advantages versus the one-time added expense.

Regional Requirements

In areas of the country that are subject to earthquakes, tornadoes, hurricanes, or floods, local codes require that wood-frame buildings be properly anchored and braced. Concrete block structures may require steel rebar and filled cells. Low-profile, shallow-pitched roofs covered with ribbed metal panels or flat tiles are less prone to wind damage than higher, steeper roofs with raised or textured "architecturally styled" shingles or tiles. Carports, breezeways, and pool cages are often lightly attached to the main house to allow for "break away" in a storm with minimal damage to the house. Consult current local building codes for details. *(See the Resources at the back of the book for more information sources.)*

Interior Remodeling

Remodeling is never as straightforward as new construction. Problems arise on every construction site, but renovation projects can seem like problem minefields at times, with booby-traps behind every musty plaster wall and under every scuffed floorboard. Put simply, you never know what you're going to find.

A remodeling plan is based on certain assumptions, e.g., "we'll be able to bolt the deck rim joist to the main house sill." These assumptions often are victims of Murphy's Law, e.g., the main house sill has been devoured by ants and won't hold a brad, much less a bolt. And so it often goes, as one simple task leads to an unpleasant discovery that requires one or two other tasks before the first "simple"

job can be completed. This points to three things: the absolute necessity of comprehensive site visits/inspections, the experience and ability to find solutions to unforeseeable problems, and a good contract with the owner.

During the site visit, probe and inspect as thoroughly as possible to identify the existing conditions, but make it clear (and put it in writing in your agreement with the owner) that the materials and labor required to deal with hidden problems and impossible-to-foresee contingencies are not included in your bid and are to be treated in the same way as any add-ons and upgrades. *(See "Your Agreement with the Owner" for more on contracts.)*

Subcontractors & Designers

Consulting with your subcontractors in the design stages can help avoid a lot of problems. During the site visit, your plumber or electrician might point out access issues; space needed for new piping, vents, or wiring; or code requirements that will have to be factored into your design.

If there are any questions regarding structural issues, such as evaluating load-bearing walls, spans, seismic bracing, and foundation anchoring in hurricane areas, you'll need an engineer to certify your plans and provide information and advice during construction.

Non-Traditional Materials & Methods

While a typical stud-framed house is sheathed with plywood, insulated with fiberglass batts, and finished with gypsum wallboard, alternative methods and materials offer specific advantages, such as reduced installation time or better insulation. For example, "timber-frame" construction uses large structural members on wide centers. The bays are then filled in with prefabricated structural insulated panels (SIPs), which are blocks of rigid foam insulation sandwiched between layers of exterior and interior roof and wall material. The typical three-phase method of sheathing, insulating, and sheetrocking is thus reduced to a one-step installation.

Although the savings in time and labor are obvious, building with SIPs requires specialized knowledge and skills. Home shows, building seminars, product manufacturers, and technical journals are the prime sources of this information, which can set you apart from your competition by increasing your productivity, speeding up your schedule, and making your services more marketable.

Many conscientious builders find themselves dissatisfied with the quality of the #2 and D-select pine available from their local suppliers. Quality has suffered as mills are forced to basically accept pretty much whatever timber comes through the gates and scrounge for more to fill the huge and growing demand. Alternatives to pine include other species such as South American cedar. The finger-joints in pine will usually show through a painted finish, but the cedar absorbs the glue better, making the joint lines much less visible.

Synthetic Products

Vinyl, wood/plastic composites, and recycled plastic decking have become popular as homeowners seek durability and low maintenance. Extruded PVC or other wood-substitute exterior trim "lumber" has also become widely used. As with anything, you and your client must weigh the pros and cons of appearance, cost, and performance. For example, PVC will never rot, but it has very little lateral stiffness and tends to conform to any unevenness in the

material to which it is fastened. The result can be an undulating fascia that requires a lot of shimming to true.

Artificial cast stone can save homeowners money if you need to face an addition foundation to match the stone one on the existing house. Cast "stone" pavers can help blend a new driveway into the surrounding landscaping. Architectural columns made of foam with a brick- or stone-like finish are sometimes used for porches and driveway entrances.

Laminate and vinyl flooring are obvious examples of synthetic materials that have gained major market share. They're available in a huge variety of patterns and textures resembling many different wood species and types of stone. Their warranties and composition also vary widely, so check the fine print.

Green Building

The "green" approach to building has taken off in new home construction and remodeling. Homeowners want healthier, more comfortable houses with lower energy and water bills – and many are concerned about a healthier environment. New standards, such as LEED™ (Leadership in Energy and Design), ENERGY STAR® (appliances and electronics), Greenspec® (building materials and products), and the Forest Stewardship Council (lumber), have made it easier to identify and specify environmentally-friendly building products.

Green building features like solar collection systems, super-efficient heating and air conditioning systems, and re-circulating hot water piping are usually easier to build in as part of a new house or major addition. But many others, such as low-flow faucets and showerheads, thermal windows, fluorescent light fixtures, or whole-house fans, can easily be incorporated into purely interior remodeling projects.

Some of the qualities you'll find in green building materials:

- They don't produce indoor air quality problems in the home and are better for people with chemical sensitivities.
- They don't degrade the environment or deplete scarce resources.
- They help minimize use of energy or water.
- They require little energy to manufacture.
- They're durable, reusable, recyclable, and/or biodegradable.
- They can be obtained locally to reduce fuel use for long-distance transportation.

Here are some examples of green building materials, products, and design approaches that your clients might want to consider. Some are easier to find than others, but manufacturers and home centers are continuing to expand their offerings. In some cases, green products may be more expensive initially, but savings in energy or water use can pay back the investment quickly.

- ENERGY STAR®-rated appliances.
- Local brick and stone.
- Cabinetry made with formaldehyde-free glues.
- MDF (molded density fiber) doors made of wood materials normally discarded by lumber mills.
- Carpet and padding made of natural or recycled materials.
- Suspended ceiling panels that are toxin-free, made of recycled materials.
- Sustainably harvested or recycled wood.
- Wood sheathing made from recycled wood fibers.
- Engineered wood products, made with smaller and faster-growing tree species. Products include finger-jointed lumber, glu-lam beams (which offer the advantage of extra strength over a long span), and prefabricated wood trusses and joists.

- Natural flooring materials, such as bamboo, linoleum, and ceramic tile (made from recycled glass), cork, recycled rubber, or recycled or wool carpeting.
- Wood flooring recycled from old buildings, or new-growth (or new "certified") wood (www.certifiedwood.org).
- Water-based urethanes for finishing floors.
- High-efficiency heating, ventilating, cooling, and hot water systems. ENERGY STAR® ventilation/thermostats.
- Radiant wood-burning stoves that burn cleaner and more efficiently than traditional fireplaces.
- Insulation with no or low levels of irritants and pollutants, such as cellulose and the new formaldehyde-free fiberglass products. Purely natural materials include Perlite and cotton.

- Low- or no-VOC (volatile organic compounds) paints to minimize unhealthy air quality.
- Quality light fixtures and bulbs that minimize headaches and eye strain. Fluorescent fixtures and bulbs (including screw-in compact fluorescent bulbs) that maximize energy savings and last much longer. ENERGY STAR®-rated lighting.
- Low-flow plumbing fixtures and faucets, re-circulating hot water systems, and faucet aerators that use less water and/or energy.
- Water filtering systems.
- Built-in recycling storage in kitchens, pantries, mudrooms, garages, or sheds.
- Light-colored, insulated roofing to reflect heat.
- Wood, plaster, and fiber cement shingles.

- Thermal windows and doors – with the correct solar heat gain, heat loss, and visual transmittance values – both for your climate and for the orientation of the room to the sun.
- "Daylighting" – placing windows to maximize natural light and views of the outdoors, and designing to diffuse or direct the light for best effect and to avoid glare.
- Overhangs to shade windows in hot, sunny climates.

You can also market your company's green practices, such as recycling as much as possible of a project's waste. Old cabinets, windows, doors, or other items may be of interest to a salvage yard or community building recycling center.

See the Resources at the back of the book for more information sources on green building.

Estimating the Project

Accurate estimates are essential to the success of every remodeling contractor. Properly done, estimates will help you not only ensure the profit you expected, but also plan the job and help in estimating future jobs. On the other hand, inaccurate estimates with calculation errors or misinformation can be costly. Problems can arise from failure to fully review the plans and specs, an inadequate site visit, careless pricing, simple math errors, and other factors.

The purpose of estimating is to calculate as accurately as possible the anticipated costs of labor, materials, and equipment, as well as your overhead costs and a reasonable profit. Putting an estimate together can take hours of work with no guarantee you'll get the job... but it's also a chance to gain profitable work. Larger contractors may bid as many as ten jobs in order to win just one. Their success often depends on having an organized system in place so they can prepare estimates efficiently and accurately. Such a system may include forms or a computer estimating program, as well as records of actual costs on recent projects.

Different Estimates for Different Uses

Preliminary or Rough Estimates

Contractors are called on to develop estimates for different situations. Homeowners, especially those you've worked for on other jobs, might ask you to provide a quick, rough cost for an addition or renovation so they can see if a project is in the realm of possibility

for them financially. This "ballpark" price will probably be based on your recent experience with similar projects, allowing for differences in project size or complications. The project estimates in this book or costs from other RSMeans publications* can also help you generate quick rough estimates.

Detailed Estimates

When it comes time to provide your client with a written bid for an actual job, you'll need to create a detailed "unit price" estimate of labor, material, equipment, and overhead and profit. Every estimate requires that you specifically define the quantity – and quality – of materials to be installed. Units of measure, such as square feet of drywall or flooring, linear feet of molding, or "each" in the case of a stand-alone item like a window, appliance, or light fixture, must also be defined. Next, the units are counted and priced.

Labor calculations require consideration of not only how long the work will take, the hourly pay rate, and benefits, but factors like a particular worker or crew's productivity, use of unfamiliar equipment, and access issues at the site that make the work go more slowly. Bids from subcontractors should be carefully reviewed to make sure they include all required work and materials.

The main references used to estimate a project are plans created by an architect or designer (if available), subcontractor quotes, vendor prices, your own experience, and details that you have noted based on an inspection of site conditions and the client's specifications. If you have questions about plans prepared by an architect or designer, get them answered at the start.

Scope of Work

To understand the scope of work, you need to identify construction methods, site conditions, and quality (including manufacturer and model numbers) and quantity of materials, fixtures, and finishes. You also need to clarify which, if any, materials or fixtures the homeowner will provide, and other items that have a cost including insurance, permits, a survey, soils testing, architect's or engineer's stamp, storage, or special equipment.

Existing Site Conditions & the Site Visit

Although a thorough site visit is essential to estimating new construction, it's even more critical in remodeling work. In new construction, the contractor can usually rely more on plans and specifications when preparing an estimate. Remodeling projects, on the other hand, are heavily dependent on existing site conditions, some of which may not be known until the work is under way.

Remodeling contractors need to carefully evaluate existing conditions, in as much detail as possible, to determine how these factors will affect the cost of the planned renovation. If there could be concealed conditions that cannot be known until the work is in progress, the estimate should include a contingency, or the contract should provide for coverage of such expenses. (See "Your Agreement with the Owner" later in Part One.)

Even if you have detailed plans for your project, you still need to anticipate any cost-related factors, such as conditions that:

- Restrict access or the work – such as road or site configurations or slopes that limit heavy equipment access, narrow hallways or windows that cause problems with material access, or the need to accommodate the owner's use of the home during the remodeling.

- Add to the work – such as the need to reinforce or rebuild the foundation, re-frame a structure to support a new load, or replace siding or a window that has water damage.

During the site visit, you'll need to envision the work to be done on the project, including items that may not be directly specified or obvious. Try to anticipate material handling problems and measure clearances for items that can't be broken down, like a long beam, a whirlpool tub, or a large L-shaped countertop. Having a plan to deal with these items will help reduce the chance of unexpected costs and change orders.

Subcontractors should also visit the site to help identify complications and to clarify their part of the job. This is a good time to clear up which trade will be responsible for things like providing support backing for bathroom fixtures, or cutting and patching holes for wiring. Contractors who are familiar with building code requirements can identify additional structural, electrical, or plumbing work that may have to be done along with the renovation.

The Site

Inspecting the land around the house might involve evaluation of soil conditions where a foundation for a new addition will be constructed and/or to plan access for heavy equipment. Determine whether soil is compacted, loose fill, etc., and note whether there is evidence of drainage problems, such as erosion, ponding, or mud in the crawl space. In some cases, it may be necessary to have the soil professionally tested by a soils engineer to find out whether special measures need to be taken before the foundation can be placed.

Also record site features such as slopes, retaining walls, and significant vegetation (such as plants indicative of wetlands that may restrict building). Note landscape features that would be affected by the construction and have to be protected or restored. Include plantings that have to be moved, temporarily or permanently. Determine the locations of the septic system and buried piping and sprinkler systems. Temporary fencing or barriers may also be needed to protect construction materials, the house if it's open at some point during the project, neighboring property, and people walking by.

From the Bottom Up

If you evaluate the existing structure from the bottom up, you can see how it's supported and trace the plumbing, heating, and electrical systems. Problems like structural weakness or water damage may need to be addressed before the project can begin. Consult an architect or engineer on questions of structural integrity.

Measurements

Every house is different, and your work has to be built around the existing conditions. Ceiling heights in older homes may vary from one part of the house to another and may be irregular because of settling. If a floor is extremely out of level, each stud in a new partition wall may have to be cut to a different length. Be sure to record dimensions to help you plan material quantities and the work involved.

Measure driveways and other exterior clearances for equipment and vehicles. Record dimensions of exterior and interior doorways, hallways, and stairways that will be your access route when bringing in materials and equipment.

Foundation

Note the existing foundation's material (concrete: poured or block, stone, brick, etc.) and condition. Examine the entire perimeter for cracks, drainage problems, or crumbling. Find out whether it's reinforced, whether lally columns are part of the support system, and the dimensions of walls and footings. If the home is in an area affected by seismic events, note the use or absence of shear clips, anchor bolts, etc. Examine sills for insect or water damage.

Framing

Take note of the type of framing used (platform, balloon, etc.), dimensions, and spacing of framing members. Examine the rafter condition and look for signs of problems such as sagging ceilings and floors, unsupported joists, and tilted walls.

Siding & Roofing

Note the age, type, size, and grade of materials used; the style of application; finish treatments; color; and condition. Record the type and condition of roofing, flashing, and gutter materials and any problems with the installation. Look for evidence of leaks on the inside. Also check the insulation type, R value, and condition, and the type and number of roof vents.

Doors & Windows

Take note of the style, type, function, and condition of windows and doors and surrounding trim. Look for signs of leakage and rot.

Interior Finishes & Cabinetry

Check out the style and materials of finishes throughout the house in consideration of their condition and compatibility with the materials planned for the new space. Even if the existing materials are in reasonably good condition, they may need to be refinished or replaced to blend effectively. If you'll need to match unusual materials in the existing house, take pictures, make sketches, and find out what you can about their origin from the homeowners.

Plumbing

The plumbing inspection starts with the water source (well or public supply) and location of the main shut-off valves, both at the street and in the house. Next, record the type (PVC, copper, etc.) and size of primary and secondary supply piping. Also note the size, number, location, and condition of drains and vents; then the water heater's type (gas, electric), age, condition, and capacity. Next are the plumbing fixtures – quantity, condition, age, and location in the house.

The age and condition of existing piping is a big factor in estimating fixture modifications and new installations. If exposed piping is corroded or pitted, concealed piping may have the same problems. Try to check the inside of pipes for scaling. Old galvanized pipes may be encrusted and restrict water flow. This problem should be addressed before new work begins.

Check gaskets, seals, and shut-off valves for general condition and function. If existing fixtures are to be replaced, rough-in dimensions should be measured to make sure they match the new fixtures. New rough-ins may require jogs and extra fittings, with more labor involved. Walls and ceilings may have to be cut and patched.

If the project involves moving fixtures to a different wall, pipes, drains, and vents may all have to be moved. During the site visit, pipes might be located by looking beneath the floor if it's accessible. You can also check in the attic and on the roof for vent pipes. In some cases, they're offset, and not directly over the pipes in the kitchen or bathroom walls.

HVAC

Elements to inspect in the heating and air conditioning systems include the type, age, and capacity (in BTUs per hour) of

the furnace; the utility used (gas, electric, oil); and whether the system is forced air or water, baseboard, radiant, etc. If an old furnace and/or piping are insulated with asbestos, there will be significant cost for modifications that would require professional removal.

Air conditioning units require similar evaluation of units and ductwork. Ductwork must be carefully planned to ensure there is adequate space in the design. Careful measurements and review of the design with subs will help identify conflicts between the ductwork, piping, electrical, and structural elements.

Electrical

Identify the home's electrical capacity, starting with the main panel (breakers or fuses) and then the sub-panels. Record the main shut-off rating in amps, and the number of circuits. Note the type of wiring (wires, volts, and amps).

Also check for the number (and working order) of electrical fixtures and outlets, including GFCIs. If there are specific problems or dangers, such as exposed wires or overloaded fuses, make note of them. Don't forget to note the location of outlets for equipment required to perform the work.

Your electrical subcontractor should be knowledgeable in both national and local electrical codes. To avoid conflicts between national and local codes, as well as complications with the building inspector after the work is completed, you may want to include in your contract a phrase similar to the following: "Perform all electrical work in compliance with applicable codes and ordinances, even when in conflict with the drawings and specifications." Any code questions or conflicts should be raised and resolved as early as possible.

Some codes now require that major appliances in the kitchen have their own circuits. (This would also apply to sauna or steam units that might be included in a spa-style bathroom.) Consult your local building authority to clarify these requirements.

If the project requires an upgrade in electrical service, the cost needs to be identified. If existing walls and ceilings are to remain in place, access holes must be made in order to snake wiring, and then the holes must be patched.

More on Cutting & Patching

Almost every remodeling job involves a good deal of cutting, patching, and repainting to match the surrounding conditions. Access holes must be opened in walls or between floors to install wire, conduit, and/or piping. If the walls or floors are fire-rated, fire-stopping caulk and sealant may be needed to seal penetrations.

For some projects, removing and re-installing new walls and ceilings is more cost-effective than cutting and patching. Not only do you get access to wiring and piping, but the new walls will be plumb and square, making tasks like cabinet installation go more smoothly.

For a partial room remodel, the original moldings and trim must be carefully removed and replaced. Any damaged pieces will have to be re-created or repaired, which takes time and can be expensive. If access holes have to be cut in a wallpapered or tiled wall, you may not be able to match the original materials to make a seamless repair. In these cases, a whole wall or room may need new finishes.

A careful site visit and inspection will often reveal unusual materials or potential complications so that you can account for their cost. For example, if a new plumbing vent has to penetrate a slate shingle roof, the requirements might include a custom-made copper sleeve and flashing, replacement of broken shingles, and even scaffolding to access the roof without damaging it. The cost would be many times what it would be for the same work on an asphalt shingle roof.

Other Items to Check

Examine the home for compliance with current codes, including for egress. Find out if there are any restrictions on the hours during which power equipment can be used. Determine whether there will be complications in the demolition part of the project, including lead paint or asbestos pipe coverings. Take note of any access restrictions inside and out, and whether there is available space for storing materials and for a dumpster or portable toilet, if needed for the job.

Demolition & Dumpster Rental

A thorough site visit includes specifically identifying and noting materials to be demolished or removed, since the costs can differ substantially from one material to another. (For example, removing gypsum plaster on metal lath is about three times more costly than nailed drywall.) Demolition may involve dismantling and removing existing materials, appliances, and fixtures; transporting them to a dumpster or truck; and hauling them to an approved dump.

To estimate demolition, contractors usually rely on experience with similar jobs, a schedule for the work, and knowledge of dump and dumpster restrictions and fees. If asbestos or other hazardous materials need to be removed, consult local authorities and a licensed subcontractor. Not only is there a health hazard, but EPA and OSHA impose stiff fines and penalties when hazardous materials are handled and discarded improperly.

Protecting Adjacent Spaces & Finished Work

During the site visit, you should also note the layout of the house and the specific requirements for protecting adjacent spaces from damage and dust during the project. Labor and materials to protect against dust, debris, and foot traffic are necessary cost items. If you're opening exterior walls or the roof, include costs for tarps and plastic sheeting.

Creating the Estimate

The following items need to be addressed in a thorough estimate:

- Quantity and quality of materials and equipment
- Existing conditions at the project site
- Availability of workers and subcontractors, their productivity, their rates, and the quality of their work
- How long the job will take and how tight the schedule is
- Effects of the weather or season – such as cold and damp, or hot and dry conditions – that may affect the schedule for placing concrete and other exterior work, as well as finishing flooring, painting, plastering, and other tasks
- Overhead directly related to this job
- The amount of your overall company overhead (including vehicles, tools, and equipment; marketing; and bookkeeping and other office expenses) that will be applied to this job

The estimate steps include:

- Quantity takeoff
- Pricing each item and multiplying by the number of items or units
- Including subcontractor quotes after you've reviewed them to make sure they include all tasks and materials
- Adding a contingency, if necessary, and overhead and profit
- Putting the estimate in the appropriate format for bidding

Overhead & Profit

Be sure your final estimate includes not only the "hard" costs (material and labor), but the right amount for "soft" costs, such as overhead, profit, insurance, and temporary items (such as dumpster, portable toilet, or scaffolding rental).

The amount to include for profit is a decision many contractors make on a case-by-case basis. For example, you might be willing to accept less profit in order to win a particular job that will boost your reputation or chances for future work. On the other hand, you might choose to increase the profit for a high-risk job that will require more time to manage.

Organizing the Estimate

Using forms, whether paper or electronic, is a helpful way to organize estimates and make sure you've included everything. Forms can be organized in different ways. For a large, complicated project, you might want to use a form to list, quantify, and price the items in each major category of work, such as carpentry, plumbing, painting, etc. – then summarize the totals on a summary estimate sheet.

The appendix of this book includes takeoff and pricing forms that list a broad range of items you may need for addition and renovation projects. Each has columns for quantifying and pricing the items, and for noting the source (vendor), model numbers, and any specifications. The forms are also available on the book's website to download and print (**http://www.rsmeans.com/ supplement/67349.asp**)

* RSMeans *Contractor Pricing Guides (Residential Square Foot Costs* and *Residential Repair & Remodeling Costs)* and home improvement cost guides (*Interior Home Improvement Costs* and *Exterior Home Improvement Costs*) are all available at home centers and bookstores.

Your Agreement with the Owner

Each project should have a contract that sets forth in a legally binding manner the expectations that you and the homeowner have of one another. The contract will help protect your financial interests, but it can also help you manage the job.

The contract should specify:

- What's being built
- When the work will take place
- The anticipated elements and quality (including material grades, manufacturers, model numbers, etc.)
- The cost to the owner
- How and when payments will be made
- How changes and disputes will be handled
- How long (and to what extent) the work is guaranteed

Types of Contracts

Different types of agreements may be used, depending on the situation and the risks. **Lump sum contracts** specify a payment amount based on a defined scope of work. You'll need to state in the contract that if the owner wants to add to or change the work, he or she will be responsible for related costs. Owners often prefer this arrangement because they know the total price up-front. You have the risk of estimating the work correctly so that it can be completed on time, for the price you specified. Progress payments may be made when certain established percentages of the work are complete.

A **cost plus fee contract** is sometimes used in order to get a project going before all the details of the work are known. It involves an agreement on the general scope of work, and that you'll be reimbursed for your actual costs plus a negotiated flat fee. This method requires that you set a reasonable fee that includes profit, that you keep accurate and detailed records of your actual costs, and that you can justify your expenses. Sometimes this type of contract has a "not-to-exceed" price.

A **labor only contract** pays you for just that – hours worked. This type of contract may be used if the owner furnishes all the materials. The advantage is not having to purchase materials, but the drawbacks include the possibility of incorrect materials, inferior quality of materials, inadequate quantities, or having to wait for the owner to obtain additional items.

What Contracts Include

Most contracts address the following items. You might modify yours to address special payment or other considerations.

- *Contact information.* Your company name, address, telephone and fax numbers, and license number. Also include the owner's name, address, and telephone number (including cell or pager numbers).
- *Scope of Work.* A description of the work you will perform. If plans have been provided by an architect or kitchen/bath designer, they are part of the scope of work. You might want to include a statement in the contract that in the event the plans do not reflect building code requirements, the work

will be done in compliance with the code. (You'll need to bring any such conflicts to the owner's attention as soon as they're discovered.)

- *A detailed list of the products and materials* that you or your subcontractors will install. (Include manufacturer, model number, colors, dimensions, and any other important information for each product.)
- *Warranties* that cover materials, products, and workmanship, including time limits and full versus limited warranty.
- *Schedule.* The planned schedule for the project, including the estimated start and finish dates, and any major milestone dates, such as completion of percentages of the work, to go along with partial payments. In addition to progress payments, the schedule may include other deadlines for the owner, such as product decisions and delivery of materials/products they plan to provide.
- *What you will be responsible for*, in addition to the construction, including obtaining permits and inspections, cleanup (daily, weekly, final), dumpster and removal of rubbish, etc.
- *Price.* This will be the total price for the entire job, for a lump sum or fixed-price contract.
- *Pay schedule.* Completion dates for portions of the work and expected payment. For example, a payment may be due when 50% of the work is complete, and another payment when it's 100% complete.

- *Conditions of the Contract*
  - Method for dealing with any changes the owner requests once the work has started. A statement indicating that changes require written authorization from the owner, and that the resulting extra expenses are the owner's responsibility. (It's important to get your client's commitment to final approval and clarification of all work, products, and materials at the start. Make sure they understand that delays and additional costs can result from changes.)
  - *Delays in the schedule.* A statement that expected start and completion dates are approximate and may be affected by unforeseen conditions (such as weather, material and equipment delays, and changes to the work), and that in these cases, the schedule will be adjusted accordingly.
  - *Method for dispute resolution.* An arbitration clause in the contract that directs you and your client to resolve a dispute, if one should arise, by mediation before any litigation.
  - *Hidden conditions.* A clause stating that you're not responsible for extra costs resulting from hidden existing conditions discovered during the work. Such conditions should be brought to the owner's attention as soon as discovered. It should also be stated that if hazardous materials are discovered, this agreement does not cover the cost of their removal or remediation.
  - *Safety.* A statement that you will make every effort to keep the work site safe, and that you're not responsible for injuries incurred by others on the site.
  - *Scope of agreement.* A statement that this contract reflects the entire agreement between you and the owner, and takes precedence over any and all previous written or oral agreements.
- *Your signature* with company name and date signed.
- *The owner's signature* with date signed.

Some owners may request these additional provisions in the agreement:

- *Certificate of Insurance* showing that you're properly covered, with your insurance company named.
- *Right of Recision* clause that allows them to withdraw from the agreement within 72 hours of signing.
- *Release of Liens* statement that protects them in the event of debts you have incurred.

The Contract as a Management Tool

The goal of the project is to meet the contract requirements. Good, solid contract documents that convey a mutual understanding and commitment to perform are the ingredients of a successful project, a satisfied customer, and a successful career. Mutual understanding is the most important point for builders and remodelers. All issues should be agreed on and understood by both parties. Changes can happen quickly when the work is in progress. Decisions made "on the fly" that don't seem important at the time can turn into major disputes at the end of the project when bills are being submitted. Many builders lose money in order to avoid dragging out a conflict. As the builder, however, you're the construction professional leading the project, and customers expect you to explain the contract and keep records of changes and decisions.

Maintenance & Warranty Information

Often, problems occur after the project is completed because the owner fails to properly care for the new space and the items in it. Even though the problems may not have anything to do with the initial construction, the customer may expect you to fix them. One way to avoid this situation is to provide the owner with written maintenance instructions when you complete the job. These can be given along with warranty information on the products you've installed. Organizations such as the National Association of Home Builders offer pre-printed booklets with maintenance guidelines for homeowners. *(See the Resources for contact information.)*

Much of the information in this section is based on guidance offered in Best Business Practices for Builders & Remodelers: An Easy-to-Use Checklist System. *See the Resources for more information.*

Typical Steps in a Remodeling Project

Additions and major renovations generally include the following activities. Their exact order may vary from what is shown here in this list of typical steps, depending on whether – and to what extent – an architect is involved in the project.

1 Client Meeting

Initial interview, discussion of owner's goals, evaluation of site issues, and review of architect's drawings, if available. Follow-up investigation at town hall of zoning issues, utility locations, etc.

2 Design

Collection of information to develop the design program, including owner input and extensive site evaluation.

3 Zoning Department

Preliminary design drawings submitted to zoning department if necessary for the particular project, and design changes made as required.

4 Detailed Working Drawings

Preparation of detailed drawings and specifications.

5 Estimate & Bid

Detailed estimate prepared for materials, labor, and equipment quantities and costs based on the contract requirements, drawings, and specifications, subcontractor quotes, and prices from material suppliers. Overhead and profit added, and bid assembled.

6 Permits

Application submitted for permit along with detailed working drawings and specifications. Consultation with building department, with modifications made to plans as necessary. Committee meetings likely if a variance is required.

7 Contract

Contractor selected by owner. Owner/contractor agreement prepared, reviewed, and signed. Deposit may be paid at this time.

8 Detailed Plan & Schedule

Re-review of detailed working drawings and any site issues that need to be addressed. Subcontractors scheduled.

9 Mobilization

Preparing the site, including removal or relocation of plantings for exterior work, furniture for interior remodeling, etc. Installation of temporary fencing or barriers as needed. Demolition, including dumpster.

10 Construction

Layout and excavation, drainage, and foundation work; framing/sheathing; plumbing, wiring and HVAC; exterior closure (roofing/siding, windows/doors); interior wall, cabinetry, and electrical/plumbing finish work; and final landscaping. Inspections at each phase.

11 Project Completion

Final cleanup and inspections, walk-through with owner, punch list, delivery of outstanding payment invoices, and maintenance/warranty information to owner.

Working with the Building Department

Any projects that involve changes to a home's plumbing, electrical, or structural systems require a permit from your town's building department. You'll need to identify all specific code requirements, as well as zoning and other issues, and schedule inspections. Doing work before obtaining the required permit is a huge risk to you and the homeowner since it's not only illegal, but unapproved work that is discovered later may have to be taken apart.

To obtain a permit, you'll need to submit an application with a set of complete working drawings. [For an addition or a project that affects the home's use (such as a professional office or rentable apartment) or outward appearance, the zoning department will first need to approve plans for the preliminary design.] The plans are checked to make sure they meet or exceed code requirements. If you've checked the plans carefully yourself to ensure they meet codes, you'll save time and avoid having to redraw them. If any changes are made from what is shown and approved on the plans, these must be submitted as modification drawings and re-approved.

The next step is picking up the stamped, approved set of plans with the permit. You'll need to keep a copy of the approved plans at the job site, where they'll be referenced for construction and by building inspectors. (Permits usually come with inspection record cards for the inspector's signature.)

Inspections are generally made at each phase of work, before it's covered. For example:

- For the foundation: when the forms are complete and the reinforcing steel is in place – before the concrete is poured.
- For framing, electrical, and plumbing/mechanical work: when the framing, sheathing, siding, and roofing are installed, along with plumbing, wiring, and vents – before the drywall is installed.

The final inspection is conducted when the project is complete.

Permit fees are set by each local jurisdiction and are based on factors such as square footage, type of rooms involved, complexity/involvement of different building systems and review requirements, and percent of project cost.

The building department can also be helpful by providing records of previous permits pulled for work done on the property, with names of architects and contractors who might have drawings or useful information about the existing structure.

Since the designer and builder are responsible for the building's safety and structural integrity, it makes sense to consult with building department officials and get the benefit of their input along the way. It's also sound business practice to establish and maintain a good working relationship with your local building, electrical, and plumbing inspectors – and it makes life more pleasant, too. Since they'll be evaluating the project plans, issuing your permits, scheduling your inspections, and signing off on your work, a cooperative, respectful, and friendly relationship can be important if problems arise down the line. When starting a job in a new town, introduce yourself and your foreman or superintendent to the inspectors and their secretaries.

Working with Homeowners

Interviewing for the Job

When homeowners interview you, they'll be trying to evaluate your skills and experience, as well as their compatibility with you. When you meet at their home, bring your licensing and insurance information, a list of several references with contact information, and quality photos of your work. If you belong to professional associations, let customers know. Try to anticipate the information they'll be looking for, and be ready to provide it in an organized way.

Ask to see the plans if an architect or designer has drawn them up for the project, or any sketches the owner has made. Ask questions and take notes. Check out the areas involved in the renovation, and identify major issues.

In some cases, it may be obvious that the project the owner wants cannot be built – or would be a poor investment – the way the owner has envisioned it. You may need to take time to consider other approaches. It's also possible that you'll see options to expand the project – for example, building a new kitchen as part of an addition to give the owner more design options. You may need to check on zoning issues and see a property survey to identify obstacles such as utilities and septic systems before proceeding any further or offering alternate design suggestions.

In your interview, let the homeowner know about your experience with similar kinds of projects. Discuss how long the project might take and how soon you could start work, which parts of the work you would be subcontracting, and if you would have another person supervising the job. Let them know about your expected method of payment, and invite them to ask other questions.

Design

If you'll be designing the new space, start with the homeowner's goals for it (including functional and aesthetic priorities) and rough budget. If an addition is planned, you'll also need to discuss changes to the existing house. By defining the scope of the project, you can help the owners identify what their budget will buy.

Once the basic design is approved, materials and products will need to be selected. If the owner is working with an architect, interior designer, certified kitchen or bath designer, or home center sales rep, you may not be involved in many material and product decisions – but your input will be important in terms of installation requirements and costs. If you're the owner's primary design consultant, you can facilitate the selection process if you have extensive knowledge of fixtures and materials – and their costs. *See the introductions, as well as the write-ups for each individual project, in Part Two and Part Three for more on design considerations.*

Financing

You may be able to help homeowners by giving them a list of banks that you know are accustomed to financing major remodeling projects. Banks should consider the future value of the home (with a completed addition or other improvement) in the appraised value.

Projects that add to a home's resale value, make it more attractive to buyers, and reduce utility bills all contribute to its value. Other factors that affect the value of a remodeling project include quality of workmanship and materials, careful blending with the existing home, and appropriateness to the neighborhood (overall size, architectural style, number of stories, etc.).

Kitchen and bath improvements have been shown to have the best payback when homes are sold. If the room is worn or outdated, or there is a distinct shortage of bathrooms and/or bedrooms, the upgrade becomes even more valuable.

Some financing options include:

- Second mortgage. Can be advantageous if the rate is low. Interest is tax-deductible.
- Home improvement loans. Interest is not tax-deductible, and the rate may be higher.
- Construction loan account with a bank, whereby payments are made throughout the project.

Clients can help head off delays by checking and making any needed corrections to their credit ratings in advance. They can contact the major credit agencies for copies of their credit report (Equifax at 800-685-1111, Experian at 888-397-3742, and TransUnion at 800-888-4213).

When the Work is Under Way

By the time you're ready to begin construction, homeowners have already experienced the stresses of financial arrangements, decisions about the scope of the project, moving or storing furniture, and possibly even making temporary alternative living arrangements. From here on, there are more potential stresses. Do your best to minimize them.

During construction, the homeowners' daily routines are disrupted, especially with large projects like adding a second story, a major addition, or a complete kitchen or bath remodel. They may also be faced with extra expenses for unexpected work, and may have to make quick product or design decisions if a planned item becomes unavailable, or if existing conditions require another approach. Owners may also be worried about neighbors' reaction to debris, trucks, dumpsters, and noise.

Here are some ways you can make life easier for your customers:

- Provide advance warning of upcoming tasks and disruptions. Be specific about when work will take place, who will do it, and what it will entail.

- Let them know when major material deliveries, large trucks, and dumpsters will be arriving, so they're prepared and can let neighbors know.

- Ask them if they prefer to have materials delivered on the lawn or on the street – and don't ask homeowners to sign for deliveries.

- Remind them in advance of progress payments.

- Introduce household members to your crew members at the start of the job.

- Address customer questions/concerns as soon as possible. Make sure your explanations are clearly understood so there won't be surprises after work is in place.

- Immediately notify the owner of unforeseen conditions and clarify expected extra costs. (Get their signature on change orders before you do the work.)

- Maintain an orderly job site. At the end of each day, sweep up and remove power tools. Don't leave exposed nails or anything that could cause injury.

- Provide a portable toilet for your crew if the homeowner does not want them using an inside bathroom.

- Make sure your employees honor special requests, such as not smoking or playing loud music in the house.

Final Completion

Well before the project finish date, go over all of the change orders, billings, and payments, and prepare the final payment invoice. Inspect the job to see what tasks still have to be completed before the final walk-through with the owner. When all punch list items have been taken care of, review the final payment invoice with the owner and answer any last questions.

Be prepared, when you receive your final payment, to give the owner product information (including specific maintenance and care requirements); warranties on cabinets, fixtures, appliances, and materials; extra paint, tiles, and so forth; and general maintenance guidelines. You might also take photos to show future customers and leave a few business cards or company brochures with the owner.

Part Two

Additions

Additions

The Project Estimates

This section of the book consists of 19 model projects for various types and sizes of room additions. Each project estimate includes:

- A tasks and materials list with unit and total costs
- Typical labor-hours (contractor and subcontractors)
- Total cost including overhead and profit*
- Some points to consider if you're planning a similar project
- A floor plan showing the layout of the model project that was estimated
- A photo showing an example of a finished project. (Photos are for illustrative purposes only; the estimates may not match every detail shown.)

"General Requirements" are also included in the estimate. For residential remodeling projects, these would typically include things like cleanup and permits. Depending on the needs of individual jobs, surveys, plot plans, and soil testing, as well as temporary power, water, or heating, might be additional costs in this category.

Each model project is designed to include typical features and materials. "Alternate" costs are also provided. These are unit costs for different materials, fixtures, or other items that you can use to adjust the estimate to more closely match your project.

These estimates are not intended for use in bidding a job, but they will give you quick, approximate prices for preliminary discussions with homeowners. They are also a good reference to make sure your own estimates are in the ballpark and that you've included all major items.

Use the Location Factors at the back of the book to adjust costs to your specific location.

Planning an Addition

Building an addition involves most of the considerations of constructing a new house. Home builders already have the skills and experience needed for these jobs. But they also need remodeling knowledge to make sure the new structure is properly supported and attached, and that the electrical, plumbing, and HVAC needs are met. Remodelers who have previously focused only on interior work will now have to think about foundations, roofing, utilities, effects of weather on the project, zoning, and a host of other issues.

Most additions are based on an approved set of plans and specifications. Having this information simplifies the process of identifying the work, materials, and equipment needed to do the job.

Once the actual construction is under way, the basic steps in most of these projects are: excavation, foundation, framing, sheathing, roofing, and then window, door, and siding installation – followed by plumbing, mechanical and electrical rough-in, insulation, wallboard, and finish work. Detailed site visits will help you clarify the extent of the work and potential complications, especially in matching or interfacing to existing work.

Following is a brief review of items to consider when planning a room addition.

Early Planning Stages

- Site access issues for excavation equipment, concrete trucks, a dumpster, and/or a crane (e.g., for placement of roof trusses). This includes evaluation of soil conditions and potential construction equipment damage to paving and landscaping.
- Restrictions related to zoning and private covenants (found on the property's deed). These may include issues such as setback requirements, restrictions on number of bedrooms or rentable apartments, septic system capacity, height of structure, footprint versus lot size restrictions, and type of roofing or siding.
- Historic district regulations.
- Location of utilities and septic system.
- Extent of clearing and hauling of trees and stumps, and landscaping.
- Existing structure(s) that must be demolished and hauled away.
- Adequate space for adjacent exterior elements, such as the driveway for a new garage.
- A survey, if a plot plan is required.

Foundations

Layout for the foundation starts with an assessment of the type, size, and condition of the existing house's foundation, along with the addition's dimensions and configuration. The existing foundation may require reinforcement and/or repairs before work on the addition can begin.

The old foundation might be concrete or any number of other materials, including concrete block or piers, brick, or stone. Depending on its age and material, the foundation may be neither level nor square. If there is any question about the existing foundation's capacity to support part or all of the new addition's load, consult a structural engineer.

Soil conditions must be determined in planning a new foundation. Loose soil or uncompacted fill, for example, may require evaluation by a soils engineer. Measures such as underpinning the existing foundation with part of the new addition foundation or supporting the new addition with a pier and grade beam foundation may be necessary, in addition to tying the new and old structure together with rebar. Expansive soil will need to be addressed by proper drainage.

Foundation depth requirements depend on the region's climate and codes. Foundations for most additions are poured reinforced concrete or slab on grade reinforced with wire mesh and surrounded by steel-reinforced concrete footings. If the existing house has a stone or brick foundation, you may have to face the addition foundation to match.

Don't forget to include items like the mudsill and rim joist materials in your estimate, plus waterproof membrane, crushed stone, filter fabric, and drainpipe for poured foundations; and sand, gravel, foam insulation, and a vapor barrier for slabs. Addition foundations are typically attached with rebar drilled and epoxied into the existing foundation.

A vented crawlspace will provide optimum space for insulation, wiring, and mechanical systems. If the addition will have a new basement underneath, be sure to plan each step and needed materials, including a new stairway. If space is at a premium on the inside, a bulkhead door may be a solution.

Framing & Roofing

Framing a new addition starts with a good foundation. Check codes for joist sizes and spacing; 2 x 8 joists at 16" O.C. are most typical. Framing the floor involves cutting through the siding of the existing house to make the connection. Next comes floor sheathing, followed by wall framing and sheathing.

Roofs on additions can be complicated, depending on their shape and how they connect to the existing house. If the roof design is fairly straightforward, consider prefabricated roof trusses, which cost more, but save on labor costs. Be sure to account for extra expenses such as

a crane that might be needed to raise trusses on a multi-story house. Also make sure the size of the trusses meets code requirements, and consider whether the need for on-site modifications would make a stick-built roof frame easier.

Other items to consider:

- Secure floor sheathing and any underlayment with adhesive, as well as nails, for a more rigid, squeak- or crack-free finish floor.

- Be sure the roof frame can support the sheathing and the roofing material, especially for heavy shingles like tile or slate. Building codes and many construction manuals provide the engineering details.

- Use the specified underlayment to maintain warranties of roof materials.

- Carefully plan and install flashing, especially with a complex roof connection involving valleys and different roof angles, as well as vent pipes, chimneys, and other penetrations.

- Consider an ice dam in regions with heavy snow. These shields, made of wide aluminum sheet or rubber membrane, must extend from the eave edge up the roof to a line or point no less than 24" inside the exterior wall line of the house.

- Select roof vents based on the owner's aesthetic concerns, the climate, and other factors. Ridge vents with channeled foam boards between rafters are often used. Solar-powered or wired-in fan systems provide extra ventilation.

Windows, Doors, & Siding

The biggest issue with windows and doors is not installing them, provided the openings are framed correctly, but rather selecting them, and minimizing changes mid-project. Choosing these elements is usually straightforward because of the need to match those on the rest of the house, but there is still the possibility of changes along the way – even if you're working from a set of fully defined plans and specifications. The owners may change their minds about specific product

features, sizes, or placement.

Another window/door issue is the light and view that one room may lose when an addition is built adjacent to it. The addition design should, of course, offer solutions for this situation, such as a skylight, light-colored finishes, added windows on another exterior wall, or large openings between rooms.

Like windows and doors, siding is typically chosen to match what is on the rest of the house. In some cases, the existing house will need repainting as well.

Electrical, Plumbing, & HVAC

The existing HVAC and electrical systems must be evaluated to determine whether supplementary equipment will be needed to serve the added space. Have your subcontractors do a thorough site visit with you to analyze the existing service in terms of both code and the needs of the new space – including special appliances and fixtures that will be added. Sunrooms and three-season rooms may require additional HVAC considerations.

Finishes

Floor, wall, and ceiling finishes offer so many choices that one of the most important tasks is to make sure that the homeowners have all the information they need to compare and make the best choices. Appearance, durability, warranties, cost, contribution to the home's overall value, warmth, and other factors will enter into it. These decisions need to be made in time to keep the overall project schedule on track.

Another consideration with additions is the height of adjoining floors. If they don't meet exactly, you'll need thresholds to transition from one room to another.

Be sure to give homeowners ample warning about ventilation requirements and drying times for paint and other volatile finishes. Also, give them detailed instructions and warranty requirements from the manufacturer or distributor for properly maintaining new flooring, countertops, and backsplashes.

New Front Entry Portico

*T**his is a relatively* small project, but one that has a big impact on a home's curb appeal. It's a great way to provide architectural styling to an otherwise plain, flat façade and, of course, offers protection from the elements. As an architectural feature, the entry portico should be designed to blend with and enhance the home's style and proportions, picking up elements like roof pitch and materials and trim. An advantage of a small-scale project like this is the modest amount of building materials, which can open up possibilities for some special details, like elaborate posts and trim, even for budget-minded homeowners.

Before you begin, evaluate the stoop. On newer homes, stoops may be an integral part of the foundation – solid, level, and ready to support the portico. Brick or concrete stoops that were installed separately, on the other hand, may have settled over time, and future movement could wreak havoc on the new portico. If the old stoop has to be replaced, the new concrete one should rest on piers, in keeping with code requirements. Brick facing may be part of your design.

Other considerations are railings – generally required if the entry involves more than two steps or is 30" above ground – and lighting in the ceiling of the portico or on either side of the door. Roof options include pitched, curved, or flat designs. The latter might include a balcony above. If it will be accessible and functional, make sure its structural design is adequate for the load.

Don't forget the house numbers, which should relate to the rest of the design and be visible from the street. Find out if the homeowner wants to place a bench, planter, or other item on the portico floor, and take its measurements into consideration in the design stage.

The estimate includes the labor and materials to construct a 6' x 12' open portico with dentil trim and a beaded ceiling. Electrical work involves a new overhead light fixture and switch. Alternate costs are provided for different types of columns, steps, and entry and storm doors.

Project Estimate

Description	Quantity		Labor		Cost per Unit		Total Cost		
	Quantity	Unit	Labor Hrs Per Unit	Labor Hrs Total	Material Per Unit	Installation Per Unit	Material Total	Installation Total	Total
Self-Performed									
Ornamental columns	4	Ea.	2	8	267	84.50	1,068	338	1,406
Framed headers	24	L.F.	0.03	0.72	1.88	1.18	45	28	73
Ceiling joists	60	L.F.	0.02	1.20	0.65	0.97	39	58	97
Roof rafters	160	L.F.	0.03	4.80	0.65	1.15	104	184	288
Outrigger rafters	16	L.F.	0.01	0.16	0.41	0.56	7	9	16
Roof deck sheathing	96	S.F.	0.01	0.96	0.68	0.48	65	46	111
Gable end sheathing	24	S.F.	0.01	0.24	1.45	0.30	35	7	42
Rake trim	16	L.F.	0.03	0.48	1.36	1.35	22	22	44
Soffit trim	24	L.F.	0.03	0.72	1.36	1.35	33	32	65
Fascia	24	L.F.	0.03	0.72	1.36	1.35	33	32	65
Rake and fascia trim	28	L.F.	0.07	1.96	2.72	2.94	76	82	158
Gable overhang soffit	16	L.F.	0.03	0.48	1.36	1.35	22	22	44
Dentils	16	L.F.	0.27	4.32	1.91	11.25	31	180	211
Gable overhang shelf	12	L.F.	0.03	0.36	1.36	1.35	16	16	32
Copper shelf flashing	12	S.F.	0.07	0.84	3.04	2.70	36	32	68
Box in header with trim	84	L.F.	0.03	2.52	1.36	1.35	114	113	227
Beaded ceiling	72	S.F.	0.05	3.60	1.54	2.25	111	162	273
Header and ceiling trim	60	L.F.	0.07	4.20	2.72	2.94	163	176	339
Drip edge	12	L.F.	0.02	0.24	0.54	0.85	6	10	16
Self-adhering underlayment	1	Sq.	0.36	0.36	50.50	14.10	51	14	65
Roof shingles	1	Sq.	2.29	2.29	69	88.50	69	89	158
Ridge shingles	6	L.F.	0.02	0.12	1.46	0.94	9	6	15
Step flashing	40	Ea.	0.01	0.40	0.13	0.16	5	6	11
Prime and paint	3	Gal.	1.38	4.14	29.50	51	89	153	242
Subcontract									
Light switch	1	Ea.	0.47	0.47	9.30	21.50	9	22	31
Electrician minimum	1	Day	8	8		365		365	365
Light fixture	1	Ea.	0.42	0.42	253	19.35	253	19	272
Dumpster	1	Week	1	1	256	33.50	256	34	290
Subtotals							2,767	2,257	5,024
General Requirements (Site Overhead)						12%	332	271	603
Subtotals							3,099	2,528	5,627
Overhead and Profit						10%	310	253	563
Subtotals							3,409	2,781	6,190

Grand Total $6,190

Note: Estimate is based on typical project materials available at home centers and may not include all elements in photo. Costs are national averages; see the Location Factors at the back of the book to adjust them to your area.

Cost per Square Foot $86

New Front Entry Portico

Alternates (Installed Costs)

	Unit	Total Cost
Columns		
6" aluminum	V.L.F.	$29
8" aluminum	V.L.F.	$39
10" aluminum	V.L.F.	$46
6" wood	V.L.F.	$31
8" wood	V.L.F.	$35
10" wood	V.L.F.	$44
8" square brick	V.L.F.	$15
12" square brick	V.L.F.	$35
16" square brick	V.L.F.	$62
12" stone	C.F.	$232
Stairs		
Cast-in-place concrete	LF Nose	$13
Brick stairs	M	$2,425
Entry Doors		
Pre-hung birch	Ea.	$370
Pre-hung pine	Ea.	$615
Pre-hung French	Ea.	$655
Storm Doors		
Wood	Ea.	$365
Aluminum	Ea.	$254

The double columns, brick and stone steps, and balcony above give this portico a substantial look.

The French doors, surrounding side lites, and half-round window bring lots of extra light into the entryway.

Side and rear entry doors can also benefit from porticos. The simple one here spruces up the entryway while providing weather protection.

Project Worksheet

	Unit	Quantity	Price per Unit	Total	Dimensions	Source/Model#/ Specs

Combination Ramp & Porch

*A*dding a ramp to an existing entryway or porch takes imagination and careful planning to maintain the home's architectural style. Building a new porch and ramp together offers a better opportunity for an attractive result that truly meets the needs of a disabled resident.

To determine the length of the ramp, start with the height above grade of the entry door. The standard slope – for use with a non-motorized wheelchair – is 1" of rise for every 12" of run. For example, if the door is 18" above grade, the ramp must be 18' long. A slope of 2" in 12" is permitted if the wheelchair is motorized.

Other requirements include handrails on both sides 34" to 38" above the ramp surface, 36" minimum between rails or curbs, and a landing at least 3' in width and 5' deep if the door swings inward and 5' square if it swings outward. (It might be worth removing an out-swinging storm door to avoid the larger landing requirement.)

The ramp should use the same decking, railing, and trim materials as the porch. Make sure the surface is slip-resistant and drains water properly.

Basic steps in this project start with laying out the posts and building a concrete pad to support the bottoms of the ramp stringers, then pouring the concrete. Next, the ledgerboard is attached to the house, and the rim and deck joists are installed. The ramp stringers are attached to the header joists with framing anchors and blocking nailed between the stringers. After laying the deck board, trim the tops of the posts, assemble and install the balustrade, and cap the posts with finials. The last step is finishing. Sand paint provides good traction for the decking.

This estimate covers the cost to construct a 40' x 8' porch that includes a 20' ramp. The lumber includes framing members, columns, roof sheathing, beadboard ceiling panels, and trim, as well as handrails and balusters. The decking is a wood/plastic composite.

See the Open Front Porch project for more on porch design and basic construction considerations.

Project Estimate

Description	Quantity		Labor		Cost per Unit		Total Cost		
	Quantity	Unit	Labor Hrs Per Unit	Labor Hrs Total	Material Per Unit	Installation Per Unit	Material Total	Installation Total	Total
Self-Performed									
Post footings	10	Ea.	2.91	29.10	16.20	105	162	1,050	1,212
Concrete stoop	1	C.Y.	0.80	0.80	192	34	192	34	226
Treated ledger bolted to house	40	L.F.	0.04	1.60	1.19	1.73	48	69	117
Floor joists and ribbons	336	L.F.	0.01	3.36	1.10	0.61	370	205	575
Joist hangers	62	Ea.	0.05	3.10	0.88	2.25	55	140	195
Posts	75	L.F.	0.04	3	1.55	1.73	116	130	246
Plastic/wood composite decking	720	L.F.	0.03	21.60	2.12	1.06	1,526	763	2,289
Headers	56	L.F.	0.03	1.68	1.88	1.18	105	66	171
Miscellaneous work at beam attachment	1	Job	4	4		169		169	169
Ceiling joists	280	L.F.	0.01	2.80	0.65	0.54	182	151	333
Ceiling joist hangers	30	Ea.	0.05	1.50	0.88	2.25	26	68	94
Strip roof shingles	4	Sq.	1.14	4.56		34.50		138	138
Rafter ledger board	40	L.F.	0.03	1.20	1.43	1.35	57	54	111
Roof rafters	558	L.F.	0.03	16.74	0.94	1.38	525	770	1,295
Roof sheathing	720	S.F.	0.01	7.20	0.68	0.48	490	346	836
Gable studs	56	L.F.	0.03	1.68	0.41	1.35	23	76	99
Gable end sheathing	72	S.F.	0.01	0.72	0.68	0.60	49	43	92
Rake trim	40	L.F.	0.04	1.60	1.58	1.69	63	68	131
Soffit	40	L.F.	0.04	1.60	1.58	1.69	63	68	131
Fascia	40	L.F.	0.04	1.60	1.58	1.69	63	68	131
Box in header (2 sides)	112	L.F.	0.04	4.48	1.85	1.88	207	211	418
Header soffit	40	L.F.	0.03	1.20	0.78	1.35	31	54	85
Furring	280	L.F.	0.02	5.60	0.31	0.97	87	272	359
Beadboard panel ceiling	320	S.F.	0.03	9.60	0.92	1.35	294	432	726
Ceiling trim	96	L.F.	0.03	2.88	0.97	1.25	93	120	213
Gable end siding	72	S.F.	0.03	2.16	3.52	1.35	253	97	350
Step flashing	50	Ea.	0.01	0.50	0.13	0.16	7	8	15
Drip edge	40	L.F.	0.02	0.80	0.54	0.85	22	34	56
Self-adhering underlayment	8	Sq.	0.36	2.88	50.50	14.10	404	113	517
Laminated roof shingles	8	Sq.	1.78	14.24	52	69	416	552	968
Handrails (top and bottom)	136	L.F.	0.03	4.08	0.53	1.13	72	154	226
Balusters	340	L.F.	0.07	23.80	0.34	3.07	116	1,044	1,160
Prime and paint	4	Gal.	1.38	5.52	29.50	51	118	204	322
Subcontract									
Dumpster	1	Week	1	1	385	33.50	385	34	419
Subtotals							6,620	7,805	14,425
General Requirements (Site Overhead)						12%	794	937	1,731
Subtotals							7,414	8,742	16,156
Overhead and Profit						10%	741	874	1,616
Subtotals							8,155	9,616	17,772

Grand Total $17,772

Note: Estimate is based on typical project materials available at home centers and may not include all elements in photo. Costs are national averages; see the Location Factors at the back of the book to adjust them to your area.

Cost per Square Foot   **$56**

Alternates (Installed Costs)

	Unit	Total Cost
Handrails		
Aluminum	L.F.	$28
Steel	L.F.	$18
Deck finish		
Anti-slip finish	S.F.	$3

Open Front Porch

Open front porches became a common architectural element starting in the late 19th century, when residents enjoyed cool breezes while communing with neighbors passing by. Air conditioning, backyard decks, and a desire for privacy all lessened their popularity, but they've made a major comeback in the past couple of decades.

Since new front porches completely change the look of the home, they're typically designed by architects or contractors who specialize in this type of work. Styles can range from Arts and Crafts bungalows with wide, tapering columns, to Victorians with simple or ornate details and even curves. A straight porch with round columns can enhance the appearance of many different house styles. Some styles, such as some contemporaries and New England saltboxes, are not well-suited to porch additions.

The proportions of an added porch must blend well with the home. A large porch may encompass two or more doorways, opening up each of the interior spaces as they flow onto the porch.

The basic steps in this project are installing footings, framing with 2 x 6s, laying the decking, and then building the roof. Tying the porch roof into the house's roof can be tricky depending on the roof pitches and condition of in-place materials. Securing the porch roof to a flat house front requires removal of siding, then cutting and patching to blend in. The porch roof pitch should allow for proper flashing below second-story windows. You'll need to figure in electrical work if you'll be adding light fixtures or GFCI outlets.

The project estimated here is a straight front porch, 8' x 35', with a granite step, tapered wood columns, and mahogany decking. The roofing is cedar shingles, and the ceiling is finished with beadboard panels. Electrical work includes six recessed light fixtures.

Project Estimate

Description	Quantity	Unit	Labor Hrs Per Unit	Labor Hrs Total	Material Per Unit	Installation Per Unit	Material Total	Installation Total	Total
Self-Performed									
Post footings	6	Ea.	2.91	17.46	16.20	105	97	630	727
Concrete footing for step	1	C.Y.	0.80	0.80	192	34	192	34	226
Granite step	18	C.F.	0.80	14.40	92.50	42.80	1,665	770	2,435
Treated ledger bolted to house	35	L.F.	0.04	1.40	1.19	1.73	42	61	103
Floor joists and ribbons	224	L.F.	0.01	2.24	1.10	0.61	246	137	383
Joist hangers	56	Ea.	0.05	2.80	0.88	2.25	49	126	175
Mahogany decking	1050	L.F.	0.03	31.50	1.43	1.23	1,502	1,292	2,794
Deck skirt	51	L.F.	0.04	2.04	1.85	1.88	94	96	190
Lattice at deck skirt	204	L.F.	0.03	6.12	0.45	1.25	92	255	347
Tapered round wood columns	6	Ea.	2.67	16.02	1275	113	7,650	678	8,328
Headers	51	L.F.	0.03	1.53	1.88	1.18	96	60	156
Miscellaneous work at beam attachment	1	Job	4	4		169		169	169
Ceiling joists	224	L.F.	0.01	2.24	0.65	0.54	146	121	267
Ceiling joist hangers	28	Ea.	0.05	1.40	0.88	2.25	25	63	88
Strip wood roof shingles	1	Sq.	1.78	1.78		53.50		54	54
Rafter ledger board	35	L.F.	0.03	1.05	1.43	1.35	50	47	97
Roof rafters	280	L.F.	0.03	8.40	0.94	1.38	263	386	649
Roof sheathing	350	S.F.	0.01	3.50	0.68	0.48	238	168	406
Gable studs	40	L.F.	0.03	1.20	0.41	1.35	16	54	70
Gable end sheathing	16	S.F.	0.01	0.16	0.68	0.60	11	10	21
Rake trim	20	L.F.	0.04	0.80	1.58	1.69	32	34	66
Soffit	51	L.F.	0.04	2.04	1.58	1.69	81	86	167
Fascia	51	L.F.	0.04	2.04	1.58	1.69	81	86	167
Box in header (2 sides)	102	L.F.	0.04	4.08	1.85	1.88	189	192	381
Header soffit	51	L.F.	0.03	1.53	0.78	1.35	40	69	109
Header trim	51	L.F.	0.03	1.53	0.97	1.25	49	64	113
Furring	245	L.F.	0.02	4.90	0.31	0.97	76	238	314
Beadboard panel ceiling	280	S.F.	0.03	8.40	0.92	1.35	258	378	636
Frieze	40	L.F.	0.02	0.80	0.67	0.70	27	28	55
Ceiling trim	86	L.F.	0.03	2.58	0.97	1.25	83	108	191
Gable end siding	16	S.F.	0.03	0.48	3.52	1.35	56	22	78
Drip edge	35	L.F.	0.02	0.70	0.54	0.85	19	30	49
Self-adhering underlayment	4	Sq.	0.36	1.44	50.50	14.10	202	56	258
Cedar roof shingles	400	S.F.	0.03	12	2.44	1.35	976	540	1,516
Prime and paint	6	Gal.	1.38	8.28	29.50	51	177	306	483
Subcontract									
Light switch	1	Ea.	0.38	0.38	5.25	17.50	5	18	23
Electrician minimum	1	Day	8	8		365		365	365
Recessed lighting	6	Ea.	0.29	1.74	59.50	13.10	357	79	436
Dumpster	1	Week	1	1	385	33.50	385	34	419
Subtotals							15,567	7,944	23,511
General Requirements (Site Overhead)						12%	1,868	953	2,821
Subtotals							17,435	8,897	26,332
Overhead and Profit						10%	1,744	890	2,633
Subtotals							19,179	9,787	28,965

Grand Total $28,965

Note: Estimate is based on typical project materials available at home centers and may not include all elements in photo. Costs are national averages; see the Location Factors at the back of the book to adjust them to your area.

Cost per Square Foot $103

Alternates (Installed Costs)

The tapered columns and matching white rockers give this porch a unified and inviting feel.

	Unit	Total Cost
Ceiling Finishes		
Knotty pine board ceiling	S.F.	$4
Rough-sawn cedar board paneling	S.F.	$4
Redwood board ceiling	S.F.	$7
Unfinished panel ceiling	S.F.	$3
Cedar finish panel ceiling	S.F.	$3
Roofing		
Aluminum shingles	Sq.	$262
Asphalt shingles	Sq.	$99
Laminated asphalt shingles	Sq.	$121
Slate shingles	Sq.	$815
Steel shingles	Sq.	$340
Clay tiles	Sq.	$465
Concrete tiles	Sq.	$335
Decking		
Pressure-treated Southern yellow pine	S.F.	$2
Cedar	L.F.	$5
Redwood	S.F.	$10
Wood/plastic composite	L.F.	$3
Electrical		
GFCI receptacle	Ea.	$69
Weatherproof cover for receptacle	Ea.	$16
Paddle fan	Ea.	$440

Prefabricated wood and polyurethane porch components offer many design possibilities. Trim, balusters and railings, and brackets are available in different styles from both home centers and special-order companies.

This wrap-around porch greatly enhances the perceived size of the home.

Project Worksheet

	Unit	Quantity	Price per Unit	Total	Dimensions	Source/Model#/ Specs

Screened Porch

 screened porch can be built over an open porch or deck, or as an entirely new addition. If you start with an open porch, you'll need to assess the condition of the foundation, floor, walls and posts, ceiling, roof, stairs, and siding. Any substandard system or element will have to be replaced or repaired, and partial walls may have to be removed, depending on the design.

The rest of the project consists of installing the screening or screen panels, and framing for and installing the screen door. You may also have wiring for an overhead paddle fan, light fixtures, and GFCI outlets. The last item is the finish trim.

If you're enclosing a deck, assess the foundation's condition and its ability to support a roof. Next, erect supporting posts, and frame out the roof and partial wall, if called for. Once the sheathing is done and the roof is finished, proceed with the other steps for the open porch conversion.

If you're building a screened porch as a new addition, you'll need a foundation and floor in addition to steps. Depending on the porch design and local codes, the foundation could be: concrete slab on grade, footings, block on strip footing, or poured concrete footings and walls. Another option is a permanent wood foundation.

The floor should be framed with pressure-treated lumber above a vapor barrier laid over the ground surface or above a vented crawl space. Since the finished floor will be exposed to some weather and moisture, use pressure-treated or other exterior lumber for the decking too, and space it to allow drainage. Screening can be attached to the underside of the deck to keep out insects. If tile or sheet flooring is planned, use exterior-grade plywood for the subfloor and/or underlayment.

Screening can also be attached directly to the outside of flat-sided support posts or installed between the posts in panels.

The project estimated here is a new 15' x 20' screened porch as an addition to a house. It's assumed that there's an existing exterior door that will access the porch. The job starts with post footings and a concrete footing for a granite step. Features include square columns, mahogany decking, a beadboard ceiling, a rubberized roof, and posts and balusters. Electrical work involves installation of six recessed fixtures and a switch.

Project Estimate

Description	Quantity		Labor		Cost per Unit		Total Cost		
	Quantity	Unit	Labor Hrs Per Unit	Labor Hrs Total	Material Per Unit	Installation Per Unit	Material Total	Installation Total	Total
Self-Performed									
Post footings	4	Ea.	2.91	11.64	16.20	105	65	420	485
Concrete footing for step	1	C.Y.	0.80	0.80	192	34	192	34	226
Granite step	24	C.F.	0.80	19.20	92.50	42.80	2,220	1,027	3,247
Treated ledger bolted to house	30	L.F.	0.04	1.20	1.19	1.73	36	52	88
Floor joists and ribbons	300	L.F.	0.01	3	1.10	0.61	330	183	513
Joist hangers	48	Ea.	0.05	2.40	0.88	2.25	42	108	150
Mahogany decking	1050	L.F.	0.03	31.50	1.43	1.23	1,502	1,292	2,794
Deck skirt	50	L.F.	0.04	2	1.85	1.88	93	94	187
Lattice at deck skirt	200	L.F.	0.03	6	0.45	1.25	90	250	340
Square wood columns	40	V.L.F.	0.25	10	18.20	10.40	728	416	1,144
Headers	50	L.F.	0.03	1.50	1.88	1.18	94	59	153
Miscellaneous work at beam attachment	1	Job	4	4		169		169	169
Ceiling joists/rafters	230	L.F.	0.01	2.30	0.65	0.54	150	124	274
Ceiling joist hangers	23	Ea.	0.05	1.15	0.88	2.25	20	52	72
Remove clapboard siding	100	S.F.	0.02	2		0.64		64	64
Roof sheathing	300	S.F.	0.01	3	0.68	0.48	204	144	348
Overhang soffit	50	L.F.	0.03	1.50	0.78	1.35	39	68	107
Overhang fascia	50	L.F.	0.03	1.50	0.78	1.35	39	68	107
Box in header (2 sides)	100	L.F.	0.04	4	1.85	1.88	185	188	373
Header soffit	50	L.F.	0.03	1.50	0.78	1.35	39	68	107
Header trim	50	L.F.	0.03	1.50	0.97	1.25	49	63	112
Furring	270	L.F.	0.02	5.40	0.31	0.97	84	262	346
Beadboard panel ceiling	300	S.F.	0.03	9	0.92	1.35	276	405	681
Frieze	30	L.F.	0.02	0.60	0.67	0.70	20	21	41
Ceiling trim	80	L.F.	0.03	2.40	0.97	1.25	78	100	178
Roof edge	50	L.F.	0.06	3	5.25	2.58	263	129	392
Rubber roof	3	Sq.	1.60	4.80	99.50	62	299	186	485
Replace clapboard siding around roof connection	1	Job	4	4		169		169	169
Gutters	50	L.F.	0.07	3.50	1.46	3.12	73	156	229
Downspouts	24	L.F.	0.04	0.96	1.95	2.08	47	50	97
Downspout elbows	6	Ea.	0.08	0.48	3.63	3.74	22	22	44
Newel posts	15	V.L.F.	0.25	3.75	18.20	10.40	273	156	429
Balusters	75	Ea.	0.32	24	42.50	13.50	3,188	1,013	4,201
Railing (top of balusters only)	45	L.F.	0.13	5.85	35	5.65	1,575	254	1,829
Screen door	1	Ea.	1.33	1.33	275	56.50	275	57	332
Screened wood frames	480	S.F.	0.04	19.20	7.05	1.80	3,384	864	4,248
Prime and paint	5	Gal.	1.38	6.90	29.50	51	148	255	403
Subcontract									
Light switch	1	Ea.	0.38	0.38	5.25	17.50	5	18	23
Electrician minimum	1	Day	8	8		365		365	365
GFCI receptacles	2	Ea.	0.65	1.30	39	30	78	60	138
Recessed lighting	6	Ea.	0.29	1.74	59.50	13.10	357	79	436
Dumpster	1	Week	1	1	256	33.50	256	34	290
Subtotals							16,818	9,598	26,416
General Requirements (Site Overhead)						12%	2,018	1,152	3,170
Subtotals							18,836	10,750	29,586
Overhead and Profit						10%	1,884	1,075	2,959
Subtotals							20,720	11,825	32,545

Grand Total $32,545

Note: Estimate is based on typical project materials available at home centers and may not include all elements in photo. Costs are national averages; see the Location Factors at the back of the book to adjust them to your area.

Cost per Square Foot $108

Alternates (Installed Costs)

	Unit	Total Cost
Ceiling Finishes		
Knotty pine board ceiling	S.F.	$4
Rough-sawn cedar board paneling	S.F.	$4
Redwood board ceiling	S.F.	$7
Unfinished panel ceiling	S.F.	$3
Cedar finish panel ceiling	S.F.	$3
Roofing		
Aluminum shingles	Sq.	$262
Asphalt shingles	Sq.	$99
Laminated asphalt shingles	Sq.	$121
Red cedar shingles	Sq.	$340
Slate shingles	Sq.	$815
Steel shingles	Sq.	$340
Clay tiles	Sq.	$465
Concrete tiles	Sq.	$335
Decking		
Pressure-treated Southern yellow pine	S.F.	$2
Cedar	L.F.	$5
Redwood	S.F.	$10
Wood/plastic composite	L.F.	$3
Electrical		
Weatherproof cover for receptacle	Ea.	$16
Paddle fan	Ea.	$440

In choosing screening, consider:

- *Aluminum – durable and less apt to sag, but susceptible to dents. Corrosion (oxidation) makes it less transparent over time – not the best choice in the city or near saltwater.*

- *Vinyl – not as strong as aluminum, but easier to install.*

- *Fiberglass – does not oxidize, but can stretch or sag out of alignment during installation.*

- *Copper – performs well, except for susceptibility to denting, and is expensive.*

Project Worksheet

	Unit	Quantity	Price per Unit	Total	Dimensions	Source/Model#/ Specs

Three-Season Porch

A *three-season porch* is halfway between an open-to-the-weather screened porch and a fully-enclosed sunroom, and a good design will incorporate the best features of both. It tends to offer more ventilation than a sunroom, often using sliding glass doors in place of windows. It may also be more casual than a sunroom, with brick floors and rustic furnishings.

If you are converting a screened-in porch to a three-season one, instead of building it as a new addition, you may need to do some preliminary work, depending on the porch's condition and design. Start by assessing the foundation, ceiling, roof, and siding.

Bringing the space to a finished condition may involve covering open decking with a solid floor, building a partial wall, and/or reconfiguring/framing around existing posts for the windows and door.

The electrical part of this project may include new wiring for lighting, GFCI outlets, and HVAC units. Some homeowners may also want to run phone, computer, speaker, or TV cables.

To maximize airflow and coolness in the summer, consider:

- Sliding glass doors and/or operable windows with screens
- Shades, blinds, or awnings on sunny exposures
- Operable or venting skylights
- Exhaust or paddle fan
- Window (or through-wall) air-conditioning unit

To provide and retain heat during the chilly weeks of spring and fall, consider:

- Insulated glass windows and exterior doors
- Wood or gas fireplace or stove
- Portable heaters
- High-R insulation in floor, walls (or partial walls), and ceiling
- Carpeting or area rugs

This project estimate is for construction of an entirely new 16' x 14' three-season porch, from the ground up. It includes excavation for a foundation and slab, footings, then framing, sheathing, siding, roofing, and decking. The ceiling is insulated, with four recessed light fixtures. The walls and ceiling are finished with gypsum wallboard and paint.

Project Estimate

Description	Quantity	Unit	Labor Hrs Per Unit	Labor Hrs Total	Material Per Unit	Installation Per Unit	Material Total	Installation Total	Total
Self-Performed									
Excavation for foundation and slab	2	Job	8	16		412		824	824
Strip footings	3	C.Y.	2.49	7.47	116	99.02	348	297	646
Foundation wall	7	C.Y.	4.36	30.52	172	199.30	1,204	1,395	2,599
Backfilling	1	Job	8	8		412		412	412
Haul away spoil	14	L.C.Y.	0.11	1.54		8.99		126	126
Spread and compact gravel for under slab	4	B.C.Y.	0.01	0.04	9.10	1	36	4	40
Concrete slab on grade	224	S.F.	0.02	4.48	1.86	0.76	417	170	587
Miscellaneous demolition at framing connections	1	Job	2	2		60.50		61	61
Structural columns at corners	24	L.F.	0.04	0.96	1.38	1.73	33	42	75
Jack studs sistered to columns and at connection	72	L.F.	0.04	2.88	0.41	1.54	30	111	141
Laminated headers	88	L.F.	0.04	3.52	6.15	1.50	541	132	673
Top plates	88	L.F.	0.02	1.76	0.41	0.85	36	75	111
Sheathing	384	S.F.	0.01	3.84	0.68	0.60	261	230	491
Ceiling joists and ribbons	242	L.F.	0.02	4.84	1.76	0.77	426	186	612
Joist hangers	13	Ea.	0.05	0.65	0.88	2.05	11	27	38
Plywood roof deck	224	SF Flr.	0.01	2.24	0.90	0.54	202	121	323
Frieze/fascia board	44	L.F.	0.02	0.88	0.67	0.70	29	31	60
Roof edge trim	44	L.F.	0.06	2.64	5.25	2.58	231	114	345
Roof deck fiberboard	224	S.F.	0.01	2.24	0.22	0.31	49	69	118
Rubber roof	3	Sq.	1.60	4.80	99.50	62	299	186	485
Deck sleepers	192	L.F.	0.01	1.92	0.55	0.54	106	104	210
Deck joists	236	L.F.	0.01	2.36	0.55	0.54	130	127	257
Composite decking	500	L.F.	0.03	15	2.12	1.06	1,060	530	1,590
Deck handrail posts	11	Ea.	0.25	2.75	14.35	10.55	158	116	274
Deck handrails	88	L.F.	0.03	2.64	0.53	1.13	47	99	146
Balusters	330	L.F.	0.07	23.10	0.34	3.07	112	1,013	1,125
Board trim around glazed openings	136	L.F.	0.03	4.08	1.36	1.35	185	184	369
Glazing and tube framing	336	S.F.	0.17	57.12	38	6.30	12,768	2,117	14,885
Ceiling insulation	224	S.F.	0.01	2.24	0.94	0.34	211	76	287
Furring	192	L.F.	0.02	3.84	0.31	0.97	60	186	246
Ceiling gypsum wallboard	224	S.F.	0.02	4.48	0.34	0.88	76	197	273
Wall gypsum wallboard	120	S.F.	0.04	4.80	0.34	1.78	41	214	255
Miscellaneous flashing and siding replacement	1	Job	4	4		155		155	155
Ceramic tile floor	224	S.F.	0.05	11.20	4.33	1.69	970	379	1,349
Painting	3	Gal.	1.38	4.14	29.50	51	89	153	242
Subcontract									
Double switch	1	Ea.	0.80	0.80	22.50	36.50	23	37	60
Electrician minimum	1	Job	4	4		184		184	184
Duplex outlets	2	Ea.	0.55	1.10	7.50	25	15	50	65
Recessed light fixtures	4	Ea.	0.29	1.16	59.50	13.10	238	52	290
Ceiling fan	1	Ea.	1	1	82	46	82	46	128
Dumpster	1	Week	1	1	256	33.50	256	34	290
Subtotals							20,780	10,666	31,447
General Requirements (Site Overhead)						12%	2,494	1,280	3,774
Subtotals							23,274	11,946	35,221
Overhead and Profit						10%	2,327	1,195	3,522
Subtotals							25,601	13,141	38,743

Grand Total $38,743

Note: Estimate is based on typical project materials available at home centers and may not include all elements in photo.
Costs are national averages; see the Location Factors at the back of the book to adjust them to your area.

Cost per Square Foot $173

Additions

Alternates (Installed Costs)

	Unit	Total Cost
Skylights		
46" x 21-1/2" venting	Ea.	$425
Flashing set for above	Ea.	$106
46" x 28" venting	Ea.	$410
Flashing set for above	Ea.	$107
57" x 44" venting	Ea.	$585
Flashing set for above	Ea.	$114
Electrical		
Paddle fan	Ea.	$440

The operable windows in this three-season room let in light and breezes.

Finish materials should be dictated by the style of the house. Concrete, stone, or ceramic tile flooring is durable and low-maintenance. If you're installing stone or tile over a wood subfloor, you may need to stiffen the framing with braces or blocks, and install a combination subfloor/ underlayment of tongue-and-groove plywood – glued and nailed or screwed to the joists – to provide a rigid, level surface for the finished floor.

Skylights and ceiling fans are popular features.

Project Worksheet

	Unit	Quantity	Price per Unit	Total	Dimensions	Source/Model#/ Specs

Greenhouse

refabricated greenhouses come in many styles and sizes. You may need to direct your clients to information sources that will help them choose a design to complement their house. The parabolic-curved aluminum-frame type is popular, but, according to one critic, calls to mind a fast-food restaurant – something to consider if it's in a highly-visible location. In terms of siting, the south or southwest side of the house is ideal, although a few hours of morning sun on the east side are sufficient for most plants.

Bare-bones, utilitarian greenhouses have aluminum or galvanized steel frames, with glass or rigid plastic panels. More stylish, higher-priced units use laminated wood frames with clad or bare wood trim (usually cedar or mahogany). High-end models start at around $20,000 and can go up to five times that amount.

Installing a prefabricated greenhouse calls for most or all of the following:

- Foundation – concrete pier, slab, or block on strip footing. (Check local codes that rule on frost line, seismic, hurricane, and other requirements.)

- Partial wall and access via exterior door. One or more sets of French doors make an elegant transition to interior rooms and let in maximum light.

- Properly prepared and flashed attachment surfaces on house.

- Flooring – brick, tile, or stone.

- Countertop and utility sink, potting bench, tool rack, storage, and shelving. If the greenhouse won't be heated, plan for a frost-proof spigot.

- Exhaust fan and other cooling and venting elements.

- Heating. (A supplemental system, such as a heat pump, may be needed for a large greenhouse.)

- Roller shades, screens, misters, and humidity controls.

- Vents and overhead paddle fan.

- Lighting and GFCI outlets.

In a northern climate, be sure the greenhouse can withstand weather extremes. In regions where hail is frequent, plastic should be substituted for glass.

A properly-sited greenhouse is an excellent source of passive-solar heat. A dark-colored interior with a brick floor absorbs heat during the day and radiates it after sundown. You can tap into this heat reservoir by installing a thermostatically-controlled exhaust fan in the house wall near the greenhouse ceiling.

This project estimate is for the installation of a 9' x 15' prefabricated greenhouse, which will be attached to an existing house. The work starts with excavating for and forming and pouring a foundation. It also includes assembly of the greenhouse, attachment to the house, and tile flooring. Electrical work involves installation of a switch, outlet, and floodlight. The house has an existing exterior door that will be used to access the new space.

Project Estimate

Description	Quantity		Labor		Cost per Unit		Total Cost		
	Quantity	Unit	Labor Hrs Per Unit	Labor Hrs Total	Material Per Unit	Installation Per Unit	Material Total	Installation Total	Total
Self-Performed									
Excavation for foundation and slab	1	Job	8	8		412		412	412
Strip footings	2	C.Y.	2.49	4.98	116	99.02	232	198	430
Foundation wall	6	C.Y.	4.36	26.16	172	199.30	1,032	1,196	2,228
Backfilling	1	Job	8	8		412		412	412
Spread and compact gravel for under slab	3	B.C.Y.	0.01	0.03	9.10	1	27	3	30
Haul away spoil	10	L.C.Y.	0.11	1.10		8.99		90	90
Concrete slab on grade	135	S.F.	0.02	2.70	1.86	0.76	251	103	353
Miscellaneous demolition at framing connections	1	Job	2	2		60.50		61	61
Stone veneer on concrete walls	144	S.F.	0.31	44.64	6.65	16.54	958	2,382	3,340
Greenhouse structure, glazing, and door	135	SF Flr.	0.15	20.25	33	6.25	4,455	844	5,299
Tile flooring	135	S.F.	0.13	17.55	4.28	4.56	578	616	1,194
Miscellaneous work at connection	1	Job	4	4		155		155	155
Subcontract									
Electrical switch gang box	1	Ea.	0.90	0.90	30	41.50	30	42	72
Electrician minimum	1	Day	8	8		365		365	365
GFCI receptacle	1	Ea.	0.65	0.65	39	30	39	30	69
Floodlight	1	Ea.	0.40	0.40	29	18.35	29	18	47
Dumpster	1	Week	1	1	256	33.50	256	34	290
Subtotals							7,887	6,961	14,847
General Requirements (Site Overhead)						12%	946	835	1,782
Subtotals							8,833	7,796	16,629
Overhead and Profit						10%	883	780	1,663
Subtotals							9,716	8,576	18,292

Grand Total $18,292

Note: Estimate is based on typical project materials available at home centers and may not include all elements in photo. Costs are national averages; see the Location Factors at the back of the book to adjust them to your area.

Cost per Square Foot $135

Alternates (Installed Costs)

	Unit	Total Cost
Flooring		
Sheet vinyl	S.F.	$5
Linoleum	S.F.	$6
12" x 12" ceramic tile	S.F.	$6
Stone	S.F.	$22
Brick	S.F.	$10
Electrical		
GFCI receptacle	Ea.	$69
Weatherproof cover for receptacle	Ea.	$16
Exhaust fan	Ea.	$112

Sunroom

*U*nlike a three-season porch, a sunroom is a fully-integrated part of the home's year-round living space, often open to adjacent rooms and sometimes with an exterior door opening onto a garden, deck, or patio. Sunrooms can be custom-built or prefabricated. "Pre-fab" units are assembled by the dealer. The basic steps in this project are:

- Site preparation: Work with the homeowner to make sure plantings are moved or protected, as needed.

- Excavation and foundation: Contact utility companies to locate pipes and lines, and arrange any needed shut-offs and re-routing.

- Floor, wall, and roof framing: Consider 2 x 6 framing to allow room for piping and wiring.

- Opening through existing wall: Discuss in advance with homeowners so they'll know when it will be open, for how long, and how you'll cover and protect the opening.

- Wiring and piping: Determine what's needed to provide heat and electrical service to the new room.

- Finish materials, light fixtures, and ceiling fans: Clarify these items early on for an accurate estimate and to protect your schedule.

- Landscaping: Identify work that you'll be responsible for.

Because you're building a heated space with walls comprised largely of windows, energy-efficient glass is essential. Glazing options include: double- or triple-pane, Argon-filled, low-emissivity (low-E), and solar reflective film (for hot southern climates).

In any climate, sunroom windows should be operable. Tilt-out awning or transom units are good options, since they provide ventilation while helping keep rain out.

For heating and cooling, a small sunroom might be hooked into the existing systems on its own thermostat without exceeding capacity. A larger room will likely require upgrading the home's systems. Sunrooms can be heated by baseboard or electric wall heaters, a gas or electric fireplace, or a ductless heat pump, and cooled by a window air-conditioner or ceiling fan.

The classic flooring choices are tile, brick, and stone. Radiant floor heat is ideal for these materials, and provides evenly distributed, comfortable warmth that's energy- and cost-efficient. Hydronic or electrical radiant systems can be installed in a wood-framed floor or a concrete slab. In the latter, the concrete stores heat and releases it steadily and evenly.

This project estimate covers the cost to construct a new sunroom addition. It starts with excavation and the new foundation, and includes removal of siding and an existing exterior door where the 12' x 16' sunroom meets the house. Other tasks are framing and sheathing, roofing (with a ridge vent, flashing, and gutters), insulation, siding, and installation of three sets of sliding glass doors, two single doors, and five transom windows. Finishes are ceramic tile flooring and painted drywall for the walls and ceilings. Electrical work includes a ceiling fan, switch, and four outlets.

Project Estimate

Description	Quantity		Labor		Cost per Unit		Total Cost		
	Quantity	Unit	Labor Hrs Per Unit	Labor Hrs Total	Material Per Unit	Installation Per Unit	Material Total	Installation Total	Total
Self-Performed									
Excavate for foundation	1	Job	8	8		412		412	412
Footings	4	C.Y.	2.94	11.76	192	116.62	768	466	1,234
Foundation wall	7	C.Y.	2.77	19.39	154	103.47	1,078	724	1,802
Backfill	1	Job	8	8		412		412	412
Remove existing wood siding	180	S.F.	0.02	3.60		0.69		124	124
Miscellaneous demolition at connection	1	Job	4	4		121		121	121
Remove existing sliding glass door	1	Ea.	1.33	1.33		40.50		41	41
Remove asphalt shingle roofing	1	Sq.	1.14	1.14		34.50		35	35
Floor frame	200	L.F.	0.02	4	1.42	0.75	284	150	434
Sill plates	44	L.F.	0.04	1.76	1.07	1.50	47	66	113
Floor sheathing	192	S.F.	0.01	1.92	0.73	0.50	140	96	236
Top and bottom plates	126	L.F.	0.02	2.52	0.41	0.85	52	107	159
Studs	280	L.F.	0.01	2.80	0.41	0.61	115	171	286
Headers over windows and doors	48	L.F.	0.05	2.40	0.94	1.99	45	96	141
Wall sheathing	440	S.F.	0.01	4.40	0.68	0.60	299	264	563
Gable roof frame	260	L.F.	0.02	5.20	0.94	0.71	244	185	429
Ceiling joists	130	L.F.	0.01	1.30	0.65	0.54	85	70	155
Ridge board	26	L.F.	0.04	1.04	1.42	1.69	37	44	81
Jack rafter nailing board	20	L.F.	0.04	0.80	0.47	1.69	9	34	43
Jack rafters	84	L.F.	0.02	1.68	0.94	0.94	79	79	158
Roof sheathing	440	S.F.	0.01	4.40	0.73	0.52	321	229	550
Self-adhering underlayment	2	Sq.	0.36	0.72	50.50	14.10	101	28	129
Roofing underlayment	300	S.F.	0.01	3	0.04	0.09	12	27	39
Asphalt shingle roofing	5	Sq.	2.29	11.45	69	88.50	345	443	788
Step flashing	20	Ea.	0.01	0.20	0.13	0.16	3	3	6
Ridge vent strip	16	L.F.	0.05	0.80	2.97	1.94	48	31	79
Siding, cedar shingles	2	Sq.	3.90	7.80	137	165	274	330	604
Exterior trim at doors, windows, rakes, soffit, and fascia	300	L.F.	0.03	9	1.36	1.35	408	405	813
Gutters	32	L.F.	0.07	2.24	1.46	3.12	47	100	147
Downspouts	20	L.F.	0.04	0.80	0.94	1.97	19	39	58
Furring	208	L.F.	0.02	4.16	0.31	0.97	64	202	266
Wall insulation	150	S.F.	0.01	1.50	0.52	0.21	78	32	110
Ceiling insulation	192	S.F.	0.01	1.92	0.53	0.21	102	40	142
Sliding glass doors	3	Opng.	5.33	15.99	2425	225	7,275	675	7,950
Single doors	2	Ea.	1.14	2.28	655	48.50	1,310	97	1,407
Transom windows over sliders	3	Ea.	0.73	2.19	435	30.50	1,305	92	1,397
Transom windows over single doors	2	Ea.	0.67	1.34	246	28	492	56	548
Gypsum wallboard	384	S.F.	0.02	7.68	0.34	0.70	131	269	400
Trim	155	L.F.	0.03	4.65	2.43	1.41	377	219	596
Paint walls and ceilings, primer	420	S.F.	0.01	4.20	0.05	0.22	21	92	113
Paint trim, primer	155	L.F.	0.01	1.55	0.03	0.46	5	71	76
Paint walls and ceilings, 2 coats	420	S.F.	0.01	4.20	0.05	0.22	21	92	113
Paint trim, 2 coats finish	300	L.F.	0.01	3	0.03	0.46	9	138	147

Project Estimate (continued)

Description	Quantity		Labor		Cost per Unit		Total Cost		
	Quantity	Unit	Labor Hrs Per Unit	Labor Hrs Total	Material Per Unit	Installation Per Unit	Material Total	Installation Total	Total
Ceramic tile floor	192	S.F.	0.05	9.60	4.33	1.69	831	324	1,155
Subcontract									
Duplex receptacles	4	Ea.	1.50	6	29	69	116	276	392
Electrical switch	1	Ea.	1.40	1.40	31	64.50	31	65	96
Ceiling fan	1	Ea.	1	1	107	46	107	46	153
Dumpster	1	Week	1	1	370	33.50	370	34	404
Subtotals							17,505	8,152	25,657
General Requirements (Site Overhead)						12%	2,101	978	3,079
Subtotals							19,606	9,130	28,736
Overhead and Profit						10%	1,961	913	2,874
Subtotals							21,567	10,043	31,610

Grand Total   **$31,610**

Note: Estimate is based on typical project materials available at home centers and may not include all elements in photo. Costs are national averages; see the Location Factors at the back of the book to adjust them to your area.

Cost per Square Foot   **$164**

Alternates (Installed Costs)

	Unit	Total Cost
Flooring		
Sheet vinyl	S.F.	$5
Linoleum	S.F.	$6
Stone	S.F.	$22
Brick	S.F.	$10
Electrical		
Weatherproof cover for receptacle	Ea.	$16
Exhaust fan	Ea.	$112
Ceiling light fixture	Ea.	$133

A sunroom's design should connect as much as possible with the landscaping surrounding the structure. Carefully consider the views from inside the room and from the gardens.

Glass roofs, often discouraged because they're hard to maintain and may not accommodate ceiling fans, can be tricky to build and are best subcontracted to greenhouse contractors or glass dealers.

Tinted glass and easy-to-operate shading systems are advised for glass roofs and skylights. Ventilating skylights and/or a thermostatically-controlled exhaust fan are useful features.

Additions

Project Worksheet

	Unit	Quantity	Price per Unit	Total	Dimensions	Source/Model#/ Specs

Bump-out Addition

*T*hese small-scale additions – often extending just 2'– 4', can have a surprising impact on the appearance and function of the space within. They're a good solution for homeowners with limited budgets, since they often can be built without an additional foundation or major roof re-framing, unlike a full-size room addition. If the existing foundation can support a bump-out, this may also be a way around setback limitations, which usually apply to the foundation footprint.

Bump-outs are often incorporated into major kitchen and bath renovations, expanding the space and sometimes adding dining nooks or space to house new fixtures. They're also used for half baths – a good investment for the homeowner in resale value – and for mudrooms, which provide both a thermal buffer zone and valuable storage space. Another use for bump-outs is adding a front entry, again providing a thermal buffer, as well as a more formal entrance. More or larger windows or French doors are typically part of these projects, brightening the area and creating a new focal point for the room. They also make great window seats.

Since bump-outs, like dormers and full additions, have a big impact on the exterior of the house, a careful, harmonious design is important. Some homeowners may want to consult an architect.

Structural issues with this project include an evaluation of the foundation, since bump-outs place additional stress on a section of it. It may be necessary to add piers to help support the foundation, or reinforcing to the foundation itself. It's best to consult an engineer on structural questions.

This project estimate covers the work involved in constructing a 10' x 3' bump-out addition to expand a kitchen for a dining nook. In this case, the work includes a foundation and footings, along with framing, roofing, insulation, and siding, as well as window and trim installation. Interior finish items are hardwood flooring, gypsum wallboard, and paint.

Project Estimate

Description	Quantity		Labor		Cost per Unit		Total Cost		
	Quantity	Unit	Labor Hrs Per Unit	Labor Hrs Total	Material Per Unit	Installation Per Unit	Material Total	Installation Total	Total
Self-Performed									
Temporary shoring partition	10	L.F.	0.13	1.30	2.86	5.40	29	54	83
Demolish exterior wall framing and interior finish	2	Job	2	4		60.50		121	121
Jack studs and opening header	1	Ea.	0.27	0.27	72	11.25	72	11	83
Remove siding	150	S.F.	0.02	3		0.69		104	104
Excavate by hand for foundation	2	Job	2	4		60.50		121	121
Concrete footing	1	C.Y.	2.49	2.49	116	99.02	116	99	216
Concrete block foundation wall	56	S.F.	0.09	5.04	2.54	3.62	142	203	345
Backfilling by hand	1	Job	2	2		60.50		61	61
Sills	14	L.F.	0.05	0.70	2.71	1.93	38	27	65
Floor joists	38	L.F.	0.01	0.38	0.94	0.61	36	23	59
Plywood subfloor	20	SF Flr.	0.01	0.20	0.73	0.50	15	10	25
Small window framing	4	Ea.	0.33	1.32	18.20	14.10	73	56	129
Large window framing	1	Ea.	0.36	0.36	59	15.35	59	15	74
Plywood sheathing	112	S.F.	0.01	1.12	0.68	0.60	76	67	143
Common roof rafters	46	L.F.	0.03	1.38	0.65	1.15	30	53	83
Ceiling joists	38	L.F.	0.01	0.38	0.65	0.54	25	21	46
Hip roof rafters	8	L.F.	0.03	0.24	0.94	1.44	8	12	20
Plywood roof sheathing	32	S.F.	0.01	0.32	0.68	0.48	22	15	37
Soffit	14	L.F.	0.04	0.56	0.61	1.61	9	23	32
Fascia	14	L.F.	0.04	0.56	2.09	1.50	29	21	50
Cornice trim	14	L.F.	0.03	0.42	1.12	1.13	16	16	32
Drip edge	14	L.F.	0.02	0.28	0.54	0.85	8	12	20
Ice barrier	1	Sq.	0.36	0.36	50.50	14.10	51	14	65
Asphalt roof shingles	1	Sq.	1.78	1.78	52	69	52	69	121
Step flashing	20	Ea.	0.01	0.20	0.13	0.16	3	3	6
Head flashing	8	S.F.	0.06	0.48	3.33	2.30	27	18	45
Small casement windows	4	Ea.	1	4	390	42.50	1,560	170	1,730
Large casement window	1	Ea.	1	1	715	42.50	715	43	758
Exterior finish plywood	28	S.F.	0.04	1.12	1.97	1.50	55	42	97
Vertical trim boards	100	L.F.	0.03	3	1.36	1.35	136	135	271
Panel trim molding	40	L.F.	0.03	1.20	0.72	1.25	29	50	79
Water table trim	14	L.F.	0.02	0.28	0.40	1.02	6	14	20
Water table	14	L.F.	0.04	0.56	1.58	1.69	22	24	46
Siding shingles	2	Sq.	4	8	179	169	358	338	696
Wall insulation	52	S.F.	0.01	0.52	0.32	0.21	17	11	28
Ceiling insulation	20	S.F.	0.01	0.20	0.78	0.25	16	5	21
Gypsum wallboard on walls	112	S.F.	0.02	2.24	0.34	0.70	38	78	116
Gypsum wallboard on ceiling	20	S.F.	0.02	0.40	0.34	0.88	7	18	25
Window trim	6	Opng.	0.80	4.80	38.50	34	231	204	435
Baseboard	14	L.F.	0.03	0.42	2.43	1.41	34	20	54
Hardwood flooring	20	S.F.	0.09	1.80	4.08	3.76	82	75	157
Finish hardwood flooring	20	S.F.	0.03	0.60	0.78	0.82	16	16	32
Paint window exterior	6	Ea.	1.60	9.60	2.73	59.50	16	357	373
Paint window interior	6	Ea.	1.60	9.60	2.38	59.50	14	357	371
Paint trim and plywood	112	S.F.	0.03	3.36	0.25	0.94	28	105	133
Prime gypsum wallboard, brushwork	80	S.F.	0.01	0.80	0.05	0.26	4	21	25
Prime gypsum wallboard, roller	112	S.F.	0.01	1.12	0.05	0.22	6	25	31
Paint gypsum wallboard, brushwork	80	S.F.	0.01	0.80	0.11	0.44	9	35	44

Project Estimate (continued)

Description	Quantity		Labor		Cost per Unit		Total Cost		
	Quantity	Unit	Labor Hrs Per Unit	Labor Hrs Total	Material Per Unit	Installation Per Unit	Material Total	Installation Total	Total
Paint gypsum wallboard, roller	112	S.F.	0.01	1.12	0.12	0.37	13	41	54
Prime and paint baseboard	14	L.F.	0.02	0.28	0.09	0.91	1	13	14
Subcontract									
Dumpster	1	Week	1	1	385	33.50	385	34	419
Subtotals							4,734	3,480	8,215
General Requirements (Site Overhead)						12%	568	418	986
Subtotals							5,302	3,898	9,201
Overhead and Profit						10%	530	390	920
Subtotals							5,832	4,288	10,121

Grand Total $10,121

Note: Estimate is based on typical project materials available at home centers and may not include all elements in photo. Costs are national averages; see the Location Factors at the back of the book to adjust them to your area.

Cost per Square Foot $506

Alternates (Installed Costs)

	Unit	Total Cost
Flooring		
Sheet vinyl	S.F.	$5
Linoleum	S.F.	$6
Stone	S.F.	$22
Brick	S.F.	$10
Floating laminate	S.F.	$6
Hardwood	S.F.	$8

A bump-out addition can have a variety of uses. This one provides a cheerful sitting and reading area.

Additions

Project Worksheet

	Unit	Quantity	Price per Unit	Total	Dimensions	Source/Model#/ Specs

12' × 16' First-Floor Addition

This type of addition is often built to house an office, playroom, or family room, or as part of a kitchen expansion. Although modestly sized, it will still have a big impact on the home's appearance and therefore may be designed by an architect. It will need to blend with the existing house in terms of windows, trim, roof pitch, and many other details. It will also need to work well on the inside, in terms of access, traffic patterns, and function of the rest of the house.

Tying into the existing house can involve complications and clearly requires a very thorough site investigation (including assessing mechanical/electrical issues) before you estimate the job. This size addition may be accommodated by the existing HVAC and electrical systems, but their capacity should be assessed at the start. You'll also want to check codes concerning setbacks and footprint-as-a-percentage-of-property restrictions, septic capacity, and other regulations.

Matching the exterior details may require some creative thinking, especially with budget constraints. If the existing house has a stone foundation, for example, you might consider cultured (or artificial) stone, which is lighter and about half the price of natural stone. Another cost-cutter is molded high-density polymer millwork in place of wood.

This project estimate is for a 12' x 16' first-floor family room addition. It includes excavation and foundation, framing, sheathing, roofing (asphalt shingles) and flashing, siding (cedar shingles), gutters/downspouts, insulation, and trim. There are also four windows and a French door. Interior items are drywall, carpet, trim, and paint. Electrical costs cover wiring and installation for four outlets and one wall switch, cable TV, a phone jack, and an Internet receptacle.

See the Introduction to the Additions section for more on foundations, framing, and other issues to consider.

Project Estimate

Description	Quantity		Labor		Cost per Unit		Total Cost		
	Quantity	Unit	Labor Hrs Per Unit	Labor Hrs Total	Material Per Unit	Installation Per Unit	Material Total	Installation Total	Total
Self-Performed									
Excavate for foundation	1	Job	8	8		412		412	412
Footings	2	C.Y.	2.94	5.88	192	116.62	384	233	617
Foundation wall	176	S.F.	0.09	15.84	2.54	3.62	447	637	1,084
Backfill	1	Job	8	8		412		412	412
Remove wood shingles	126	S.F.	0.02	2.52		0.69		87	87
Floor frame	192	L.F.	0.02	3.84	1.42	0.75	273	144	417
Sill plates	96	L.F.	0.04	3.84	1.07	1.50	103	144	247
Floor sheathing	192	S.F.	0.01	1.92	0.73	0.50	140	96	236
Top and bottom plates	144	L.F.	0.02	2.88	0.41	0.85	59	122	181
Studs	320	L.F.	0.01	3.20	0.41	0.61	131	195	326
Headers over windows and doors	36	L.F.	0.05	1.80	0.94	1.99	34	72	106
Wall sheathing	384	S.F.	0.01	3.84	0.68	0.60	261	230	491
Remove roof shingles	1	Sq.	1.14	1.14		34.50		35	35
Jack rafter nailer	1	L.F.	0.04	0.04	0.94	1.69	1	2	3
Gable roof frame	314	L.F.	0.02	6.28	0.65	0.68	204	214	418
Ceiling joists	156	L.F.	0.01	1.56	0.65	0.54	101	84	185
Ridge board	24	L.F.	0.04	0.96	0.94	1.50	23	36	59
Roof sheathing	360	S.F.	0.01	3.60	0.73	0.52	263	187	450
Exterior trim	144	L.F.	0.04	5.76	1.58	1.69	228	243	471
Roofing underlayment	4	S.F.	0.01	0.04	0.04	0.09			
Asphalt shingle roofing	4	Sq.	2.29	9.16	69	88.50	276	354	630
Additional labor for roof at connection	1	Job	4	4		155		155	155
Wall flashing	16	S.F.	0.06	0.96	0.62	2.14	10	34	44
Ridge vent strip	16	L.F.	0.05	0.80	2.97	1.94	48	31	79
Siding, cedar shingles	3	Sq.	3.90	11.70	137	165	411	495	906
Gutters	34	L.F.	0.07	2.38	1.46	3.12	50	106	156
Downspouts	20	L.F.	0.04	0.80	0.94	1.97	19	39	58
Wall insulation	400	S.F.	0.01	4	0.52	0.21	208	84	292
Ceiling insulation	200	S.F.	0.01	2	0.53	0.21	106	42	148
French door	1	Ea.	4	4	1400	169	1,400	169	1,569
Double-hung windows	3	Ea.	0.89	2.67	385	37.50	1,155	113	1,268
Casement window	1	Ea.	0.94	0.94	560	40	560	40	600
Gypsum wallboard	648	S.F.	0.02	12.96	0.34	0.70	220	454	674
Carpet	207	S.F.	0.02	4.14	1.51	0.69	313	143	456
Carpet pad	207	S.F.	0.01	2.07	0.28	0.23	58	48	106
Interior trim	170	L.F.	0.03	5.10	2.43	1.41	413	240	653
Paint walls and ceilings, primer	420	S.F.	0.01	4.20	0.05	0.22	21	92	113
Paint door and frame, primer	1	Ea.	1.33	1.33	2.01	49.50	2	50	52
Paint window, incl. frame and trim, primer	3	Ea.	0.57	1.71	0.32	21	1	63	64
Paint trim, primer	155	L.F.	0.01	1.55	0.03	0.46	5	71	76
Paint walls and ceilings, 2 coats	420	S.F.	0.01	4.20	0.05	0.22	21	92	113
Paint door and frame, 2 coats	1	Ea.	1.33	1.33	2.01	49.50	2	50	52
Paint window, incl. frame and trim, 2 coats	3	Ea.	0.57	1.71	0.32	21	1	63	64
Paint trim, 2 coats finish	170	L.F.	0.01	1.70	0.03	0.46	5	78	83
Paint exterior trim	144	L.F.	0.01	1.44	0.07	0.46	10	66	76

Project Estimate (continued)

Description	Quantity		Labor		Cost per Unit		Total Cost		
	Quantity	Unit	Labor Hrs Per Unit	Labor Hrs Total	Material Per Unit	Installation Per Unit	Material Total	Installation Total	Total
Subcontract									
Baseboard radiation	30	L.F.	0.28	8.40	7.35	11.60	221	348	569
Thermostat	1	Ea.	1	1	29.50	47	30	47	77
Copper pipe	100	L.F.	0.10	10	2.36	4.76	236	476	712
Copper fittings	20	Ea.	0.42	8.40	1.25	19.55	25	391	416
Duplex receptacles	4	Ea.	1.50	6	29	69	116	276	392
Wall switch	1	Ea.	1.40	1.40	31	64.50	31	65	96
Cable TV receptacle	1	Ea.	0.50	0.50	14.50	23	15	23	38
Computer receptacle	1	Ea.	0.50	0.50	14.50	23	15	23	38
Phone jack	1	Ea.	0.31	0.31	8.70	14.10	9	14	23
Dumpster	1	Week	1	1	385	33.50	385	34	419
Subtotals							9,050	8,454	17,504
General Requirements (Site Overhead)						12%	1,086	1,014	2,100
Subtotals							10,136	9,468	19,604
Overhead and Profit						10%	1,014	947	1,960
Subtotals							11,150	10,415	21,564

Grand Total $21,564

Note: Estimate is based on typical project materials available at home centers and may not include all elements in photo. Costs are national averages; see the Location Factors at the back of the book to adjust them to your area.

Cost per Square Foot   **$112**

Alternates (Installed Costs)

	Unit	Total Cost
Roofing		
Aluminum shingles	Sq.	$262
Laminated asphalt shingles	Sq.	$121
Red cedar shingles	Sq.	$340
Slate shingles	Sq.	$815
Steel shingles	Sq.	$340
Clay tiles	Sq.	$465
Concrete tiles	Sq.	$335
Standing seam copper roofing	Sq.	$755
Siding		
Aluminum	S.F.	$3
Fiber-cement	S.F.	$3
Vinyl	S.F.	$2
Cedar clapboard	S.F.	$5
Rough-sawn vertical cedar	S.F.	$5
Texture 1-11	S.F.	$4
Flooring		
Floating laminate	S.F.	$6
Sheet vinyl	S.F.	$5
Linoleum	S.F.	$6
12" x 12" ceramic tile	S.F.	$6
Stone	S.F.	$22
Lighting		
Ceiling light fixture	Ea.	$133
Molding		
Crown molding	L.F.	$3

Inform homeowners early of steps involved in the work. This project can intrude heavily upon their daily lives, especially if it involves the kitchen.

Project Worksheet

	Unit	Quantity	Price per Unit	Total	Dimensions	Source/Model#/ Specs

20' × 25' First-Floor Addition

his type of addition often houses a new family room and expanded kitchen, or a new master suite. As with all additions, and especially ones of this size, the design is of foremost importance. To protect the homeowner's investment, the addition needs to blend with the existing house in both scale and style. The enlarged house should also fit with the sizes of other homes in the neighborhood.

If the project is a new family room/ kitchen, it could easily involve a team of designers – architect, structural engineer, interior designer, kitchen specialist, and maybe even a lighting designer. This will add to the project management/ coordination tasks. If you're the primary designer as well as the builder, here are some issues and possible design

features you'll want to discuss with the homeowner:

- Degree of openness between family room and kitchen
- Columns, arches, or angled walls
- Cathedral or vaulted ceiling
- Gas- or wood-burning fireplace – and size/type of surrounding materials
- Types of doors and windows and skylights (including desired level of natural light and ventilation)
- Heating/cooling issues from sunlight
- Visibility between areas and for TV viewing
- Wiring for cable TV, home theater components, computers, etc.
- Space to house a large TV and electronic equipment

- Kitchen elements, including functional layout for the household's needs (eating, entertaining, bill-paying or studying, baking center, display areas for china or artwork, pets' feeding areas, etc.); whether there will be a pantry, island, or breakfast nook; types of counters, sinks, cabinets/accessories, flooring, and appliances

If the space will be used as a master suite, a similar team of designers could be involved – in this case, an architect, interior designer, and bath or lighting specialist. In discussing the project with your client, consider these possible features:

- Bath with separate shower and tub (if a whirlpool, 220-volt electrical will be needed) and dual vanities or pedestal sinks

- Walk-in closets
- Sitting area with fireplace
- Skylights
- French doors to patio
- Cathedral ceiling
- Natural light, ventilation
- Heat/cooling issues from sunlight
- Wiring for cable TV, computers, etc.

This project estimate is based on a 20' x 25' first-floor addition, housing a new kitchen and family room. Items involved in building the structure include excavation/foundation; framing and sheathing; roofing/gutters; French doors and three double-hung windows; and floor, ceiling, and wall treatments. Fitting out the island kitchen requires installation of mid-priced stock cabinets, solid-surface countertops, appliances, and ceramic tile flooring, as well as finish painting. Subcontracted plumbing involves piping and installation of the kitchen sink and dishwasher. Electrical includes wiring and outlets, four under-cabinet light fixtures, and eight recessed light fixtures.

Project Estimate

Description	Quantity	Unit	Labor Hrs Per Unit	Labor Hrs Total	Material Per Unit	Installation Per Unit	Material Total	Installation Total	Total
Self-Performed									
Excavate for foundation	1	Job	8	8		412		412	412
Footing	4	C.Y.	2.94	11.76	192	116.62	768	466	1,234
Foundation wall	272	S.F.	0.09	24.48	2.54	3.62	691	985	1,676
Backfill	1	Job	8	8		412		412	412
Floor frame	380	L.F.	0.02	7.60	1.42	0.75	540	285	825
Sill plates	68	L.F.	0.04	2.72	1.07	1.50	73	102	175
Floor sheathing	480	S.F.	0.01	4.80	0.73	0.50	350	240	590
Top and bottom plates	204	L.F.	0.02	4.08	0.41	0.85	84	173	257
Studs	604	L.F.	0.01	6.04	0.41	0.61	248	368	616
Headers over openings	52	L.F.	0.05	2.60	0.94	1.99	49	103	152
Wall sheathing	624	S.F.	0.01	6.24	0.68	0.60	424	374	798
Roof frame	608	L.F.	0.02	12.16	0.65	0.68	395	413	808
Ceiling joists	380	L.F.	0.01	3.80	0.65	0.54	247	205	452
Ridge board	24	L.F.	0.04	0.96	0.94	1.50	23	36	59
Roof sheathing	768	S.F.	0.01	7.68	0.73	0.52	561	399	960
Roofing underlayment	800	S.F.	0.01	8	0.04	0.09	32	72	104
Roofing, asphalt shingles	8	Sq.	2.29	18.32	69	88.50	552	708	1,260
Wall flashing	16	S.F.	0.06	0.96	0.62	2.14	10	34	44
Ridge vent strip	24	L.F.	0.05	1.20	2.97	1.94	71	47	118
Siding, cedar shingles	7	Sq.	3.90	27.30	137	165	959	1,155	2,114
Exterior trim	200	L.F.	0.04	8	1.58	1.69	316	338	654
Gutters	48	L.F.	0.07	3.36	1.46	3.12	70	150	220
Downspouts	20	L.F.	0.04	0.80	0.94	1.97	19	39	58
Wall insulation	544	S.F.	0.01	5.44	0.52	0.21	283	114	397
Ceiling insulation	480	S.F.	0.01	4.80	0.53	0.21	254	101	355
French doors	2	Ea.	4	8	1400	169	2,800	338	3,138
Double-hung window	2	Ea.	0.89	1.78	385	37.50	770	75	845
Interior partitions	16	L.F.	0.16	2.56	3.68	6.75	59	108	167
Heavy timber columns and beams	44	L.F.	0.07	3.08	13.70	2.82	603	124	727
Gypsum wallboard	1280	S.F.	0.02	25.60	0.34	0.70	435	896	1,331
Hardwood flooring	480	S.F.	0.09	43.20	4.08	3.76	1,958	1,805	3,763
Kitchen wall cabinets	7	Ea.	0.70	4.90	197	30	1,379	210	1,589
Kitchen sink base cabinets	1	Ea.	0.81	0.81	315	34	315	34	349
Kitchen oven cabinet	1	Ea.	2	2	650	84.50	650	85	735
Kitchen base cabinets	6	Ea.	0.79	4.74	345	33.50	2,070	201	2,271
Kitchen wall cabinet over refrigerator	1	Ea.	0.70	0.70	197	30	197	30	227
Solid surface countertop	24	L.F.	0.80	19.20	65.50	34	1,572	816	2,388
Solid surface kitchen sink	1	Ea.	4	4	445	169	445	169	614
Valance board trim	4	L.F.	0.04	0.16	9.25	1.71	37	7	44
Kitchen crown molding	12	L.F.	0.03	0.36	1.12	1.13	13	14	27

Project Estimate (continued)

Description	Quantity	Unit	Labor Hrs Per Unit	Labor Hrs Total	Material Per Unit	Installation Per Unit	Material Total	Installation Total	Total
Built-in oven	1	Ea.	2	2	435	92	435	92	527
Range hood	1	Ea.	2	2	42.50	86	43	86	129
Refrigerator	1	Ea.	2	2	580	60.50	580	61	641
Microwave oven	1	Ea.	2	2	94	92	94	92	186
Dishwasher	1	Ea.	5	5	620	232	620	232	852
Interior trim	172	L.F.	0.03	5.16	2.43	1.41	418	243	661
Paint gypsum wallboard, primer	1280	S.F.	0.01	12.80	0.05	0.22	64	282	346
Paint French doors, primer	2	Ea.	1.33	2.66	2.01	49.50	4	99	103
Paint window, incl. frame and trim, primer	2	Ea.	0.57	1.14	0.32	21	1	42	43
Paint trim, primer	172	L.F.	0.01	1.72	0.03	0.46	5	79	84
Paint walls and ceilings, 2 coats	1280	S.F.	0.01	12.80	0.05	0.22	64	282	346
Paint French doors	2	Ea.	1.33	2.66	2.01	49.50	4	99	103
Paint window, incl. frame and trim, 2 coats	2	Ea.	0.57	1.14	0.32	21	1	42	43
Paint trim, 2 coats finish	172	L.F.	0.01	1.72	0.03	0.46	5	79	84
Paint exterior trim	200	L.F.	0.01	2	0.07	0.46	14	92	106
Zero-clearance gas fireplace	1	Ea.	11.43	11.43	2975	485	2,975	485	3,460
Subcontract									
Kitchen faucet and drain	1	Ea.	0.80	0.80	56.50	37	57	37	94
Plumbing for kitchen sink	2	Ea.	7.48	14.96	143	310	286	620	906
Plumbing for dishwasher	1	Ea.	7.92	7.92	141	330	141	330	471
Baseboard radiation	40	L.F.	0.28	11.20	7.35	11.60	294	464	758
Thermostat	1	Ea.	1	1	29.50	47	30	47	77
Copper pipe	50	L.F.	0.10	5	2.36	4.76	118	238	356
Copper fittings	20	Ea.	0.42	8.40	1.25	19.55	25	391	416
Under-cabinet lighting	4	Ea.	0.33	1.32	58.50	15.30	234	61	295
Recessed lighting fixtures	8	Ea.	0.29	2.32	59.50	13.10	476	105	581
GFCI receptacles	3	Ea.	0.65	1.95	39	30	117	90	207
Duplex receptacles	12	Ea.	1.50	18	29	69	348	828	1,176
Electrical switches	6	Ea.	1.40	8.40	31	64.50	186	387	573
Dumpster	1	Week	1	1	415	33.50	415	34	449
Subtotals							28,376	18,662	47,038
General Requirements (Site Overhead)						12%	3,405	2,239	5,645
Subtotals							31,781	20,901	52,683
Overhead and Profit						10%	3,178	2,090	5,268
Subtotals							34,959	22,991	57,951

Grand Total $57,951

Note: Estimate is based on typical project materials available at home centers and may not include all elements in photo. Costs are national averages; see the Location Factors at the back of the book to adjust them to your area.

Cost per Square Foot $121

The addition's exterior should tie into the architecture of the existing house.

Alternates (Installed Costs)

	Unit	Total Cost
Roofing		
Aluminum shingles	Sq.	$262
Red cedar shingles	Sq.	$340
Laminated asphalt shingles	Sq.	$121
Slate shingles	Sq.	$815
Steel shingles	Sq.	$340
Clay tiles	Sq.	$465
Concrete tiles	Sq.	$335
Standing seam copper roofing	Sq.	$755
Siding		
Aluminum	S.F.	$3
Fiber-cement	S.F.	$3
Vinyl	S.F.	$2
Cedar clapboard	S.F.	$5
Rough-sawn vertical cedar	S.F.	$5
Texture 1-11	S.F.	$4
Flooring		
Floating laminate	S.F.	$6
Sheet vinyl	S.F.	$5
Linoleum	S.F.	$6
12" x 12" ceramic tile	S.F.	$6
Stone	S.F.	$22
Hardwood	S.F.	$8
Lighting		
Ceiling light fixture	Ea.	$133
Molding		
Crown molding	L.F.	$3

Island seating saves space in this combined family room/kitchen. High-end appliances, "furniture" style cabinetry, and continuous wood flooring help keep the room unified.

A 20' x 25' addition can be used for one large, open room, like the family room with fireplace and cathedral ceiling shown here.

The cost for a kitchen/ family room addition can range widely with the vast price differences in materials, appliances, and fixtures. Costs can quickly increase with exterior features like natural stone foundations and custom windows, and with interior items like high-end sinks and finish materials, appliances, and custom cabinetry. You can help guide your client to savings in some areas that will allow splurges in others.

20' × 25' First-Floor Addition

Project Worksheet

	Unit	Quantity	Price per Unit	Total	Dimensions	Source/Model#/ Specs

Project Worksheet

	Unit	Quantity	Price per Unit	Total	Dimensions	Source/Model#/ Specs

12' × 16' Second-Floor Bedroom Addition

dding a standard extra bedroom like the one in this project may not give quite as good a return on investment in resale value as a master suite – unless the existing home has a clear shortage compared to other homes in the area. But if staying in their location is important to a growing family, this improvement can have tremendous value by enhancing their everyday lives.

The fundamental construction issue is the first-floor framing and foundation, and whether additional support will be needed for a second story. Careful site visits (with your electrician and possibly plumber and air conditioning/furnace contractor) will help uncover potential complications and define the extent of the work.

Existing mechanical and electrical systems will need to be assessed to determine whether they can service the additional space. If the home has a septic system,

there may also be zoning restrictions on the total number of bedrooms based on its size.

The first tasks in this project include roof removal, appropriate reinforcement of ceiling joists, and wall and roof framing and sheathing. The exterior second-story wall that the addition joins onto will need preparation, and an opening will need to be cut and framed into a hallway to connect the addition to the rest of the second floor. You may be able to use an existing window opening as part of the new doorway.

The next steps are partitioning for a closet and any built-ins, insulating, electrical and plumbing rough-in (for heating), then drywall, trim, and finishes. If the space below is unheated, such as a screened porch, you'll need to insulate the floor as well as the new walls and ceiling. Extra insulation and staggered framing may also be needed between the

new space and an adjoining bathroom for sound reduction.

Take into account planning and execution time for any complex roof angles and valleys that will be part of this project. And don't forget time and costs for demolition of the old roof and protection of the exposed interior during construction.

This project estimate lists the costs to construct a 12' x 16' second-floor room addition. It includes demolition and removal of siding, roofing, sheathing, studs, and a window, as well as gutters and downspouts. The rest of the exterior costs are for framing and sheathing, roofing (asphalt shingles), siding (cedar shingles), a picture window and two double-hung units, and new gutters/downspouts. Interior items include insulation, drywall, carpet, trim, building a clothes closet, and painting. For electrical, there are four outlets, wiring, and a switch.

Project Estimate

Description	Quantity	Unit	Labor Hrs Per Unit	Labor Hrs Total	Material Per Unit	Installation Per Unit	Material Total	Installation Total	Total
Self-Performed									
Remove existing roof shingles	3	Sq.	1.14	3.42		34.50		104	104
Remove existing roof sheathing	288	S.F.	0.01	2.88		0.35		101	101
Remove existing roof rafters	240	L.F.	0.02	4.80		0.58		139	139
Remove existing rake, soffit, and fascia	126	L.F.	0.01	1.26		0.22		28	28
Remove existing masonry/stucco siding	200	S.F.	0.06	12		1.73		346	346
Remove existing plywood sheathing	64	S.F.	0.01	0.64		0.43		28	28
Remove existing gable end studs	52	L.F.	0.01	0.52		0.24		12	12
Remove window	1	Ea.	0.40	0.40		12.10		12	12
Miscellaneous demolition at window removal	1	Job	2	2		60.50		61	61
Remove existing gutter and downspouts as necessary	40	L.F.	0.03	1.20		1.01		40	40
Debris removal	20	C.Y.	0.87	17.40		26		520	520
Miscellaneous protection during construction	10	Job	2	20		84.50		845	845
Sister new joists to existing ceiling framing	160	L.F.	0.02	3.20	1.42	0.75	227	120	347
Floor sheathing	192	S.F.	0.01	1.92	0.73	0.50	140	96	236
Top and bottom plates	120	L.F.	0.02	2.40	0.41	0.85	49	102	151
Studs	320	L.F.	0.01	3.20	0.41	0.61	131	195	326
Header over windows	22	L.F.	0.05	1.10	0.94	1.99	21	44	65
Gable studs	52	L.F.	0.02	1.04	0.41	0.75	21	39	60
Wall sheathing	384	S.F.	0.01	3.84	0.68	0.60	261	230	491
Gable roof frame	240	L.F.	0.02	4.80	0.65	0.68	156	163	319
Ceiling joists	160	L.F.	0.01	1.60	0.65	0.54	104	86	190
Furring	156	L.F.	0.02	3.12	0.31	0.97	48	151	199
Closet partitions	16	L.F.	0.16	2.56	3.68	6.75	59	108	167
Ridge board	12	L.F.	0.04	0.48	0.94	1.50	11	18	29
Roof sheathing	320	S.F.	0.01	3.20	0.73	0.52	234	166	400
Rake, rake trim, soffit, and fascia	128	L.F.	0.04	5.12	1.58	1.69	202	216	418
Drip edge	24	L.F.	0.02	0.48	0.54	0.85	13	20	33
Roofing underlayment	320	S.F.	0.01	3.20	0.04	0.09	13	29	42
Asphalt shingle roofing	4	Sq.	2.29	9.16	69	88.50	276	354	630
Ridge vent strip	12	L.F.	0.05	0.60	2.97	1.94	36	23	59
Housewrap	400	S.F.	0.01	4	0.20	0.09	80	36	116
Brick veneer	400	S.F.	0.18	72	3.61	7	1,444	2,800	4,244
Lintels	14	L.F.	0.11	1.54	7.15	4.86	100	68	168
Gutters	24	L.F.	0.07	1.68	1.46	3.12	35	75	110
Downspouts and elbows	40	L.F.	0.04	1.60	0.94	1.97	38	79	117
Bi-passing closet doors	1	Opng.	1.60	1.60	520	67.50	520	68	588
Room entry door	1	Ea.	0.84	0.84	292	35.50	292	36	328
Closet door trim	2	Opng.	1.60	3.20	28	67.50	56	135	191
Room entry door trim	2	Opng.	1.36	2.72	24	57.50	48	115	163
Wall insulation	320	S.F.	0.01	3.20	0.52	0.21	166	67	233
Ceiling insulation	200	S.F.	0.01	2	0.53	0.21	106	42	148
Picture window	1	Ea.	1.45	1.45	345	61.50	345	62	407
Double-hung windows	2	Ea.	0.89	1.78	385	37.50	770	75	845
Gypsum wallboard	696	S.F.	0.02	13.92	0.34	0.70	237	487	724
Carpet	192	S.F.	0.02	3.84	1.51	0.69	290	132	422
Carpet pad	192	S.F.	0.01	1.92	0.28	0.23	54	44	98
Baseboard trim	76	L.F.	0.03	2.28	2.43	1.41	185	107	292
Closet shelf and pole	8	L.F.	0.13	1.04	2.40	5.65	19	45	64
Paint walls and ceilings, primer	696	S.F.	0.01	6.96	0.05	0.22	35	153	188
Paint doors and frames, primer	3	Ea.	1.33	3.99	2.01	49.50	6	149	155

12' × 16' Second-Floor Bedroom Addition

Project Estimate (continued)

Description	Quantity	Unit	Labor Hrs Per Unit	Labor Hrs Total	Material Per Unit	Installation Per Unit	Material Total	Installation Total	Total
Paint window, incl. frame and trim, primer	3	Ea.	0.57	1.71	0.32	21	1	63	64
Paint trim, primer	206	L.F.	0.01	2.06	0.03	0.46	6	95	101
Paint walls and ceilings, 2 coats	696	S.F.	0.01	6.96	0.05	0.22	35	153	188
Paint doors and frames, 2 coats	3	Ea.	1.33	3.99	2.01	49.50	6	149	155
Paint window, incl. frame and trim, 2 coats	3	Ea.	0.57	1.71	0.32	21	1	63	64
Paint trim, 2 coats finish	206	L.F.	0.01	2.06	0.03	0.46	6	95	101
Subcontract									
Baseboard radiation	30	L.F.	0.28	8.40	7.35	11.60	221	348	569
Copper pipe	20	L.F.	0.10	2	2.36	4.76	47	95	142
Copper fittings	10	Ea.	0.42	4.20	1.25	19.55	13	196	209
Duplex receptacles	4	Ea.	1.50	6	29	69	116	276	392
Wall switch	1	Ea.	1.40	1.40	31	64.50	31	65	96
Electrician minimum	1	Job	4	4		184		184	184
Dumpster	1	Week	1	1	370	33.50	370	34	404
Subtotals							7,681	10,987	18,668
General Requirements (Site Overhead)						12%	922	1,318	2,240
Subtotals							8,603	12,305	20,908
Overhead and Profit						10%	860	1,231	2,091
Subtotals							9,463	13,536	22,999

Grand Total

Note: Estimate is based on typical project materials available at home centers and may not include all elements in photo. Costs are national averages; see the Location Factors at the back of the book to adjust them to your area.

Grand Total $22,999

Cost per Square Foot $120

Alternates (Installed Costs)

	Unit	Total Cost
Roofing		
Red cedar shingles	Sq.	$340
Laminated asphalt shingles	Sq.	$121
Slate shingles	Sq.	$815
Steel shingles	Sq.	$340
Clay tiles	Sq.	$465
Concrete tiles	Sq.	$335
Siding		
Aluminum	S.F.	$3
Fiber-cement	S.F.	$3
Vinyl	S.F.	$2
Cedar clapboard	S.F.	$5
Rough-sawn vertical cedar	S.F.	$5
Texture 1-11	S.F.	$4
Flooring		
Floating laminate	S.F.	$6
12" × 12" ceramic tile	S.F.	$6
Stone	S.F.	$22
Hardwood	S.F.	$8
Lighting		
Ceiling light fixture	Ea.	$133
Molding		
Crown molding	L.F.	$3
Fireplace		
Pre-manufactured zero-clearance gas fireplace	Ea.	$3,450

Homeowners may want to consult with an architect on a project like this since it has such a big effect on the home's exterior appearance.

The addition's windows (style, size, and placement), roof line, overhang, trim, siding, and roofing materials must blend with those of the existing house. On a very old home, you may need approval for the changes from a local historic commission.

Project Worksheet

	Unit	Quantity	Price per Unit	Total	Dimensions	Source/Model#/ Specs

20' x 25.5' Second-Floor Master Suite Addition

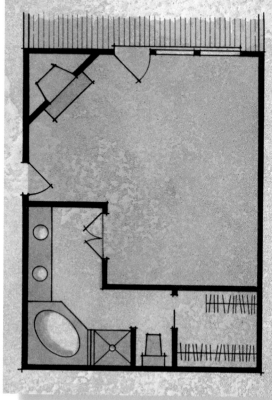

Realtors generally agree that a new master suite will make a strong contribution to a home's resale value. (The key is making sure it doesn't create a house much larger than others in the neighborhood.) These additions are often built over an attached garage or one-story wing of the house, typically adding about 500 S.F. of new interior space. A successful addition must blend with the existing house's roof line, style of overhang, and other architectural features.

Today's master suites often have vaulted ceilings and include walk-in closets; a sitting area; a large bath with two vanities or pedestal sinks, and separate tub and shower; and amenities such as a fireplace, balcony, or skylights. Many homeowners will want to work with an architect

and other specialists (interior, bath, and lighting) to define their plans.

A first step in this project is evaluation of the first-floor framing to assess its ability to support the new load. The first-floor roof must be removed, and the ceiling joists reinforced. If they're 2 x 8s or larger and supported by a center beam, reinforcement should be minimal. If they're 2 x 6s, substantial reinforcement will be needed.

Next is the plywood decking, then new wall and roof framing and sheathing. When the exterior is complete and weathertight, a doorway opening can be cut from the new addition to the house interior. Interior partitioning, insulation, electrical, and plumbing are next, followed by drywall, trim, and finishes. Insulation goes not only in the new walls

and ceiling, but the floor below if the addition is above an unheated garage.

The estimate shown here is based on a 20' x 25.5' addition. Labor and materials cover everything from the demolition of existing roofing, siding, and a window – to framing and sheathing, roofing (asphalt shingles), siding (cedar shingles), and gutters/downspouts. In addition to insulation, drywall, and painting, there are many special interior items, including a gas fireplace and multi-fixture bath, as well as a pocket door on the closet. The electrical work includes not only wiring and outlets for the bedroom and bath, but a bath ventilation fan, whirlpool tub hookup, recessed fixtures, and phone and CATV jacks.

Refer to the Introduction to the Additions section for more project tips.

Project Estimate

Description	Quantity		Labor		Cost per Unit		Total Cost		
	Quantity	Unit	Labor Hrs Per Unit	Labor Hrs Total	Material Per Unit	Installation Per Unit	Material Total	Installation Total	Total
Self-Performed									
Remove existing roof shingles	7	Sq.	1.14	7.98		34.50		242	242
Remove existing roof sheathing	640	S.F.	0.01	6.40		0.35		224	224
Remove existing roof rafters	512	L.F.	0.02	10.24		0.58		297	297
Remove existing rake, soffit, and fascia	144	L.F.	0.01	1.44		0.22		32	32
Remove existing siding	304	S.F.	0.02	6.08		0.69		210	210
Remove existing plywood sheathing	100	S.F.	0.01	1		0.43		43	43
Remove existing gable end studs	105	L.F.	0.01	1.05		0.24		25	25
Remove window	1	Ea.	0.40	0.40		12.10		12	12
Miscellaneous demolition at window removal	1	Job	2	2		60.50		61	61
Sister new joists to existing ceiling framing	448	L.F.	0.02	8.96	1.42	0.75	636	336	972
Floor sheathing	510	S.F.	0.01	5.10	0.73	0.50	372	255	627
Top and bottom plates	200	L.F.	0.02	4	0.41	0.85	82	170	252
Studs	560	L.F.	0.01	5.60	0.41	0.61	230	342	572
Header over windows	24	L.F.	0.05	1.20	0.94	1.99	23	48	71
Gable studs	105	L.F.	0.02	2.10	0.41	0.75	43	79	122
Wall sheathing	624	S.F.	0.01	6.24	0.68	0.60	424	374	798
Truss roof frame	11	Ea.	0.77	8.47	106	42.45	1,166	467	1,633
Furring	420	L.F.	0.02	8.40	0.31	0.97	130	407	537
Roof sheathing	640	S.F.	0.01	6.40	0.73	0.52	467	333	800
Rake, rake trim, soffit, and fascia	144	L.F.	0.04	5.76	1.58	1.69	228	243	471
Drip edge	40	L.F.	0.02	0.80	0.54	0.85	22	34	56
Roofing underlayment	640	S.F.	0.01	6.40	0.04	0.09	26	58	84
Asphalt shingle roofing	7	Sq.	2.29	16.03	69	88.50	483	620	1,103
Ridge vent strip	20	L.F.	0.05	1	2.97	1.94	59	39	98
Siding, cedar shingles	7	Sq.	3.90	27.30	137	165	959	1,155	2,114
Gutters	40	L.F.	0.07	2.80	1.46	3.12	58	125	183
Downspouts and elbows	40	L.F.	0.04	1.60	0.94	1.97	38	79	117
New room entry door	1	Ea.	0.84	0.84	292	35.50	292	36	328
Room entry door trim	2	Opng.	1.36	2.72	24	57.50	48	115	163
Wall insulation	524	S.F.	0.01	5.24	0.52	0.21	272	110	382
Ceiling insulation	510	S.F.	0.01	5.10	0.53	0.21	270	107	377
Deck door	1	Ea.	1.14	1.14	655	48.50	655	49	704
Bathroom entry door	1	Pr.	2.29	2.29	1350	96.50	1,350	97	1,447
Bathroom door lockset	1	Ea.	0.67	0.67	58.50	28	59	28	87
Closet pocket door	1	Ea.	1.52	1.52	237	64.50	237	65	302
Double-hung windows	2	Ea.	0.89	1.78	385	37.50	770	75	845
Partitions	50	L.F.	0.16	8	3.68	6.75	184	338	522
Gypsum wallboard	1325	S.F.	0.02	26.50	0.34	0.70	451	928	1,379
Zero-clearance gas fireplace	1	Ea.	11.43	11.43	2975	485	2,975	485	3,460
Ceramic tile bathroom floor	160	S.F.	0.08	12.80	3.45	2.74	552	438	990
Hardwood flooring	354	S.F.	0.09	31.86	4.08	3.76	1,444	1,331	2,775
Baseboard trim	165	L.F.	0.03	4.95	2.43	1.41	401	233	634
Closet shelf and pole	12	L.F.	0.13	1.56	2.40	5.65	29	68	97
Paint walls and ceilings, primer	1325	S.F.	0.01	13.25	0.05	0.22	66	292	358
Paint doors and frames, primer	5	Ea.	1.33	6.65	2.01	49.50	10	248	258
Paint window, incl. frame and trim, primer	2	Ea.	0.57	1.14	0.32	21	1	42	43
Paint trim, primer	296	L.F.	0.01	2.96	0.03	0.46	9	136	145
Paint walls and ceilings, 2 coats	1325	S.F.	0.01	13.25	0.05	0.22	66	292	358
Paint doors and frames, 2 coats	5	Ea.	1.33	6.65	2.01	49.50	10	248	258
Paint window, incl. frame and trim, 2 coats	2	Ea.	0.57	1.14	0.32	21	1	42	43
Paint trim, 2 coats finish	296	L.F.	0.01	2.96	0.03	0.46	9	136	145

Project Estimate (continued)

Description	Quantity	Unit	Labor Hrs Per Unit	Labor Hrs Total	Material Per Unit	Installation Per Unit	Material Total	Installation Total	Total
Subcontract									
Whirlpool tub	1	Ea.	16	16	3825	670	3,825	670	4,495
Rough plumbing for whirlpool	1	Ea.	7.73	7.73	182	325	182	325	507
Lavatories	2	Ea.	2.50	5	605	104	1,210	208	1,418
Rough plumbing for lavatories	2	Ea.	6.96	13.92	124	290	248	580	828
Shower stall	1	Ea.	2.91	2.91	510	121	510	121	631
Rough plumbing for shower	1	Ea.	7.80	7.80	268	325	268	325	593
Toilet	1	Ea.	0.01	0.01	223		223		223
Rough plumbing for toilet	1	Ea.	5.25	5.25	210	219	210	219	429
Miscellaneous plumbing at connections to old	1	Job	4	4		167		167	167
Baseboard radiation	70	L.F.	0.28	19.60	7.35	11.60	515	812	1,327
Thermostat	1	Ea.	1	1	29.50	47	30	47	77
Copper pipe	50	L.F.	0.10	5	2.36	4.76	118	238	356
Copper fittings	1	Ea.	0.42	0.42	1.25	19.55	1	20	21
Connection at boiler	1	Job	13.71	13.71		555		555	555
Duplex receptacles	9	Ea.	1.50	13.50	29	69	261	621	882
Wall switches	2	Ea.	1.40	2.80	31	64.50	62	129	191
GFCI receptacles	3	Ea.	0.65	1.95	21.50	30	65	90	155
Telephone jack	1	Ea.	0.31	0.31	8.70	14.10	9	14	23
Cable TV jack	1	Ea.	0.50	0.50	14.50	23	15	23	38
Recessed lighting fixtures	2	Ea.	0.29	0.58	59.50	13.10	119	26	145
Bathroom vent fan	1	Ea.	0.67	0.67	129	30.50	129	31	160
Whirlpool tub hookup	1	Ea.	1.60	1.60	110	73.50	110	74	184
Dumpster	1	Week	1	1	415	33.50	415	34	449
Subtotals							24,132	17,578	41,710
General Requirements (Site Overhead)						12%	2,896	2,109	5,005
Subtotals							27,028	19,687	46,715
Overhead and Profit						10%	2,703	1,969	4,672
Subtotals							29,731	21,656	51,387

Grand Total   **$51,387**

Note: Estimate is based on typical project materials available at home centers and may not include all elements in photo. Costs are national averages; see the Location Factors at the back of the book to adjust them to your area.

Cost per Square Foot   **$101**

A whirlpool tub and custom vanity add elegance to this master suite bathroom.

Alternates (Installed Costs)

	Unit	Total Cost
Roofing		
Aluminum shingles	Sq.	$262
Red cedar shingles	Sq.	$340
Laminated asphalt shingles	Sq.	$121
Slate shingles	Sq.	$815
Steel shingles	Sq.	$340
Clay tiles	Sq.	$465
Concrete tiles	Sq.	$335
Standing seam copper roofing	Sq.	$755
Siding		
Aluminum	S.F.	$3
Fiber-cement	S.F.	$3
Vinyl	S.F.	$2
Cedar clapboard	S.F.	$5
Rough-sawn vertical cedar	S.F.	$5
Texture 1-11	S.F.	$4
Flooring		
Floating laminate	S.F.	$6
Sheet vinyl	S.F.	$5
Linoleum	S.F.	$6
12″ x 12″ ceramic tile	S.F.	$6
Stone	S.F.	$22
Lighting		
Ceiling light fixture	Ea.	$133
Molding		
Crown molding	L.F.	$3

Don't overlook extra costs for this sizeable project, including scaffolding rental and dumpster and hauling fees.

If your project is over a garage, be sure to check local code requirements for fire separation. If not already in place, you may have to add two layers of 5/8" fire-code-rated gypsum board to the garage ceiling.

A furniture-quality vanity cabinet serves as a nice transition from the bedroom to the bath in this master suite.

20' × 25.5' Second-Floor Master Suite Addition

Project Worksheet

	Unit	Quantity	Price per Unit	Total	Dimensions	Source/Model#/Specs

Project Worksheet

	Unit	Quantity	Price per Unit	Total	Dimensions	Source/Model#/ Specs

Adding a Second Story

Ranch-style houses got their start in the 1950s and provided basic, economical homes as the baby boom took off. They're still out there in abundance, and they provide some strong points for homeowners ready to remodel. Often the foundation and framing of these homes are adequate to support a second story. And because they tend to be basic and unadorned, you can create an entirely new style for the house in keeping with the region, the homeowner's preferences, and their budget.

If the foundation and framing are capable of supporting a second story, the homeowners double their living space without the cost of an additional foundation, and don't have to give up yard space. Given their typical age, ranch homes may also have mature plantings that make the property that much more worth the remodeling investment.

Potential problems with this project include zoning restrictions on height, neighbors whose views would be affected, and the expense and challenge of reconfiguring the first floor of the house to accommodate a set of stairs and for any other changes needed to make the house flow and look right.

Since it is such a major project, an architect may be involved. A structural engineer may need to determine whether the foundation and framing can support the second floor. If greater support is needed, this should be clarified in detail at the start. The project requires careful site visits and consultations with your plumber and electrician.

This project estimate covers the cost of removing the old roof on an existing house and building a 30' x 22' second story, including two bedrooms and a three-fixture bath. The project involves demolition of a hallway and closet on the first floor and construction of a new stairway in that space to access the second floor. Some of the major materials are asphalt roofing, cedar shingle siding, and six double-hung windows.

Project Estimate

Description	Quantity	Unit	Labor Hrs Per Unit	Labor Hrs Total	Material Per Unit	Installation Per Unit	Material Total	Installation Total	Total
Self-Performed									
Temporary weather protection	10	Job	4	40		169		1,690	1,690
Remove existing roof shingles	9	Sq.	1.14	10.26		34.50		311	311
Remove existing roof sheathing	840	S.F.	0.01	8.40		0.35		294	294
Remove existing roof rafters	672	L.F.	0.02	13.44		0.58		390	390
Remove existing rake, soffit, and fascia	232	L.F.	0.01	2.32		0.22		51	51
Remove existing siding	120	S.F.	0.02	2.40		0.69		83	83
Remove existing plywood sheathing	120	S.F.	0.01	1.20		0.43		52	52
Remove existing gable end studs	128	L.F.	0.01	1.28		0.24		31	31
Remove existing gutters and downspouts	60	L.F.	0.03	1.80		1.01		61	61
Sister new joists to existing ceiling framing	528	L.F.	0.02	10.56	1.42	0.75	750	396	1,146
Floor sheathing	660	S.F.	0.01	6.60	0.73	0.50	482	330	812
Top and bottom plates	312	L.F.	0.02	6.24	0.41	0.85	128	265	393
Studs	520	L.F.	0.02	10.40	0.41	0.83	213	432	645
Face framing for dormers	6	Ea.	0.33	1.98	23.50	14.10	141	85	226
Cheek stud framing for dormers	144	L.F.	0.02	2.88	0.41	0.94	59	135	194
Dormer top plates	120	L.F.	0.02	2.40	0.41	0.85	49	102	151
Dormer roof rafters	180	L.F.	0.02	3.60	0.65	0.85	117	153	270
Gable studs	128	L.F.	0.02	2.56	0.41	0.75	52	96	148
Wall sheathing	1222	S.F.	0.01	12.22	0.68	0.60	831	733	1,564
Gable roof frame	1200	L.F.	0.02	24	0.65	0.68	780	816	1,596
Ceiling joists	528	L.F.	0.01	5.28	0.65	0.54	343	285	628
Furring	720	L.F.	0.02	14.40	0.31	0.97	223	698	921
Ridge board	30	L.F.	0.04	1.20	0.94	1.50	28	45	73
Roof sheathing	1560	S.F.	0.01	15.60	0.73	0.52	1,139	811	1,950
Rake, rake trim, soffit, and fascia	272	L.F.	0.04	10.88	1.58	1.69	430	460	890
Drip edge	100	L.F.	0.02	2	0.54	0.85	54	85	139
Roofing underlayment	1260	S.F.	0.01	12.60	0.04	0.09	50	113	163
Ice barrier	3	Sq.	0.36	1.08	50.50	14.10	152	42	194
Asphalt shingle roofing	16	Sq.	2.29	36.64	69	88.50	1,104	1,416	2,520
Ridge vent strip	30	L.F.	0.05	1.50	2.97	1.94	89	58	147
Housewrap	1300	S.F.	0.01	13	0.20	0.09	260	117	377
Corner boards	112	L.F.	0.04	4.48	1.58	1.69	177	189	366
Step flashing	300	Ea.	0.01	3	0.13	0.16	39	48	87
Lead flashing	20	S.F.	0.06	1.20	3.33	2.30	67	46	113
Asphalt shingles for patching existing roof	1	Sq.	2.29	2.29	69	88.50	69	89	158
Additional labor for patching roof	1	Sq.	0.50	0.50		19.40		19	19
Siding, cedar shingles	13	Sq.	3.90	50.70	137	165	1,781	2,145	3,926
Gutters	42	L.F.	0.07	2.94	1.46	3.12	61	131	192
Downspouts	80	L.F.	0.04	3.20	0.94	1.97	75	158	233
Interior partitions	84	L.F.	0.16	13.44	3.68	6.75	309	567	876
New bi-passing closet doors	2	Opng.	1.60	3.20	520	67.50	1,040	135	1,175
New room entry door	3	Ea.	0.84	2.52	292	35.50	876	107	983
Closet door trim	4	Opng.	1.60	6.40	28	67.50	112	270	382
Room entry door trim	6	Opng.	1.36	8.16	24	57.50	144	345	489
Wall insulation	1042	S.F.	0.01	10.42	0.52	0.21	542	219	761
Ceiling insulation	900	S.F.	0.01	9	0.53	0.21	477	189	666
Double-hung windows	6	Ea.	0.89	5.34	385	37.50	2,310	225	2,535
Gypsum wallboard	2614	S.F.	0.02	52.28	0.34	0.70	889	1,830	2,719
Underlayment	660	SF Flr.	0.01	6.60	1.34	0.48	884	317	1,201
Miscellaneous demolition and reconstruction for stairway	2	Job	4	8		169		338	338
Stair stringers	42	L.F.	0.12	5.04	1.42	5.20	60	218	278
Stair balusters	26	Ea.	0.29	7.54	6.95	12.05	181	313	494

Project Estimate (continued)

Description	Quantity	Unit	Labor Hrs Per Unit	Labor Hrs Total	Material Per Unit	Installation Per Unit	Material Total	Installation Total	Total
Stair newel posts	3	Ea.	1.14	3.42	42	48.50	126	146	272
Stair railings	14	L.F.	0.13	1.82	35	5.65	490	79	569
Stair risers	42	L.F.	0.13	5.46	6.35	5.30	267	223	490
Stair treads	13	Ea.	0.44	5.72	32	18.80	416	244	660
Carpet	660	S.F.	0.02	13.20	1.51	0.69	997	455	1,452
Carpet pad	660	S.F.	0.01	6.60	0.28	0.23	185	152	337
Ceramic tile bathroom flooring	63	S.F.	0.06	3.78	3.45	2.19	217	138	355
Baseboard trim	250	L.F.	0.03	7.50	2.43	1.41	608	353	961
Closet shelf and pole	20	L.F.	0.13	2.60	2.40	5.65	48	113	161
Paint walls and ceilings, primer	2614	S.F.	0.01	26.14	0.05	0.22	131	575	706
Paint doors and frames, primer	7	Ea.	1.33	9.31	2.01	49.50	14	347	361
Paint window, incl. frame and trim, primer	6	Ea.	0.57	3.42	0.32	21	2	126	128
Paint trim, primer	448	L.F.	0.01	4.48	0.03	0.46	13	206	219
Paint walls and ceilings, 2 coats	2614	S.F.	0.01	26.14	0.05	0.22	131	575	706
Paint doors and frames, 2 coats	7	Ea.	1.33	9.31	2.01	49.50	14	347	361
Paint window, incl. frame and trim, 2 coats	6	Ea.	0.57	3.42	0.32	21	2	126	128
Paint trim, 2 coats finish	448	L.F.	0.01	4.48	0.03	0.46	13	206	219
Vanity countertop	3	L.F.	0.27	0.81	31	11.25	93	34	127
Vanity base	1	Ea.	1	1	232	42.50	232	43	275
Subcontract									
Electrical disconnections/shut-off	1	Job	4	4		184		184	184
Plumbing disconnections/shut-off	1	Job	2	2		93		93	93
HVAC disconnections/shut-off	1	Job	13.71	13.71		555		555	555
Bathtub	1	Ea.	3.64	3.64	1775	152	1,775	152	1,927
Rough plumbing for bathtub	1	Ea.	7.73	7.73	182	325	182	325	507
Vanity sink	1	Ea.	2.50	2.50	234	104	234	104	338
Rough plumbing for vanity sink	1	Ea.	6.96	6.96	124	290	124	290	414
Toilet	1	Ea.	3.02	3.02	186	126	186	126	312
Rough plumbing for toilet	1	Ea.	5.86	5.86	485	245	485	245	730
Service calls for electrical connections to existing and start-up	4	Job	4	16		167		668	668
Baseboard radiation	70	L.F.	0.42	29.40	30.50	17.70	2,135	1,239	3,374
Connection to boiler	1	Job	5	5		210		210	210
Copper pipe for heating supply and return	80	L.F.	0.14	11.20	6.85	6.65	548	532	1,080
Miscellaneous copper fittings	40	Ea.	0.53	21.20	4.69	25	188	1,000	1,188
Thermostat	1	Ea.	0.62	0.62	19.80	28.50	20	29	49
Electrical service upgrade	1	Ea.	8.89	8.89	1100	410	1,100	410	1,510
Electrical service mast	1	Ea.	5.33	5.33	237	245	237	245	482
Duplex receptacles	13	Ea.	1.50	19.50	29	69	377	897	1,274
Electrical switches	4	Ea.	1.40	5.60	31	64.50	124	258	382
GFCI receptacles	2	Ea.	0.65	1.30	39	30	78	60	138
Telephone jacks	2	Ea.	0.31	0.62	8.70	14.10	17	28	45
Cable TV jacks	2	Ea.	0.50	1	9.35	23	19	46	65
Internet connection jacks	2	Ea.	0.50	1	9.35	23	19	46	65
Light fixture at top of stairs	1	Ea.	0.32	0.32	259	14.70	259	15	274
Service calls for plumbing connections to existing and start-up	4	Job	4	16		184		736	736
Dumpster	2	Week	1	2	455	33.50	910	67	977
Subtotals							30,583	31,582	62,165
General Requirements (Site Overhead)						12%	3,670	3,790	7,460
Subtotals							34,253	35,372	69,625
Overhead and Profit						10%	3,425	3,537	6,963
Subtotals							37,678	38,909	76,588

Grand Total $76,588

Note: Estimate is based on typical project materials available at home centers and may not include all elements in photo. Costs are national averages; see the Location Factors at the back of the book to adjust them to your area.

Cost per Square Foot $116

Additions

Alternates (Installed Costs)

	Unit	Total Cost
Roofing		
Aluminum shingles	Sq.	$262
Red cedar shingles	Sq.	$340
Laminated asphalt shingles	Sq.	$121
Slate shingles	Sq.	$815
Steel shingles	Sq.	$340
Clay tiles	Sq.	$465
Concrete tiles	Sq.	$335
Standing seam copper roofing	Sq.	$755
Siding		
Aluminum	S.F.	$3
Fiber-cement	S.F.	$3
Vinyl	S.F.	$2
Cedar clapboard	S.F.	$5
Rough-sawn vertical cedar	S.F.	$5
Texture 1-11	S.F.	$4
Flooring		
Floating laminate	S.F.	$6
Sheet vinyl	S.F.	$5
Linoleum	S.F.	$6
12" x 12" ceramic tile	S.F.	$6
Stone	S.F.	$22
Hardwood	S.F.	$8
Lighting		
Ceiling light fixture	Ea.	$133
Molding		
Crown molding	L.F.	$3
Fireplace		
Pre-manufactured zero-clearance gas fireplace	Ea.	$3,450

You'll want to work closely with the homeowners to prepare them for each step of the work, especially since they may have to move out of the house during construction. One possibility for reducing construction time is using pre-built trusses for the roof.

Adding A Second Story

Project Worksheet

	Unit	Quantity	Price per Unit	Total	Dimensions	Source/Model#/ Specs

Adding A Second Story

Project Worksheet

	Unit	Quantity	Price per Unit	Total	Dimensions	Source/Model#/ Specs

Project Estimate (continued)

Description	Quantity		Labor		Cost per Unit		Total Cost		
	Quantity	Unit	Labor Hrs Per Unit	Labor Hrs Total	Material Per Unit	Installation Per Unit	Material Total	Installation Total	Total
Carpet pad	78	S.Y.	0.05	3.90	7.40	2.06	577	161	738
Carpet	78	S.Y.	0.11	8.58	20	4.12	1,560	321	1,881
Stair stringers	42	L.F.	0.12	5.04	1.76	5.20	74	218	292
Stair railing	2	Ea.	1.86	3.72	490	79	980	158	1,138
Stair risers	43	L.F.	0.12	5.16	3.36	5.10	144	219	363
Stair skirt board	28	L.F.	0.15	4.20	3.19	6.15	89	172	261
Stair treads, oak	40	L.F.	0.15	6	32	6.25	1,280	250	1,530
18" base cabinet	1	Ea.	0.69	0.69	292	29	292	29	321
24" base cabinets	2	Ea.	0.72	1.44	345	30.50	690	61	751
Sink base cabinet	1	Ea.	0.79	0.79	345	33.50	345	34	379
Corner base cabinet	1	Ea.	0.97	0.97	510	41	510	41	551
Over-stove and over-refrigerator cabinets	2	Ea.	0.70	1.40	241	30	482	60	542
24" wall cabinets	4	Ea.	0.79	3.16	270	33.50	1,080	134	1,214
Corner wall cabinet	1	Ea.	0.97	0.97	252	41	252	41	293
Island cabinets	2	Ea.	0.85	1.70	520	36	1,040	72	1,112
Solid surface countertops	21	L.F.	1.07	22.47	114	45	2,394	945	3,339
Solid surface integral kitchen sinks	2	Ea.	4	8	445	169	890	338	1,228
Prime and paint window exteriors	4	Ea.	1.33	5.32	2.73	49.50	11	198	209
Prime and paint interior doors	3	Ea.	3.20	9.60	12.05	119	36	357	393
Prime and paint window interiors	4	Ea.	1.33	5.32	2.38	49.50	10	198	208
Stair finish	14	L.F.	0.47	6.58	2.74	17.45	38	244	282
Handrail finish	28	L.F.	0.06	1.68	0.28	2.04	8	57	65
Prime and paint exterior trim	352	L.F.	0.03	10.56	0.15	0.94	53	331	384
Paint baseboard trim	200	L.F.	0.01	2	0.03	0.35	6	70	76
Prime gypsum wallboard	3466	S.F.	0.01	34.66	0.05	0.22	173	763	936
Paint gypsum wallboard	3466	S.F.	0.01	34.66	0.12	0.37	416	1,282	1,698
Built-in oven	1	Ea.	2	2	435	92	435	92	527
Range hood	1	Ea.	2	2	42.50	86	43	86	129
Refrigerator	1	Ea.	2	2	580	60.50	580	61	641
Microwave oven	1	Ea.	2	2	94	92	94	92	186
Dishwasher	1	Ea.	5	5	620	232	620	232	852
Subcontract									
Rough plumbing for kitchen sinks	2	Ea.	6.96	13.92	124	290	248	580	828
Baseboard radiation	80	L.F.	0.28	22.40	7.35	11.60	588	928	1,516
Thermostat	1	Ea.	1	1	29.50	47	30	47	77
Copper pipe	120	L.F.	0.10	12	2.36	4.76	283	571	854
Copper fittings	30	Ea.	0.42	12.60	1.25	19.55	38	587	625
Connection at boiler	1	Job	13.71	13.71		555		555	555
Electrical sub-panel	1	Ea.	8.70	8.70	590	400	590	400	990
Switch devices	6	Ea.	0.47	2.82	9.30	21.50	56	129	185
Three-way switch	2	Ea.	0.55	1.10	13.35	25	27	50	77
Duplex receptacles	11	Ea.	0.55	6.05	7.50	25	83	275	358
GFCI receptacles	4	Ea.	0.65	2.60	21.50	30	86	120	206
Telephone jack	2	Ea.	0.31	0.62	8.70	14.10	17	28	45
Cable TV and Internet connections	4	Ea.	0.50	2	14.50	23	58	92	150
Recessed light fixtures	7	Ea.	0.29	2.03	59.50	13.10	417	92	509
Dumpster	1	Week	1	1	415	33.50	415	34	449
Subtotals							41,016	27,765	68,781
General Requirements (Site Overhead)						12%	4,922	3,332	8,254
Subtotals							45,938	31,097	77,035
Overhead and Profit						10%	4,594	3,110	7,704
Subtotals							50,532	34,207	84,739

Grand Total $84,739

Note: Estimate is based on typical project materials available at home centers and may not include all elements in photo. Costs are national averages; see the Location Factors at the back of the book to adjust them to your area.

Cost per Square Foot $93

Additions

Alternates (Installed Costs)

	Unit	Total Cost
Roofing		
Aluminum shingles	Sq.	$262
Red cedar shingles	Sq.	$340
Laminated asphalt shingles	Sq.	$121
Slate shingles	Sq.	$815
Steel shingles	Sq.	$340
Clay tiles	Sq.	$465
Concrete tiles	Sq.	$335
Standing seam copper roofing	Sq.	$755
Siding		
Aluminum	S.F.	$3
Fiber-cement	S.F.	$3
Vinyl	S.F.	$2
Cedar clapboard	S.F.	$5
Rough-sawn vertical cedar	S.F.	$5
Texture 1-11	S.F.	$4
Flooring		
Floating laminate	S.F.	$6
Sheet vinyl	S.F.	$5
Linoleum	S.F.	$6
12" x 12" ceramic tile	S.F.	$6
Stone	S.F.	$22
Hardwood	S.F.	$8
Lighting		
Ceiling light fixture	Ea.	$133
Molding		
Crown molding	L.F.	$3
Fireplace		
Pre-manufactured zero-clearance gas fireplace	Ea.	$3,450

Depending on the existing layout, the addition may be side-by-side with the house (for example, on homes with the gable end facing front), or may be at a right angle at the back of the house. If facing front, the addition may jog back a bit and include complementary features such as a new porch and French doors.

Any time a new second story is involved, you need to check height restrictions imposed by local zoning. You may also have to deal with objections from neighbors whose views may be affected.

Historically significant homes need approval from the local authority.

Project Worksheet

Additions

	Unit	Quantity	Price per Unit	Total	Dimensions	Source/Model#/ Specs

Project Worksheet

	Unit	Quantity	Price per Unit	Total	Dimensions	Source/Model#/ Specs

Garage Addition/Expansion

emodeling a one-car garage to a two-car space not only provides everyday convenience, but is a good investment in resale value. With the popularity of SUVs and trucks, some older one-car garages (10' or narrower) can't accommodate even one vehicle comfortably – one more reason to consider an expansion.

One-car garages are generally 12' x 22', and two-car garages somewhere between 22'–24' x 22'–27' – preferably at least 24' x 24'. The owner's needs to store extras like a boat, equipment, tools, bikes, and other items will determine what's best for each project plan. Single-width garage doors are usually 8' or 9' wide, and 7'–8' high – 8' is best for large SUVs, most pickups, and vans. (Get exact measurements for larger vehicles.) It's best to allow 18" from the top of the door to the finished garage ceiling for a garage door opener. Like all additions, an expanded garage should be in harmony with the scale and architectural features of the existing home. Roof pitch is typically determined by the owner's plans for storage or future finishing of space above the vehicles, but you also want to make sure the new roof blends with the home's roof slope(s).

Possible extra costs for this project:

- Clearing and hauling away trees, stumps, large rocks, etc.
- A new or expanded driveway
- Landscaping and walkways
- Storage space in the garage. Clarify the type and quality of any shelves, cabinets, or other storage systems the owner wants installed.
- Special flooring for a "designer" garage

- Extra support and a plywood floor for attic-type storage above vehicles
- Electrical outlets, interior and exterior light fixtures, and a smoke detector
- Piping for an outdoor faucet

When planning garage access and the driveway, you and the owner will need to discuss the required turning radius, loss of yard space, and any other issues relevant to a particular lot.

This project estimate covers the costs to add a second bay to a single-car garage. The work includes grading and a new concrete slab, framing and sheathing, siding and asphalt shingle roofing, plus gutters and downspouts. One new window is being added, along with a new matching single garage door. Painting costs are for the new garage door and trim. Electrical work includes a new circuit breaker, light fixture/switch, and receptacle.

Project Estimate

Description	Quantity		Labor		Cost per Unit		Total Cost		
	Quantity	Unit	Labor Hrs Per Unit	Labor Hrs Total	Material Per Unit	Installation Per Unit	Material Total	Installation Total	Total
Self-Performed									
Edge forms for floor slab	56	L.F.	0.05	2.80	0.32	1.94	18	109	127
Concrete floor slab	473	S.F.	0.02	9.46	1.24	0.71	587	336	923
Anchor bolts	14	Ea.	0.04	0.56	0.75	1.70	11	24	35
Wall framing	56	L.F.	0.13	7.28	2.86	5.40	160	302	462
Headers over openings	28	L.F.	0.05	1.40	1.76	2.25	49	63	112
Sheathing for walls	569	S.F.	0.01	5.69	0.94	0.61	535	347	882
Ridge board	18	L.F.	0.03	0.54	0.97	1.23	17	22	39
Roof framing, rafters	594	L.F.	0.02	11.88	0.65	0.85	386	505	891
Hip and valley rafters	36	L.F.	0.03	1.08	0.94	1.24	34	45	79
Joists	396	L.F.	0.01	3.96	0.65	0.54	257	214	471
Gable framing	120	L.F.	0.03	3.60	0.41	1.24	49	149	198
Sheathing for roof	432	S.F.	0.01	4.32	0.68	0.48	294	207	501
Sub-fascia	34	L.F.	0.07	2.38	0.94	3	32	102	134
Felt paper	5	Sq.	0.22	1.10	3.75	9.15	19	46	65
Roofing, asphalt shingles	5	Sq.	1.60	8	47.50	62	238	310	548
Drip edge	34	L.F.	0.02	0.68	0.33	0.85	11	29	40
Fascia	34	S.F.	0.06	2.04	3.25	2.58	111	88	199
Soffit	34	S.F.	0.04	1.36	1.36	1.61	46	55	101
Gutters and downspouts	34	L.F.	0.07	2.38	1.46	3.12	50	106	156
Window	1	Ea.	0.80	0.80	256	34	256	34	290
Garage door	1	Ea.	2.67	2.67	870	113	870	113	983
Siding, cedar shingles	569	S.F.	0.03	17.07	1.23	1.31	700	745	1,445
Paint garage door and window trim, primer	50	S.F.	0.01	0.50	0.03	0.46	2	23	25
Paint, garage door and window trim, 2 coats	50	S.F.	0.02	1	0.06	0.74	3	37	40
Subcontract									
Circuit breaker, 20A	1	Ea.	0.67	0.67	11.10	30.50	11	31	42
Non-metallic sheathed cable	60	L.F.	0.03	1.80	0.20	1.47	12	88	100
Switch	1	Ea.	0.47	0.47	9.30	21.50	9	22	31
Duplex receptacle	1	Ea.	0.65	0.65	21.50	30	22	30	52
Lighting outlet box and wire	1	Ea.	0.32	0.32	11.50	14.70	12	15	27
Light fixture	1	Ea.	0.20	0.20	28.50	9.20	29	9	38
Dumpster	1	Week	1	1	415	33.50	415	34	449
Subtotals							5,245	4,240	9,485
General Requirements (Site Overhead)						12%	629	509	1,138
Subtotals							5,874	4,749	10,623
Overhead and Profit						10%	587	475	1,062
Subtotals							6,461	5,224	11,685

Grand Total $11,685

Note: Estimate is based on typical project materials available at home centers and may not include all elements in photo. Costs are national averages; see the Location Factors at the back of the book to adjust them to your area.

Cost per Square Foot $25

Alternates (Installed Costs)

	Unit	Total Cost
Storage Space		
Plywood subfloor	SF Flr.	$1
Pull-down stairway	Ea.	$234
Electrical		
GFCI receptacle	Ea.	$69

Double Attached Carport

*I*n areas where vehicle security is not an issue, a carport is an economical way to gain shelter from rain, sun, snow, ice, and hailstorms. Carports are sometimes built in front of (as extensions to) an existing garage. This arrangement provides a protected place for loading and unloading a vehicle, and shelter for a third or fourth car.

Whether attached or free-standing, carports should be designed to harmonize with the home and/or existing garage. Roofing material and pitch, as well as supports, light fixtures, and any other details, should blend with what is there already. Carports are typically visible from the street if not screened with shrubs or trees. This high visibility makes attention to architectural detail even more beneficial for these structures.

A simple carport can be constructed with 4 x 4 pressure-treated posts set in concrete, a roof framed with pressure-treated 2 x 6s, 24" on center, and doubled headers. Siding on the house or garage wall will need to be cut back to the sheathing, and flashing put in place. Once the joists and headers are installed, the plywood roof sheathing can be put up.

Drip edge (or a gutter and downspout) should be installed on all open sides of the carport roof. Rolled roofing can be used on a nearly-flat roof pitch.

This project estimate provides costs for a 22' x 22' double carport, attached to the side of a house. Tasks include preparation and patching of the house wall; installation of anchors/posts and a concrete slab; framing, sheathing, and roofing (asphalt shingles); and flashing. Priming and painting of posts and trim are also priced. Electrical items include a GFCI outlet and a lighting junction box, fixture, and switch.

Project Estimate

Description	Quantity		Labor		Cost per Unit		Total Cost		
	Quantity	Unit	Labor Hrs Per Unit	Labor Hrs Total	Material Per Unit	Installation Per Unit	Material Total	Installation Total	Total
Self-Performed									
Remove siding	100	S.F.	0.02	2		0.69		69	69
Post footings	6	Ea.	3.20	19.20	21.50	116	129	696	825
Hand grading	53	S.Y.	0.03	1.59		1.12		59	60
Slab formwork	66	L.F.	0.05	3.30	0.32	1.94	21	128	149
Vapor barrier	5	Sq.	0.22	1.10	4.50	9.15	23	46	69
Slab on grade	484	S.F.	0.02	9.68	1.27	0.78	615	378	993
Column/post anchors	6	Ea.	0.04	0.24	0.75	1.70	5	10	15
Column/posts	48	L.F.	0.05	2.40	2.71	1.93	130	93	223
Joists/collar ties	374	L.F.	0.04	14.96	1.07	1.50	400	561	961
Furring	363	L.F.	0.02	7.26	0.31	0.97	113	352	465
Plywood ceiling	484	S.F.	0.04	19.36	1.41	1.61	682	779	1,461
Headers	66	L.F.	0.05	3.30	2.71	1.93	179	127	306
Ridge	24	L.F.	0.04	0.96	1.07	1.50	26	36	62
Rafters	476	L.F.	0.03	14.28	0.82	1.35	390	643	1,033
Roof sheathing	616	S.F.	0.01	6.16	0.68	0.48	419	296	715
Gable studs	60	L.F.	0.02	1.20	0.41	0.94	25	56	81
Gable end sheathing	80	S.F.	0.01	0.80	0.68	0.60	54	48	102
Rake, rake trim, soffit, fascia, and trim	166	L.F.	0.04	6.64	1.58	1.69	262	281	543
Drip edge	44	L.F.	0.02	0.88	0.33	0.85	15	37	52
Flashing at connection	50	Ea.	0.01	0.50	0.13	0.16	7	8	15
Patch siding and shingles for gable end	2	Sq.	3.33	6.66	179	141	358	282	640
Ventilation louver	1	Ea.	0.53	0.53	28.50	22.50	29	23	52
Asphalt roof shingles	7	Sq.	1.45	10.15	42	56.50	294	396	690
Paint trim and columns	358	L.F.	0.01	3.58	0.07	0.46	25	165	190
Prime ceiling	484	S.F.	0.01	4.84	0.11	0.46	53	223	276
Paint ceiling, 2 coats	484	S.F.	0.02	9.68	0.18	0.73	87	353	440
Gutters	44	L.F.	0.07	3.08	1.46	3.12	64	137	201
Downspouts and elbows	40	L.F.	0.04	1.60	0.94	1.97	38	79	117
Subcontract									
Circuit breaker	1	Ea.	0.67	0.67	11.10	30.50	11	31	42
Wiring	60	L.F.	0.03	1.80	0.20	1.47	12	88	100
Switch	1	Ea.	0.47	0.47	9.30	21.50	9	22	31
GFCI receptacle	1	Ea.	0.65	0.65	39	30	39	30	69
Lighting junction box	1	Ea.	0.32	0.32	11.50	14.70	12	15	27
Light fixture	1	Ea.	0.20	0.20	28.50	9.20	29	9	38
Dumpster	1	Week	1	1	385	33.50	385	34	419
Subtotals							4,940	6,590	11,531
General Requirements (Site Overhead)						12%	593	791	1,384
Subtotals							5,533	7,381	12,915
Overhead and Profit						10%	553	738	1,292
Subtotals							6,086	8,119	14,207

Grand Total $14,207

Note: Estimate is based on typical project materials available at home centers and may not include all elements in photo. Costs are national averages; see the Location Factors at the back of the book to adjust them to your area.

Cost per Square Foot **$29**

Alternates (Installed Costs)

	Unit	Total Cost
Electrical		
Weatherproof cover for receptacle	Ea.	$16
2-Lamp floodlight	Ea.	$66

Two-Car Garage

iting a new garage, whether attached or free-standing, involves consideration of several factors, in addition to convenient entry to the house. You must take into account the location of underground utilities, setback requirements, existing or planned landscaping, and the slope of the land.

Attached garages can join directly to the house or breezeway, or can angle behind the house – a good solution for narrow lots. (Driveways are usually allowed within setback-restricted areas.) If the garage will sit side-by-side with the house, with no connecting structure, it looks better if the garage's front wall sits back 2' or more behind the front of the house.

Like room additions, new garages must blend with the home's architecture,

with appropriate roof pitch, sheathing materials, windows, doors, and trim. It's also important to consider how the garage will affect views and take away light from the existing house.

Two-car garages are typically between 22' x 22' and 24' x 24'. If the property allows, the homeowner may want a larger structure for a workshop, office, or studio. If the existing house is small, you'll want to keep the garage size to the practical minimum and design the structure to minimize its apparent size. Don't shrink the size of the bays and garage doors too much, however. The current owner may have a Mini, but may one day want to sell the house to someone with a large SUV.

Single bay garage doors are usually 8' or 9' wide, and 7' high. They should be 8' high for large SUVs, most pickup trucks, and vans. (If the homeowner wants to store larger items or equipment, such as a boat, you'll need to get exact measurements.) Allow 18" from the top of the door to the finished garage ceiling for electric openers.

This project estimate is for a 22' x 22' two-car garage with two garage doors, three windows, and a pre-hung entry door. Costs cover a concrete slab, framing and sheathing, asphalt roof shingles, siding, gutters and downspouts, and priming/painting the finished structure. Subcontracted electrical work includes wiring and installation of a circuit breaker and light fixture and switch.

Project Estimate

Description	Quantity		Labor		Cost per Unit		Total Cost		
	Quantity	Unit	Labor Hrs Per Unit	Labor Hrs Total	Material Per Unit	Installation Per Unit	Material Total	Installation Total	Total
Self-Performed									
Excavate and backfill for foundation	2	Job	8	16		412		824	824
Concrete footing	5	C.Y.	2.80	14	135	111.59	675	558	1,233
Cast in place foundation wall	352	S.F.	0.11	38.72	3.78	4.53	1,331	1,595	2,926
Grading	576	S.F.	0.03	17.28		1.12		645	645
Concrete floor slab	484	S.F.	0.02	9.68	1.24	0.71	600	344	944
Anchor bolts	20	Ea.	0.04	0.80	0.75	1.70	15	34	49
Wall framing	88	L.F.	0.13	11.44	2.86	5.40	252	475	727
Headers over openings	40	L.F.	0.05	2	1.76	2.25	70	90	160
Sheathing for walls	816	S.F.	0.01	8.16	0.94	0.61	767	498	1,265
Ridge board	24	L.F.	0.03	0.72	0.97	1.23	23	30	53
Roof framing, rafters	684	L.F.	0.02	13.68	0.65	0.68	445	465	910
Joists	374	L.F.	0.01	3.74	0.65	0.54	243	202	445
Gable framing	204	L.F.	0.03	6.12	0.41	1.24	84	253	337
Sheathing for roof	792	S.F.	0.01	7.92	0.68	0.48	539	380	919
Felt paper	8	Sq.	0.22	1.76	3.75	9.15	30	73	103
Roofing, asphalt shingles	8	Sq.	1.60	12.80	47.50	62	380	496	876
Drip edge	44	L.F.	0.02	0.88	0.33	0.85	15	37	52
Rake, rake soffit, fascia, fascia soffit	232	L.F.	0.04	9.28	1.58	1.69	367	392	759
Corner boards, garage door trim, and water table	270	L.F.	0.03	8.10	1.36	1.35	367	365	732
Frieze board	116	L.F.	0.02	2.32	0.67	0.70	78	81	159
Gutters	44	L.F.	0.07	3.08	1.46	3.12	64	137	201
Downspouts and elbows	20	L.F.	0.04	0.80	0.94	1.97	19	39	58
Small window	1	Ea.	0.80	0.80	256	34	256	34	290
Garage doors	2	Ea.	2	4	1575	84.50	3,150	169	3,319
Entrance door	1	Ea.	1	1	315	42.50	315	43	358
Double-hung windows	2	Ea.	0.80	1.60	310	34	620	68	688
Siding, cedar shingles	816	S.F.	0.03	24.48	3.52	1.35	2,872	1,102	3,974
Prime and paint trim	648	L.F.	0.03	19.44	0.15	0.94	97	609	706
Paint siding, primer	816	S.F.	0.01	8.16	0.11	0.46	90	375	465
Paint siding, 2 coats	816	S.F.	0.02	16.32	0.18	0.73	147	596	743
Prime and paint entry door	1	L.F.	0.03	0.03	0.19	1.12		1	1
Prime and paint windows	3	Ea.	1.60	4.80	2.73	59.50	8	179	187
Prime and paint garage door	2	Ea.	1.33	2.66	6.20	49.50	12	99	111
Shutters	1	Pr.	0.80	0.80	145	34	145	34	179
Subcontract									
Electrician minimum	1	Job	4	4		184		184	184
Circuit breaker, 20A	1	Ea.	0.67	0.67	11.10	30.50	11	31	42
Non-metallic sheathed cable	60	L.F.	0.03	1.80	0.20	1.47	12	88	100
Switch	1	Ea.	0.47	0.47	9.30	21.50	9	22	31
Duplex receptacle	1	Ea.	0.65	0.65	21.50	30	22	30	52
Lighting outlet box and wire	1	Ea.	0.32	0.32	11.50	14.70	12	15	27
Light fixture	1	Ea.	0.20	0.20	28.50	9.20	29	9	38
Dumpster	1	Week	1	1	385	33.50	385	34	419
Subtotals							14,556	11,735	26,291
General Requirements (Site Overhead)						12%	1,747	1,408	3,155
Subtotals							16,303	13,143	29,446
Overhead and Profit						10%	1,630	1,314	2,945
Subtotals							17,933	14,457	32,391

Grand Total $32,391

Cost per Square Foot $67

Note: Estimate is based on typical project materials available at home centers and may not include all elements in photo. Costs are national averages; see the Location Factors at the back of the book to adjust them to your area.

Two-Car Garage

Alternates (Installed Costs)

	Unit	Total Cost
Electrical		
GFCI receptacle	Ea.	$69
Weatherproof cover for receptacle	Ea.	$16
2-lamp floodlight	Ea.	$66
Electrical sub-panel	Ea.	$990
Switch device	Ea.	$31
Duplex receptacle	Ea.	$33
Telephone jack	Ea.	$23
Fluorescent light fixture	Ea.	$105
Garage door opener	Ea.	$445
Roofing		
Aluminum shingles	Sq.	$262
Red cedar shingles	Sq.	$340
Laminated asphalt shingles	Sq.	$121
Slate shingles	Sq.	$815
Steel shingles	Sq.	$340
Clay tiles	Sq.	$465
Concrete tiles	Sq.	$335
Standing seam copper roofing	Sq.	$755
Siding		
Aluminum	S.F.	$3
Fiber-cement	S.F.	$3
Vinyl	S.F.	$2
Cedar clapboard	S.F.	$5
Rough-sawn vertical cedar	S.F.	$5
Texture 1-11	S.F.	$4

A second-story addition over the breezway connects with the large living space above this garage.

Garage additions are often combined with other projects, such as a new porch and/or a breezeway converted to interior space. Be sure to clarify the extent of remodeling work to be done to the existing house. New paving and landscaping are other major aspects of a project like this that should not be overlooked.

Things to Consider:

- *If the homeowner plans to use the space above the ceiling joists for storage or to finish it later for living space, you might want to use 2 x 8 joists.*

- *Insulating glass or deluxe airtight units are unnecessary for a garage unless it will be heated. If so, it will need full insulation in the walls and ceiling. You might omit windows entirely if security is a major concern.*

- *Check code requirements for fire separation and other safety issues.*

Project Worksheet

	Unit	Quantity	Price per Unit	Total	Dimensions	Source/Model#/ Specs

Garage with Master Suite Above

If the lot size is adequate, and the surrounding neighborhood has large enough homes, this major addition can be a sound investment in resale value. Early planning and design include investigation of issues such as setback and other zoning restrictions, available yard space, and neighboring houses whose views may be affected. If the home uses a septic system, there may be restrictions on added bedrooms. There are also specific code requirements for constructing a sleeping area over spaces where vehicles are housed.

Architects are frequently involved in designing additions of this size and complexity. They can help ensure that the new structure will be in harmony with

the home's proportions and architectural features, and that it will meet structural and code requirements and the homeowner's specific needs.

While this structure must be attached and appropriately connect to the existing living spaces, there are other siting considerations, such as underground utilities, driveway location and turning radius, and landscaping. Attached garages generally sit side-by-side with the house or breezeway, but may also angle behind the house.

Two-car garages are typically between 22' x 22' and 24' x 24', providing ample space for a master suite above with a walk-in closet and a bath. If the main house is of ample proportions and the lot size is large enough, a bigger addition may be desired, allowing for a workshop

or office below and a more spacious master suite.

This project estimate is for the construction of a 24' x 24' double attached garage with a master suite above. Costs include all the items required to build the structure, from a concrete foundation and slab to framing, roofing, and siding, and window/skylight and door installation. Interior work includes not only insulation, drywall, trim and paint, but a whirlpool tub with tile floor, stairs, and closets. Electrical work includes a new sub-panel, wiring, six recessed light fixtures, 13 receptacles (three GFCI), and a floodlight.

See the Two-car Garage and Second-Floor Master Suite Addition projects for more on typical design and construction issues.

Project Estimate

Description	Quantity		Labor		Cost per Unit		Total Cost		
	Quantity	Unit	Labor Hrs Per Unit	Labor Hrs Total	Material Per Unit	Installation Per Unit	Material Total	Installation Total	Total
Self-Performed									
Excavate and backfill for foundation	2	Job	8	16		412		824	824
Concrete footing	4	C.Y.	2.80	11.20	135	111.59	540	446	986
Concrete foundation	12	C.Y.	2.77	33.24	154	103.47	1,848	1,242	3,090
Anchor bolts	18	Ea.	0.25	4.50	1.42	10.40	26	187	213
Gravel under slab	576	S.F.	0.01	5.76	0.18	0.17	104	98	202
Slab on grade	576	S.F.	0.02	11.52	1.86	0.76	1,071	438	1,509
Remove existing siding	100	S.F.	0.02	2		0.69		69	69
Treated wood sill	72	L.F.	0.05	3.60	2.71	1.93	195	139	334
Garage door framing	2	Ea.	0.27	0.54	72	11.25	144	23	167
Garage window framing	2	Ea.	0.33	0.66	21.50	14.10	43	28	71
Bedroom double window framing	1	Ea.	0.33	0.33	28	14.10	28	14	42
Bedroom picture window framing	1	Ea.	0.36	0.36	59	15.35	59	15	74
Wall framing plates for both levels	432	L.F.	0.02	8.64	0.41	0.85	177	367	544
Exterior wall studs for both levels	1008	L.F.	0.01	10.08	0.41	0.61	413	615	1,028
Exterior wall sheathing	1440	S.F.	0.01	14.40	0.68	0.60	979	864	1,843
Composite wood joists	576	S.F.	0.01	5.76	2.23	0.37	1,284	213	1,497
Plywood subfloor	1	SF Flr.	0.01	0.01	0.90	0.54	1	1	2
Ceiling joists	456	L.F.	0.01	4.56	0.94	0.61	429	278	707
Roof rafters	532	L.F.	0.02	10.64	0.94	0.71	500	378	878
Roof sheathing	672	S.F.	0.01	6.72	0.68	0.48	457	323	780
Gable studs	144	L.F.	0.02	2.88	0.41	0.67	59	96	155
Rake board	64	L.F.	0.04	2.56	1.58	1.69	101	108	209
Rake trim	64	L.F.	0.02	1.28	0.40	1.02	26	65	91
Soffit and fascia	96	L.F.	0.04	3.84	1.85	1.88	178	180	358
Corner boards and garage door trim	204	L.F.	0.03	6.12	1.36	1.35	277	275	552
Exterior wall trim band	24	L.F.	0.03	0.72	1.36	1.35	33	32	65
Small window	1	Ea.	1	1	715	42.50	715	43	758
Garage and suite entry doors	2	Ea.	1	2	224	42.50	448	85	533
Garage and suite entry locksets	2	Ea.	0.57	1.14	30	24	60	48	108
Mulled window unit	5	Ea.	1	5	390	42.50	1,950	213	2,163
Drip edge	48	L.F.	0.02	0.96	0.54	0.85	26	41	67
Ice barrier	2	Sq.	0.36	0.72	50.50	14.10	101	28	129
Roof underlayment	5	Sq.	0.13	0.65	3.75	4.84	19	24	43
Asphalt roof shingles	7	Sq.	1.60	11.20	41.50	62	291	434	725
Roof window	1	Ea.	1	1	365	42.50	365	43	408
Flashing set for roof window	1	Ea.	1.60	1.60	39.50	67.50	40	68	108
Vapor barrier	1440	S.F.	0.01	14.40	0.12	0.08	173	115	288
Exterior wall insulation	1440	S.F.	0.01	14.40	0.32	0.21	461	302	763
Red cedar clapboard siding	1440	S.F.	0.01	14.40	0.32	0.21	461	302	763
Floor and ceiling insulation	576	S.F.	0.01	5.76	0.78	0.29	449	167	616
Interior partitions	66	L.F.	0.12	7.92	1.76	5.20	74	218	292
Stair stringers	42	L.F.	0.12	5.04	1.76	5.20	74	218	292
Furring	912	L.F.	0.02	18.24	0.31	0.97	283	885	1,168
Gypsum wallboard on ceilings	576	S.F.	0.02	11.52	0.34	0.88	196	507	703
Gypsum wallboard on walls	2496	S.F.	0.02	49.92	0.34	0.70	849	1,747	2,596
Interior wood doors	3	Ea.	0.84	2.52	292	35.50	876	107	983
Door trim sets	8	Opng.	1.36	10.88	24	57.50	192	460	652
Small window trim sets	3	Opng.	0.80	2.40	38.50	34	116	102	218
Large window trim set	1	Opng.	1.33	1.33	68.50	56.50	69	57	126
Baseboard trim	200	L.F.	0.03	6	2.43	1.41	486	282	768
Closet shelf and pole	2	Ea.	0.40	0.80	9.55	16.90	19	34	53
Flooring underlayment	576	SF Flr.	0.01	5.76	1.34	0.48	772	276	1,048

Project Estimate (continued)

Additions

Description	Quantity		Labor		Cost per Unit		Total Cost		
	Quantity	Unit	Labor Hrs Per Unit	Labor Hrs Total	Material Per Unit	Installation Per Unit	Material Total	Installation Total	Total
Ceramic tile flooring in bathroom	133	S.F.	0.06	7.98	3.45	2.19	459	291	750
Carpet pad	64	S.Y.	0.05	3.20	7.40	2.06	474	132	606
Carpet	64	S.Y.	0.11	7.04	20	4.12	1,280	264	1,544
Stair railing	2	Ea.	1.86	3.72	490	79	980	158	1,138
Stair risers	43	L.F.	0.12	5.16	3.36	5.10	144	219	363
Stair skirt board	28	L.F.	0.15	4.20	3.19	6.15	89	172	261
Stair treads, oak	40	L.F.	0.15	6	32	6.25	1,280	250	1,530
Bathroom vanity	1	Ea.	1.40	1.40	650	59	650	59	709
Solid surface vanity top	6	L.F.	0.80	4.80	104	34	624	204	828
Medicine cabinet/mirror	1	Ea.	1.33	1.33	370	56.50	370	57	427
Garage doors	2	Ea.	3.03	6.06	850	128	1,700	256	1,956
Garage door openers	2	Ea.	1	2	460	42.50	920	85	1,005
Prime and paint window exteriors	4	Ea.	1.33	5.32	2.73	49.50	11	198	209
Prime and paint interior doors	4	Ea.	3.20	12.80	12.05	119	48	476	524
Prime and paint window interiors	4	Ea.	1.33	5.32	2.38	49.50	10	198	208
Stair finish	14	L.F.	0.47	6.58	2.74	17.45	38	244	282
Handrail finish	28	L.F.	0.06	1.68	0.28	2.04	8	57	65
Prime siding	1440	S.F.	0.01	14.40	0.11	0.46	158	662	820
Paint siding, 2 coats	1440	S.F.	0.02	28.80	0.18	0.73	259	1,051	1,310
Prime and paint exterior trim	428	L.F.	0.03	12.84	0.15	0.94	64	402	466
Paint garage doors	2	Ea.	2	4	6.20	74	12	148	160
Paint baseboard trim	200	L.F.	0.01	2	0.03	0.35	6	70	76
Prime gypsum wallboard	3072	S.F.	0.01	30.72	0.05	0.22	154	676	830
Paint gypsum wallboard	1	S.F.	0.01	0.01	0.12	0.37			
Subcontract									
Rough plumbing for toilet	1	Ea.	5.86	5.86	485	245	485	245	730
Rough plumbing for lavatories	2	Ea.	6.96	13.92	124	290	248	580	828
Rough plumbing for shower	1	Ea.	7.80	7.80	268	325	268	325	593
Whirlpool bath	1	Ea.	16	16	2925	670	2,925	670	3,595
Rough plumbing for whirlpool bath	1	Ea.	7.73	7.73	182	325	182	325	507
Lavatories	2	Ea.	2.50	5	605	104	1,210	208	1,418
Shower stall	1	Ea.	2.91	2.91	510	121	510	121	631
Toilet	1	Ea.	3.02	3.02	645	126	645	126	771
10' electric baseboard heaters	6	Ea.	2.42	14.52	105	111	630	666	1,296
Electrical sub-panel	1	Ea.	8.70	8.70	590	400	590	400	990
Switch devices	2	Ea.	0.47	0.94	9.30	21.50	19	43	62
Three-way switch	1	Ea.	0.55	0.55	13.35	25	13	25	38
Duplex receptacles	10	Ea.	0.55	5.50	7.50	25	75	250	325
GFCI receptacles	3	Ea.	0.65	1.95	21.50	30	65	90	155
Telephone jack	2	Ea.	0.31	0.62	8.70	14.10	17	28	45
Cable TV and Internet connections	2	Ea.	0.50	1	14.50	23	29	46	75
Recessed light fixtures	6	Ea.	0.29	1.74	59.50	13.10	357	79	436
Bathroom vent fan	1	Ea.	0.67	0.67	129	30.50	129	31	160
Wall-mounted exterior light fixtures	2	Ea.	2.29	4.58	204	105	408	210	618
Floodlight	1	Ea.	0.40	0.40	29	18.35	29	18	47
Dumpster	1	Week	1	1	385	33.50	385	34	419
Subtotals							37,494	24,973	62,467
General Requirements (Site Overhead)						12%	4,499	2,997	7,496
Subtotals							41,993	27,970	69,963
Overhead and Profit						10%	4,199	2,797	6,996
Subtotals							46,192	30,767	76,959

Grand Total $76,959

Note: Estimate is based on typical project materials available at home centers and may not include all elements in photo. Costs are national averages; see the Location Factors at the back of the book to adjust them to your area.

Cost per Square Foot $134

Alternates (Installed Costs)

	Unit	Total Cost
Electrical		
Weatherproof cover for receptacle	Ea.	$16
2-lamp floodlight	Ea.	$66
Electrical sub-panel	Ea.	$990
Switch device	Ea.	$31
Duplex receptacle	Ea.	$33
Telephone jack	Ea.	$23
Fluorescent light fixture	Ea.	$105
Garage door opener	Ea.	$445
Ceiling canopy-style light fixture	Ea.	$62
Chandelier	Ea.	$272
Bathroom heat lamp	Ea.	$83
Smoke detector	Ea.	$58
Flooring		
Floating laminate	S.F.	$6
Sheet vinyl	S.F.	$5
Linoleum	S.F.	$6
12" x 12" ceramic tile	S.F.	$6
Stone	S.F.	$22
Hardwood	S.F.	$8
Roofing		
Aluminum shingles	Sq.	$262
Red cedar shingles	Sq.	$340
Laminated asphalt shingles	Sq.	$121
Slate shingles	Sq.	$815
Steel shingles	Sq.	$340
Clay tiles	Sq.	$465
Concrete tiles	Sq.	$335
Standing seam copper roofing	Sq.	$755
Siding		
Aluminum	S.F.	$3
Fiber-cement	S.F.	$3
Vinyl	S.F.	$2
Cedar clapboard	S.F.	$5
Rough-sawn vertical cedar	S.F.	$5
Texture 1-11	S.F.	$4

A stone countertop and elegant light fixtures are details that enhance a home's value.

These projects often involve additional work, from modifications to the home's adjoining spaces to landscaping and a new or upgraded driveway. For example, the new structure will block light and views from some parts of the house, and this could lead to added skylights or new configurations in the existing home.

If there was previously no garage at all, there may be no driveway, or it may not be large enough or in the correct location. Clarify the work up-front so you and the homeowner are on the same page from the start in terms of cost and schedule.

Garage with Master Suite Above

Project Worksheet

	Unit	Quantity	Price per Unit	Total	Dimensions	Source/Model#/ Specs

Project Worksheet

	Unit	Quantity	Price per Unit	Total	Dimensions	Source/Model#/ Specs

Cabana with Bath

 *abanas, or pool-*houses, like the one shown above, provide a place to change clothes, take shelter from the sun, and have access to refreshments and a shower. While cabanas may not be the best investment in terms of a home's resale value, they can certainly add to the enjoyment of owners who spend a lot of time relaxing and entertaining in their pool area.

Some cabanas have no plumbing or may offer just an outdoor shower and/or a bar sink, but full or half baths are not uncommon. The more elaborate cabanas include full spa treatment, with whirlpool tubs and steam rooms.

Plumbing considerations for a new cabana include a separate hot water heater, which can be turned off in winter in climates with below-freezing temperatures. The cabana must be properly insulated and heated (or the pipes drained and winterized) to prevent pipes from bursting.

If a sauna will be included, it requires drainage and 220-volt current. Other electrical amenities include GFCI outlets for lighting and appliances, and interior and exterior light fixtures. Speaker wiring and phone cabling are another option.

This project estimate is for the construction of a new cabana with full bath, sauna, bar sink, and recessed and outdoor lighting. Tasks include everything from excavation and foundation work through framing, roofing, siding, trim, and all interior finishes, including tile flooring. Subcontracted items are plumbing the bath, and electrical work with a sub-panel, wiring, light fixture, switches and four GFCI outlets.

Project Estimate

Description	Quantity		Labor		Cost per Unit		Total Cost		
	Quantity	Unit	Labor Hrs Per Unit	Labor Hrs Total	Material Per Unit	Installation Per Unit	Material Total	Installation Total	Total
Self-Performed									
Excavation for foundation	1	Job	8	8		412		412	412
Concrete footings	4	C.Y.	2.49	9.96	116	99.02	464	396	860
CMU foundation wall	240	S.F.	0.09	21.60	2.54	3.62	610	869	1,479
Backfilling/grading	1	Job	8	8		412		412	412
Gravel for under slab	4	S.F.	0.01	0.04	0.26	0.19	1	1	2
Slab on grade	192	S.F.	0.02	3.84	1.95	0.78	374	150	524
Treated sills	60	L.F.	0.03	1.80	0.53	1.23	32	74	106
Door framing	1	Ea.	0.25	0.25	17.35	10.55	17	11	28
Window framing	2	Ea.	0.33	0.66	23.50	14.10	47	28	75
Wall framing, plates	180	L.F.	0.02	3.60	0.41	0.85	74	153	227
Wall framing, studs	320	L.F.	0.01	3.20	0.41	0.61	131	195	326
Plywood sheathing	448	S.F.	0.01	4.48	0.68	0.60	305	269	574
Ceiling joists	156	L.F.	0.01	1.56	0.65	0.54	101	84	185
Roof rafters	260	L.F.	0.02	5.20	0.65	0.85	169	221	390
Eyebrow dormer framing	20	L.F.	0.03	0.60	0.65	1.15	13	23	36
Roof sheathing	240	S.F.	0.01	2.40	0.68	0.48	163	115	278
Eyebrow dormer sheathing	32	S.F.	0.01	0.32	0.68	0.42	22	13	35
Miscellaneous framing for eyebrow dormer	16	L.F.	0.03	0.48	0.41	1.35	7	22	29
Rake	40	L.F.	0.04	1.60	1.58	1.69	63	68	131
Rake trim	40	L.F.	0.02	0.80	0.40	1.02	16	41	57
Fascia	32	L.F.	0.04	1.28	2.09	1.50	67	48	115
Soffit	32	L.F.	0.04	1.28	1.58	1.69	51	54	105
Drip edge	32	L.F.	0.02	0.64	0.54	0.85	17	27	44
Felt underlayment	3	Sq.	0.13	0.39	3.75	4.84	11	15	26
Asphalt shingles	3	Sq.	1.78	5.34	52	69	156	207	363
Entry door	1	Pr.	2.29	2.29	1175	96.50	1,175	97	1,272
Windows	2	Ea.	1	2	715	42.50	1,430	85	1,515
Vapor barrier	448	S.F.	0.01	4.48	0.20	0.09	90	40	130
Red cedar siding shingles	5	Sq.	3.20	16	206	135	1,030	675	1,705
Interior partitions	22	L.F.	0.16	3.52	4.05	6.75	89	149	238
Vanity sink base cabinet	1	Ea.	0.80	0.80	202	34	202	34	236
Vanity storage base cabinet	1	Ea.	1.40	1.40	370	59	370	59	429
Solid surface vanity countertop	6	L.F.	0.80	4.80	65.50	34	393	204	597
Prefabricated sauna	1	Ea.	13	13	4225	460	4,225	460	4,685
Wall insulation	448	S.F.	0.01	4.48	0.32	0.21	143	94	237
Ceiling insulation	192	S.F.	0.01	1.92	0.78	0.25	150	48	198
Wall gypsum wallboard	368	S.F.	0.02	7.36	0.34	0.70	125	258	383
Ceiling gysum wallboard	192	S.F.	0.02	3.84	0.34	0.88	65	169	234
Door trim molding	5	Opng.	1.36	6.80	24	57.50	120	288	408
Window trim molding	2	Opng.	0.80	1.60	38.50	34	77	68	145
Ceramic tile base	120	L.F.	0.12	14.40	3.23	4	388	480	868
Ceramic tile floor	192	S.F.	0.08	15.36	3.45	2.74	662	526	1,188
Prime and paint door trim	1	L.F.	0.03	0.03	0.19	1.12		1	1
Prime and paint doors	2	Ea.	1.60	3.20	14.15	59.50	28	119	147
Prime and paint windows	2	Ea.	1.60	3.20	2.73	59.50	5	119	124
Prime and paint siding	450	S.F.	0.02	9	0.15	0.73	68	329	397
Prime and paint exterior trim	72	L.F.	0.03	2.16	0.15	0.94	11	68	79
Cut in gypsum wallboard, primer	176	S.F.	0.01	1.76	0.05	0.26	9	46	55
Prime gypsum wallboard, roller	560	S.F.	0.01	5.60	0.05	0.22	28	123	151
Cut in gypsum wallboard, paint	176	S.F.	0.01	1.76	0.11	0.44	19	77	96
Paint gypsum wallboard, roller	560	S.F.	0.01	5.60	0.12	0.37	67	207	274
Paint trim	60	L.F.	0.02	1.20	0.09	0.91	5	55	60

Project Estimate (continued)

Description	Quantity		Labor		Cost per Unit		Total Cost		
	Quantity	Unit	Labor Hrs Per Unit	Labor Hrs Total	Material Per Unit	Installation Per Unit	Material Total	Installation Total	Total
Subcontract									
Bar sink	1	Ea.	2.50	2.50	234	104	234	104	338
Rough plumbing for bar sink	1	Ea.	6.96	6.96	124	290	124	290	414
Shower stall	1	Ea.	2.91	2.91	510	121	510	121	631
Rough plumbing for shower	1	Ea.	7.80	7.80	268	325	268	325	593
Toilet	1	Ea.	3.02	3.02	186	126	186	126	312
Rough plumbing for toilet	1	Ea.	5.25	5.25	210	219	210	219	429
Vanity sink	1	Ea.	2.86	2.86	465	119	465	119	584
Electrical sub-panel	1	Ea.	6.72	6.72	540	310	540	310	850
Switches	3	Ea.	0.47	1.41	9.30	21.50	28	65	93
GFCI receptacles	4	Ea.	0.65	2.60	39	30	156	120	276
Sauna electrical connection	1	Ea.	1.25	1.25	63.50	57.50	64	58	122
Phone jack	1	Ea.	0.31	0.31	8.70	14.10	9	14	23
Recessed light fixture	4	Ea.	0.29	1.16	59.50	13.10	238	52	290
Outdoor light fixture	2	Ea.	2.29	4.58	204	105	408	210	618
Dumpster	1	Week	1	1	385	33.50	385	34	419
Subtotals							17,710	10,953	28,663
General Requirements (Site Overhead)						12%	2,125	1,314	3,440
Subtotals							19,835	12,267	32,103
Overhead and Profit						10%	1,984	1,227	3,210
Subtotals							21,819	13,494	35,313

Grand Total

Grand Total   **$35,313**

Note: Estimate is based on typical project materials available at home centers and may not include all elements in photo. Costs are national averages; see the Location Factors at the back of the book to adjust them to your area.

Cost per Square Foot   **$184**

This cabana features a bar-style seating area and built-in grill.

Alternates (Installed Costs)

	Unit	Total Cost
Flooring		
Floating laminate	S.F.	$6
Sheet vinyl	S.F.	$5
Linoleum	S.F.	$6
12″ x 12″ ceramic tile	S.F.	$6
Stone	S.F.	$22
Roofing		
Aluminum shingles	Sq.	$262
Red cedar shingles	Sq.	$340
Laminated asphalt shingles	Sq.	$121
Slate shingles	Sq.	$815
Steel shingles	Sq.	$340
Clay tiles	Sq.	$465
Concrete tiles	Sq.	$335
Standing seam copper roofing	Sq.	$755
Siding		
Aluminum	S.F.	$3
Fiber-cement	S.F.	$3
Vinyl	S.F.	$2
Cedar clapboard	S.F.	$5
Rough-sawn vertical cedar	S.F.	$5
Texture 1-11	S.F.	$4
Plumbing		
Electric hot water heater	Ea.	$455
Rough plumbing for outdoor shower	Ea.	$595
Mixing valve for outdoor shower	Ea.	$179
Shower head for outdoor shower	Ea.	$87
Appliances		
Under-cabinet microwave oven	Ea.	$660
Under-counter refrigerator	Ea.	$550

Under-counter refrigerators and ample counter space make this pool cabana a great asset for entertaining.

Part Three

Renovations

Interior Renovations

The Project Estimates

This section of the book consists of 16 different model projects. Each estimate includes:

- A tasks and materials list with unit and total costs
- Typical labor-hours (contractor and subcontractors)
- Total cost including overhead and profit*
- A floor plan showing the layout of the model project that was estimated
- Some points to consider if you're planning a similar project
- A photo showing an example of a finished project. (Photos are for illustrative purposes only; the estimates may not match every detail shown.)

"General Requirements" are also included in the estimate. For residential remodeling projects, these would typically include things like cleanup and permits. Depending on the needs of individual jobs, surveys, plot plans, and soil testing, as well as temporary power, water, or heating, might be additional costs in this category.

Use the Location Factors at the back of the book to adjust costs to your specific location.

Each model project is designed to include typical features and materials. "Alternate" costs are also provided. These are installed costs for different materials, fixtures, or other items that you can use to adjust the estimate to more closely match your project.

These estimates are not intended for use in bidding a job. Instead, refer to them when you need quick, approximate prices for early discussions with a client – or later to check your budget or bid estimates to make sure you've included all major items.

Planning Interior Remodeling Projects

Before undertaking any interior project, you'll want to assess the home's structural, mechanical, and electrical systems and determine their condition. Neither you nor the homeowner will want leaks, doors that won't close, a sloping floor, or poorly functioning fixtures to take away from the finished result. Here are some things to check in the existing house:

- Foundation and framing – overall condition, especially cracks and other signs of settling in walls, floors, and doorways.
- Roof – signs of leaks and damage. If the roof is older than 20 years or has missing or curled shingles, a new roof may be needed. Isolated problems should be corrected, including improperly installed or worn-out flashing.
- Windows – overall condition and signs of water damage.
- Siding – overall condition, water damage.
- Electrical system – age, capacity, and adherence to current code, including safety provisions. Determine whether

the system can handle extra circuits needed for the remodel. Don't forget extra voltage requirements of new appliances and fixtures, such as whirlpool tubs.

- HVAC system – condition and age of existing equipment and whether it can handle the extra load if you're creating new living space.
- Plumbing – whether the water pressure is adequate for the existing fixtures, and the effect of additional fixtures that may be added as part of the remodeling project. Locate piping and make sure it's in good shape, up-to-date, and has proper shut-off valves. These factors affect the difficulty of fixture replacements or relocations – not to mention future performance of the client's new bath or kitchen. Determine whether pipes will need to be moved in order to move or open up a wall or finish a ceiling at full height.
- Hazardous materials – if affected by demolition. Removal of asbestos or mold involves extra cost for professional handling.
- Access – narrow rooms, stairs or hallways, or lack of an exterior door for a basement conversion, which can complicate and add time to the work. Plan carefully for delivery of large items like shower stalls or tubs – for example, having them delivered when a roof or wall is opened up, or a large rough opening is cut for windows or doors. Old fixtures may have to be dismantled or broken up to be removed.

Check local zoning and building code requirements early in the planning stages. Issues like headroom, egress and stairs, separation between a garage and a sleeping area, window height, ventilation, framing, wiring, and plumbing (including septic system capacity) could cause complications.

Converting Basements, Attics, & Garages to Living Space

Three of the main considerations in converting these spaces to living areas are:

- Is the area large enough?
- Is there adequate headroom?
- Can convenient, code-compliant access be provided?

Each of these conversions has its own additional issues.

Basement Conversions

Dampness is a common basement problem that needs to be addressed early in the project. Depending on the severity of water infiltration, the solution could be application of waterproofing materials – or something much more complicated and costly, such as installing a sump pump or drain system outside of the foundation.

Basements usually make good offices, play areas, home theaters, or exercise areas, but cannot normally be used for bedrooms unless they're "walk-outs," partly at grade level. If used for a professional office, the client may want a separate entrance, which may require exterior stairs, paving, and landscaping. The stairs to the main floor need to be code-compliant.

If a new bath or kitchen will be installed in a finished basement, find out if a pump or special types of plumbing fixtures will be needed to overcome gravity issues. Also note whether pipes or ductwork will need to be re-routed to ensure adequate headroom. Support columns are another basement issue. Drop ceilings may be needed to provide future access to pipes and wiring. An existing exterior door will enable materials to be moved into and out of the space during the remodel.

Attic Conversions

Attics can be good spaces for children's bedrooms or playrooms, home offices, and home theaters. In addition to adequate headroom, you need to check the floor joists and framing members to make sure there is enough capacity for the new loads. You'll also need a code-compliant stairway. If the existing attic has no stairs, or folding pull-down ones, you may need to steal some space from the floor below for a new stairway. Proper insulation will have to be installed while still maintaining headroom.

Garage Conversions

Even though these projects involve finishing interior space, you and the homeowner need to also consider the structure's outside appearance. For instance, if garage door(s) are eliminated, it may look odd to have the driveway going right up to the new wall. Be sure to clarify any additional work like paving and landscaping that the client may want.

Closing in Outdoor Spaces

Like room additions, projects such as enclosing a porch or breezeway involve changes to the home's exterior appearance. It's essential that the style, materials, and color of windows, trim, and siding blend with the rest of the structure.

Kitchens & Baths

Any remodeling project that involves a new or upgraded kitchen or bath takes on another dimension – both in planning time and the large number of different materials, fixtures, appliances, vendors, subcontractors, and possibly designers.

It's well-established that of all home improvements, both kitchens and baths add the most value to a house, but they also tend to be the most expensive. Great care needs to be taken at every step, and client decision-making deadlines must be integrated into the schedule.

The National Kitchen & Bath Association offers helpful recommendations on kitchen and bath design and layout, including specific dimensions for various kitchen sizes. *(See the Resources section for contact information)*. Also look for *Kitchen & Bath Project Costs* (available at home centers and bookstores), a book that outlines 35 different kitchen and bath projects – each with a detailed cost estimate. It includes material and installation standards, design tips, and estimating guidance.

Opening Up a Wall

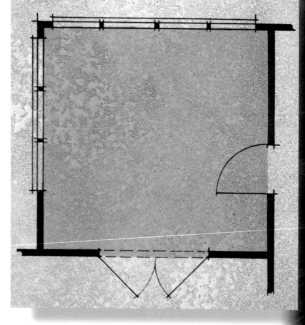

Most homeowners who want to remodel are interested in expanding their space – either literally, with additional square footage, or visually, by creating a more open feeling. Connecting two rooms with interior French doors can lighten the space and extend the line of sight, making the house seem larger.

To determine whether a wall is load-bearing, many contractors start with a general rule: if it runs perpendicular to the ceiling joists, it's load-bearing; if it runs parallel to the joists, it's not. There are exceptions, of course, and a structural engineer should be consulted if there's any doubt. For a large opening in a load-bearing wall, you'll be erecting a temporary support wall, which will be left in place until the permanent support system is constructed.

Include time and materials for cleanup and dust and debris control in your estimate. You'll need coverings for doorways and ducts, furniture and rugs (ideally removed prior to construction) and floors.

When you do the demolition work, remove and save anything salvageable – doors, casing, molding, and trim – to recycle or reuse. Matching the existing casing and molding is no problem in newer homes, but can be a challenge in some older homes with antique trim. One of the most difficult trims to reproduce is the stained hardwood in Victorian or Arts and Crafts homes. In these cases, a custom order from a specialty millwork shop may be the only solution. Clients interested in authentic restorations tend to be understanding of the extra expense.

The project estimated here starts with removal of existing baseboard, molding, and drywall for a new door opening. The next steps are building (and later removing) temporary supports; framing the new opening; installing new interior French doors; and then replacing the baseboard and crown molding. The last tasks are patching the floor and painting.

Project Estimate

Description	Quantity		Labor		Cost per Unit		Total Cost		
	Quantity	Unit	Labor Hrs Per Unit	Labor Hrs Total	Material Per Unit	Installation Per Unit	Material Total	Installation Total	Total
Self-Performed									
Temporary support walls	16	L.F.	0.16	2.56	3.68	6.75	59	108	167
Remove ceiling molding	24	L.F.	0.02	0.48		0.48		12	12
Remove wood baseboard	24	L.F.	0.01	0.24		0.40		10	10
Remove gypsum wallboard	80	S.F.	0.01	0.80		0.24		19	19
Remove existing studs and sole plate	46	L.F.	0.01	0.46		0.24		11	11
Debris removal	2	C.Y.	0.97	1.94		29.50		59	59
Framing, king studs	16	L.F.	0.01	0.16	0.41	0.61	7	10	17
Framing, trimmer (jack) studs	16	L.F.	0.01	0.16	0.41	0.61	7	10	17
Framing, door header	6	L.F.	0.03	0.18	2.84	1.23	17	7	24
Remove temporary support walls	128	S.F.	0.01	1.28		0.40		51	51
French door jamb	21	L.F.	0.04	0.84	6.40	1.80	134	38	172
French doors	2	Ea.	0.94	1.88	255	40	510	80	590
Door opening casing trim, pine	42	L.F.	0.04	1.68	2.01	1.57	84	66	150
Patch floor	6	S.F.	0.05	0.30	6.80	1.99	41	12	53
Re-install old wood trim	1	Job	2	2		84.50		85	85
Paint door frame and trim, brush, primer, and 2 coats	21	L.F.	0.02	0.42	0.06	0.58	1	12	13
Paint doors	2	Ea.	4	8	5.90	148	12	296	308
Paint old baseboard, brush, 2 coats	12	L.F.	0.02	0.24	0.06	0.74	1	9	10
Paint old ceiling molding, brush, 2 coats	24	L.F.	0.02	0.48	0.11	0.74	3	18	21
Paint wall surface, cut in w/ brush, 2 coats	40	S.F.	0.01	0.40	0.11	0.44	4	18	22
Paint entire wall surface, roller, 2 coats	200	S.F.	0.01	2	0.12	0.37	24	74	98
Door handles and hardware	2	Ea.	0.80	1.60	145	34	290	68	358
Subcontract									
Dumpster	1	Week	1	1	256	33.50	256	34	290
Subtotals							1,450	1,107	2,557
General Requirements (Site Overhead)						12%	174	133	307
Subtotals							1,624	1,240	2,864
Overhead and Profit						10%	162	124	286
Subtotals							1,786	1,364	3,150

Grand Total $3,150

Note: Estimate is based on typical project materials available at home centers and may not include all elements in photo. Costs are national averages; see the Location Factors at the back of the book to adjust them to your area.

Alternates (Installed Costs)

	Unit	Total Cost
Alternate Doors and Frames		
Pine door jamb	Ea.	$170
Lauan mahogany flush door slab	Ea.	$83
Birch face flush door slab	Ea.	$95
Oak face flush door slab	Ea.	$131
Walnut face flush door slab	Ea.	$211
Molded hardbord paneled door slab	Ea.	$102
Six-panel pine door slab	Ea.	$228
Two-panel pine door slab	Ea.	$425
Hand-carved fir door slab	Ea.	$585
Hand-carved mahogany door slab	Ea.	$860

New Set of Stairs

I *n remodeling, "new* stairs" can mean anything from refurbishing old stairs to installing brand new ones in a more convenient location or to serve a new addition. Any stairs within living space must be code-compliant. Since stairs are always a focal point, they deserve careful planning in terms of the space they occupy, layout, style, and finishes.

What to consider:

- Stair runs depend on riser height (usually between 7-1/2"–8") and tread depth (usually 9"–10", but can be as much as 12") – both controlled by local codes. A 13-step set of stairs (with 7-1/2" risers and 10" runs) will require

a space 10'-10" long by 3' wide (the code minimum) from the floor below. With ceilings higher than 8', stair runs have to be longer.

- The area at the top and bottom of the staircase should be in proportion to surrounding spaces.

- Existing basement stairs may not have adequate headroom for living space conversions. To address this, you'll need to extend the run into the living space or add turns and landings.

- Handrail height is typically 34"–38", and it must extend from top to bottom posts. Wall handrails are required if the stairs are more than 44" wide. The space between balusters is usually 3"–4". Dimensions are controlled by local codes.

- Material selection is based on visibility and other factors, e.g., engineered wood stringers for stability, and plywood (cabinet grade) for treads and risers on carpeted stairs – versus hardwoods for exposed stairs.

- When rebuilding old stairs, fix the squeaks caused by movement between wood pieces or a nail and wood. Use square-drive finish nails and construction adhesive to attach risers and treads firmly to stringers.

This project estimate covers the complete removal of an old set of wood stairs and construction of new ones. Tasks include demolition/removal of stair carpet, all stair parts, and gypsum wallboard and building and finishing new stairs and an accompanying shelf.

Project Estimate

Description	Quantity		Labor		Cost per Unit		Total Cost		
	Quantity	Unit	Labor Hrs Per Unit	Labor Hrs Total	Material Per Unit	Installation Per Unit	Material Total	Installation Total	Total
Self-Performed									
Remove stairway carpeting	13	Ea.	0.05	0.65		1.46		19	19
Remove stairway padding and tackless strips	13	Ea.	0.05	0.65		1.46		19	19
Remove wall-mounted handrail	20	L.F.	0.04	0.80		1.69		34	34
Remove balusters	65	L.F.	0.02	1.30		0.50		33	33
Remove post to post handrail	20	L.F.	0.04	0.80		1.69		34	34
Remove newel posts	4	L.F.	0.25	1		7.55		30	30
Remove treads	10	Ea.	0.25	2.50		10.55		106	106
Remove landing treads	28	S.F.	0.08	2.24		2.52		71	71
Remove risers	14	Ea.	0.18	2.52		7.70		108	108
Remove skirt boards	40	L.F.	0.04	1.60		1.76		70	70
Remove gypsum wallboard	240	S.F.	0.01	2.40		0.24		58	58
Remove stringer support wall	80	S.F.	0.01	0.80		0.40		32	32
Remove stair stringers	60	L.F.	0.03	1.80		0.93		56	56
Miscellaneous demolition	1	Job	2	2		60.50		61	61
Shelf wall framing	6	L.F.	0.16	0.96	3.68	6.75	22	41	63
Stringer wall framing	20	L.F.	0.16	3.20	3.68	6.75	74	135	209
Stringers	60	L.F.	0.12	7.20	1.76	5.20	70	208	278
Stringer support walls	12	L.F.	0.16	1.92	3.68	6.75	44	81	125
Landing framing	22	L.F.	0.01	0.22	0.94	0.61	21	13	34
Gypsum wallboard	240	S.F.	0.02	4.80	0.34	0.70	82	168	250
Skirt boards	40	L.F.	0.15	6	3.80	6.50	152	260	412
Stair risers	42	L.F.	0.12	5.04	3.36	5.10	141	214	355
Newel posts	4	Ea.	1.33	5.32	350	56.50	1,400	226	1,626
Stair treads	10	Ea.	0.44	4.40	32	18.80	320	188	508
Tread nosing returns	10	L.F.	0.01	0.10	4.29		43		43
Stair landings and winders	28	S.F.	0.44	12.32	11.35	18.80	318	526	844
Balusters	15	Ea.	0.32	4.80	42.50	13.50	638	203	841
Post-to-post handrail	20	L.F.	0.15	3	48	6.15	960	123	1,083
Handrail goosenecks	3	L.F.	0.15	0.45	48	6.15	72	9	81
Wall-mounted handrail	20	L.F.	0.15	3	48	6.15	960	123	1,083
Skirt and riser scotia molding	90	L.F.	0.03	2.70	0.88	1.25	79	113	192
Wainscot	60	S.F.	0.12	7.20	21.50	5.20	1,290	312	1,602
Shelf	8	S.F.	0.44	3.52	11.35	18.80	91	150	241
Shelf trim	6	L.F.	0.03	0.18	2.43	1.41	15	8	23
Prime and paint gypsum wallboard, brushwork	60	S.F.	0.02	1.20	0.17	0.58	10	35	45
Prime and paint gypsum wallboard, roller	180	S.F.	0.01	1.80	0.18	0.46	32	83	115
Prime and paint new woodwork	380	L.F.	0.02	7.60	0.17	0.91	65	346	411
Protective coat on treads, railings, and shelf	290	S.F.	0.02	5.80	0.08	0.74	12	107	119
Subcontract									
Dumpster	1	Week	1	1	256	33.50	256	34	290
Subtotals							7,167	4,437	11,604
General Requirements (Site Overhead)						12%	860	532	1,392
Subtotals							8,027	4,969	12,996
Overhead and Profit						10%	803	497	1,300
Subtotals							8,830	5,466	14,296

Grand Total $14,296

Note: Estimate is based on typical project materials available at home centers and may not include all elements in photo.
Costs are national averages; see the Location Factors at the back of the book to adjust them to your area.

New Set of Stairs

Alternates (Installed Costs)

Stair Parts

	Unit	Total Cost
Simple pine balusters, 30″	Ea.	$16
Ornate pine balusters, 30″	Ea.	$34
Simple birch balusters, 30″	Ea.	$19
Ornate birch balusters, 30″	Ea.	$43
Simple pine balusters, 42″	Ea.	$18
Ornate pine balusters, 42″	Ea.	$44
Simple birch balusters, 42″	Ea.	$25
Ornate birch balusters, 42″	Ea.	$56
Simple starting newel post	Ea.	$91
Ornate starting newel post	Ea.	$405
Simple landing post	Ea.	$182
Ornate landing post	Ea.	$470
Simple oak railing	L.F.	$41
Ornate oak railing	L.F.	$54
Beech risers	L.F.	$12
Fir risers	L.F.	$7
Oak risers	L.F.	$12
Pine risers	L.F.	$8
Pine stairway skirtboard	L.F.	$9
3′ long oak stair treads	Ea.	$53
3′ long beech stair treads	Ea.	$59
3′ long plywood stair treads	Ea.	$29
3′ long maple stair treads	Ea.	$59
3′ long pine/fir stair treads	Ea.	$36

This set of stairs tucks between two rooms, providing access to a new second-story.

Rules of Thumb

- *Maintain consistent dimensions. This is important to building inspectors, and codes require that there be no more than 3/4″ variation in tread depths and riser heights.*

- *It's best not to exceed 8″ on riser heights or 12″ tread depth for a comfortable step.*

- *Follow the 17″–18″ formula: riser height and tread depth, added together, should equal this number.*

- *Always check and follow local code requirements.*

Spiral stair tread depth is 7.5″, measured 12″ from the narrow end, with a riser height no more than 9.5″. Headroom is 6'-6″. Handrail heights are similar to regular stairs. Most spiral stair kits are economical and fairly easy to install. Some builders offer homeowners the option of a trap door built into the floor above to allow for future moving of large objects between the spaces.

Project Worksheet

	Unit	Quantity	Price per Unit	Total	Dimensions	Source/Model#/ Specs

Gable Dormer

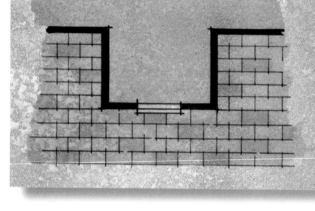

This is a common remodeling project, whether to add a window and headroom in an upstairs room, or as part of an attic conversion. Dormers are integral to most attic conversions, as they provide not only light and air circulation, but help meet code requirements for windows and an emergency exit. Ideally, there would be windows facing each other on each side of the house to provide cross-ventilation.

In terms of design, there are typically two or more gable dormers on one side of a house, especially if they are smaller dormers. While the homeowner may need only one dormer to open up the space in one room, it's important to consider the overall look of the home.

Gable dormers tend to be easier to install than shed dormers because of their smaller size, but they still involve a lot of angle cuts. They also require installation of roof valleys and proper flashing to avoid future leaks.

Basically, the project involves determining the dormer location, cutting into and removing the roofing materials, cutting the rafter(s) and heading them off, then framing the dormer walls, ceiling joists, and rafters. If you're cutting into an engineered truss, you may need guidance from an engineer on proper support. After the frame is in place, the sheathing and roofing felt go on, then the siding, insulation, and interior finish materials.

Don't forget to include weather protection in your planning for this project. You should be able to cover the opening for a gable dormer with a tarp – something you'll want to do whenever you'll be away from the site. Make sure it's well-secured so the wind won't blow it off.

The project estimated here is construction of a new 4' gable dormer on a wood frame house with clapboard siding. Major materials items are framing and trim lumber, sheathing, insulation, housewrap, siding, shingles, an ice barrier, a new window, flashing, drywall, and paint.

Project Estimate

Description	Quantity		Labor		Cost per Unit		Total Cost		
	Quantity	Unit	Labor Hrs Per Unit	Labor Hrs Total	Material Per Unit	Installation Per Unit	Material Total	Installation Total	Total
Self-Performed									
Miscellaneous interior demolition	1	Job	2	2		84.50		85	85
Remove asphalt shingles	3	Sq.	1.14	3.42		34.50		104	104
Remove plywood roof sheathing	272	S.F.	0.01	2.72		0.35		95	95
Cut and remove rafters	24	L.F.	0.02	0.48		0.58		14	14
Install new rafters (sistered onto old rafters)	44	L.F.	0.02	0.88	0.94	0.90	41	40	81
Install new rafter headers	24	L.F.	0.04	0.96	0.94	1.69	23	41	64
Re-install plywood sheathing (re-use existing)	1	Job	4	4		169		85	85
Frame dormer side walls	12	L.F.	0.16	1.92	4.05	6.75	49	81	130
Frame dormer front wall	1	Ea.	0.33	0.33	23.50	14.10	24	14	38
Ceiling joists	24	L.F.	0.01	0.24	0.65	0.54	16	13	29
Dormer roof rafters	48	L.F.	0.03	1.44	0.65	1.15	31	55	86
Valley jack rafters	10	L.F.	0.03	0.30	0.65	1.33	7	13	20
Ridge board	10	L.F.	0.04	0.40	0.94	1.50	9	15	24
Sheathing on walls	80	S.F.	0.01	0.80	0.68	0.60	54	48	102
Sheathing on roof	64	S.F.	0.01	0.64	0.68	0.48	44	31	75
Front gable trim blocking	22	L.F.	0.04	0.88	0.65	1.52	14	33	47
Soffit trim	24	L.F.	0.04	0.96	0.61	1.61	15	39	54
Fascia trim	24	L.F.	0.03	0.72	1.65	1.35	40	32	72
Frieze boards	6	L.F.	0.03	0.18	0.78	1.35	5	8	13
Corner boards	16	L.F.	0.04	0.64	1.65	1.69	26	27	53
Cornice trim	24	L.F.	0.03	0.72	2.16	1.35	52	32	84
Drip edge	16	L.F.	0.02	0.32	0.54	0.85	9	14	23
Ice barrier	1	Sq.	0.36	0.36	50.50	14.10	51	14	65
Laminated asphalt shingles	1	Sq.	2.29	2.29	69	88.50	69	89	158
Dormer window	1	Ea.	0.89	0.89	292	37.50	292	38	330
Lead flashing	6	S.F.	0.06	0.36	3.33	2.30	20	14	34
Step flashing	40	Ea.	0.01	0.40	0.13	0.16	5	6	11
Housewrap	80	S.F.	0.01	0.80	0.13	0.08	10	6	16
Clapboard siding	80	S.F.	0.03	2.40	3.52	1.35	282	108	390
Insulation	168	S.F.	0.01	1.68	0.46	0.34	77	57	134
Gypsum wallboard	168	S.F.	0.02	3.36	0.34	0.70	57	118	175
Miscellaneous gypsum wallboard patching	1	Job	8	8		340		340	340
Window trim	1	Opng.	1.33	1.33	68.50	56.50	69	57	126
Baseboard trim	20	L.F.	0.03	0.60	2.43	1.41	49	28	77
Interior trim painting	34	L.F.	0.02	0.68	0.09	0.91	3	31	34
Interior gypsum wallboard painting, brushwork	44	S.F.	0.02	0.88	0.17	0.58	7	26	33
Interior gypsum wallboard painting, roller	168	S.F.	0.01	1.68	0.18	0.46	30	77	107
Exterior trim painting	94	L.F.	0.01	0.94	0.07	0.46	2	14	16
Exterior siding painting	80	S.F.	0.02	1.60	0.29	0.85	23	68	91
Exterior window painting	1	Ea.	1.33	1.33	2.73	49.50	3	50	53
Subcontract									
Dumpster	1	Week	1	1	385	33.50	385	34	419
Subtotals							1,893	2,094	3,987
General Requirements (Site Overhead)						12%	227	251	478
Subtotals							2,120	2,345	4,465
Overhead and Profit						10%	212	235	447
Subtotals							2,332	2,580	4,912

Grand Total $4,912

Note: Estimate is based on typical project materials available at home centers and may not include all elements in photo. Costs are national averages; see the Location Factors at the back of the book to adjust them to your area.

Cost per Square Foot $182

Gable Dormer

Alternates (Installed Costs)

	Unit	Total Cost
Roofing		
Aluminum shingles	Sq.	$262
Asphalt shingles	Sq.	$99
Red cedar shingles	Sq.	$340
Slate shingles	Sq.	$815
Steel shingles	Sq.	$340
Clay tiles	Sq.	$465
Concrete tiles	Sq.	$335
Standing seam copper roofing	Sq.	$755
Siding		
Aluminum	S.F.	$3
Fiber-cement	S.F.	$3
Vinyl	S.F.	$2
Rough-sawn vertical cedar	S.F.	$5
Texture 1-11	S.F.	$4
Three coat stucco	S.F.	$4

Gable dormers add interest to a variety of roofs.

Project Worksheet

	Unit	Quantity	Price per Unit	Total	Dimensions	Source/Model#/ Specs

Shed Dormer

Second-story

remodeling projects often include shed dormers – an economical way to expand living space or add a small room, such as a bathroom or walk-in closets. Shed dormers are easier to frame than gable dormers because they don't require as many angled cuts and detailed work. The challenges are structural issues and keeping the inside of the house dry.

Since the dormer roof extends from the ridge of the existing roof to a point near or directly over the exterior wall, the existing roof's pitch needs to be steep enough for the shed dormer to look right.

Shallow pitches also limit the weight (and materials) of the dormer roof and, in cold climates, increase the risk of ice dams. The right combination of properly installed flashing, insulation, and soffit

ventilation can help prevent these problems.

Flat-roof shed dormers are often built on the back of a house, where they won't interfere with the home's curb appeal, but will have a major effect in terms of opening up the interior space to full ceiling height. A gutter and downspout should be added if the dormer is over a doorway.

Since shed dormer construction involves cutting many rafters or trusses, you'll need to plan the roof's structural support system beforehand. Usual measures include provision of vertical supports for the ridge board, as well as kneewalls to brace the trusses or rafters you won't be cutting.

Weather protection is an important part of this project. You need to cover the

exposed interior whenever you're not working on the new dormer. Be sure to have large enough tarps ready. You can overlap and secure them with a 1 x 3 strip of furring, which can be screwed to the roof, over the ridge. You can make a seal around new vertical framing members with heavy plastic sheeting secured around them with duct tape and tacked down on the roof.

The project estimated here is the construction of a 12' shed dormer on a wood frame house. It involves demolition of existing roofing and siding, framing the dormer, installing two new windows, and finish work inside and out. Materials range from framing and trim lumber to insulation, siding, roofing, flashing, drywall, and paint. If you don't have roof brackets and planks, you'll need to add them to your material list.

Project Estimate

Description	Quantity	Unit	Labor Hrs Per Unit	Labor Hrs Total	Material Per Unit	Installation Per Unit	Material Total	Installation Total	Total
Self-Performed									
Remove interior gypsum wallboard ceiling	216	S.F.	0.02	4.32		0.60		130	130
Remove furring from ceiling framing	216	S.F.	0.01	2.16		0.06		13	13
Remove asphalt shingles	6	Sq.	1.14	6.84		34.50		207	207
Remove plywood roof sheathing	448	S.F.	0.01	4.48		0.35		157	157
Cut and remove rafters	162	L.F.	0.02	3.24		0.58		94	94
Install new rafters (sistered onto old rafters)	44	L.F.	0.02	0.88	0.94	0.90	41	40	81
Install new rafter headers	48	L.F.	0.04	1.92	0.94	1.69	45	81	126
Re-install plywood sheathing (re-use existing)	1	Job	4	4		169		42	42
Frame dormer side walls	28	L.F.	0.16	4.48	4.05	6.75	113	189	302
Frame dormer front wall	12	L.F.	0.16	1.92	4.05	6.75	49	81	130
Ceiling joists	100	L.F.	0.01	1	0.65	0.54	65	54	119
Dormer roof rafters	160	L.F.	0.03	4.80	0.65	1.15	104	184	288
Sheathing on walls	180	S.F.	0.01	1.80	0.68	0.60	122	108	230
Sheathing on roof	168	S.F.	0.01	1.68	0.68	0.48	114	81	195
Soffit trim	14	L.F.	0.04	0.56	0.61	1.61	9	23	32
Fascia trim	14	L.F.	0.03	0.42	1.65	1.35	23	19	42
Frieze boards	14	L.F.	0.03	0.42	0.78	1.35	11	19	30
Corner boards	24	L.F.	0.04	0.96	1.65	1.69	40	41	81
Cornice trim	48	L.F.	0.03	1.44	2.16	1.35	104	65	169
Drip edge	12	L.F.	0.02	0.24	0.54	0.85	6	10	16
Ice barrier	1	Sq.	0.36	0.36	50.50	14.10	51	14	65
Laminated asphalt shingles	2	Sq.	2.29	4.58	69	88.50	138	177	315
Dormer window	2	Ea.	0.89	1.78	292	37.50	584	75	659
Lead flashing	14	S.F.	0.06	0.84	3.33	2.30	47	32	79
Step flashing	50	Ea.	0.01	0.50	0.13	0.16	7	8	15
Housewrap	180	S.F.	0.01	1.80	0.13	0.08	23	14	37
Clapboard siding	180	S.F.	0.03	5.40	3.52	1.35	634	243	877
Insulation	300	S.F.	0.01	3	0.46	0.34	138	102	240
Gypsum wallboard	300	S.F.	0.02	6	0.34	0.70	102	210	312
Miscellaneous gypsum wallboard patching	2	Job	8	16		340		680	680
Window trim	2	Opng.	1.33	2.66	68.50	56.50	137	113	250
Interior trim painting	34	L.F.	0.02	0.68	0.09	0.91	3	31	34
Interior gypsum wallboard painting, brushwork	79	S.F.	0.02	1.58	0.17	0.58	13	46	59
Interior gypsum wallboard painting, roller	300	S.F.	0.01	3	0.18	0.46	54	138	192
Exterior trim painting	114	L.F.	0.01	1.14	0.07	0.46	3	17	20
Exterior siding painting	180	S.F.	0.02	3.60	0.29	0.85	52	153	205
Exterior window painting	2	Ea.	1.33	2.66	2.73	49.50	5	99	104
Subcontract									
Dumpster	1	Week	1	1	385	33.50	385	34	419
Subtotals							3,222	3,824	7,046
General Requirements (Site Overhead)						12%	387	459	846
Subtotals							3,609	4,283	7,892
Overhead and Profit						10%	361	428	789
Subtotals							3,970	4,711	8,681

Grand Total $8,681

Note: Estimate is based on typical project materials available at home centers and may not include all elements in photo. Costs are national averages; see the Location Factors at the back of the book to adjust them to your area.

Cost per Square Foot $161

Shed Dormer

Alternates (Installed Costs)

	Unit	Total Cost
Roofing		
Aluminum shingles	Sq.	$262
Red cedar shingles	Sq.	$340
Laminated asphalt shingles	Sq.	$121
Slate shingles	Sq.	$815
Steel shingles	Sq.	$340
Clay tiles	Sq.	$465
Concrete tiles	Sq.	$335
Standing seam copper roofing	Sq.	$755
Siding		
Aluminum	S.F.	$3
Fiber-cement	S.F.	$3
Vinyl	S.F.	$2
Rough-sawn vertical cedar	S.F.	$5
Texture 1-11	S.F.	$4
Three coat stucco	S.F.	$4

Shed dormers can be dressed up to become interesting architectural features in their own right, as shown here.

This full shed dormer softens a steep roof.

Project Worksheet

	Unit	Quantity	Price per Unit	Total	Dimensions	Source/Model#/ Specs

Vaulted Ceiling

This project doesn't add more living space, but it makes the most of living in the space. If the homeowner's budget or the site don't allow for an addition or even a bump-out, a vaulted ceiling is a great way to make the space feel larger and more open. A transom or eyebrow window, or skylights, will take the space one step further by adding light and a view that will attract the eye upward, for full appreciation of the open area.

Any large expanse of ceiling requires high-quality drywall installation and finishing. If the drywall panels are not absolutely flat, and the seams flush and smooth, imperfections will show up. Take pains to make sure the first panel is positioned perfectly on the ceiling, so all those that follow will be in correct alignment.

Basically, the project involves removing ceiling light fixtures, wallboard, and ceiling joists, then installing tie beams, new light fixtures, insulation, and gypsum wallboard. A thorough roof inspection should precede this project. Any needed repairs to shingles or flashing should be made in advance, and the roof tested for weather-tightness.

Elaborate variations on vaulted ceilings are becoming more popular, partly because of the availability of bendable 1/4" drywall. Keep in mind the extra cost (about 50% more than standard gypsum board). In addition to skylights, transom or other specialty windows, added features for this project might include a ceiling fan and light fixtures.

This project estimate itemizes the costs to remove a 20' x 14' ceiling in a one-story house with a low-pitch gable roof, followed by construction of a new vaulted ceiling. The project includes wiring and installation of recessed ceiling light fixtures and painting. It is assumed that the roof is in good condition and weather-tight.

Project Estimate

Description	Quantity		Labor		Cost per Unit		Total Cost		
	Quantity	Unit	Labor Hrs Per Unit	Labor Hrs Total	Material Per Unit	Installation Per Unit	Material Total	Installation Total	Total
Self-Performed									
Remove gypsum wallboard ceiling	280	S.F.	0.02	5.60		0.60		168	168
Remove furring	280	S.F.	0.01	2.80		0.06		17	17
Remove ceiling insulation	190	C.F.	0.01	1.90		0.17		32	32
Remove ceiling joists	210	L.F.	0.02	4.20		0.51		107	107
Install collar ties/ceiling joists	128	L.F.	0.01	1.28	0.94	0.61	120	78	198
Rafter breather vents	30	Ea.	0.09	2.70	0.34	3.76	10	113	123
Install ceiling insulation	320	S.F.	0.01	3.20	0.78	0.29	250	93	343
Install furring	280	L.F.	0.02	5.60	0.31	0.97	87	272	359
Install gypsum wallboard ceiling	320	S.F.	0.02	6.40	0.34	0.88	109	282	391
Cut in painting, brushwork	112	S.F.	0.02	2.24	0.17	0.58	19	65	84
Ceiling painting, roller	320	S.F.	0.01	3.20	0.18	0.46	58	147	205
Subcontract									
Electrician minimum	1	Job	4	4		184		184	184
Wiring for new light fixtures	4	Ea.	0.25	1	5.20	11.50	21	46	67
Recessed light fixtures	4	Ea.	0.27	1.08	39.50	12.25	158	49	207
Dumpster	1	Week	1	1	385	33.50	385	34	419
Subtotals							1,217	1,687	2,904
General Requirements (Site Overhead)						12%	146	202	348
Subtotals							1,363	1,889	3,252
Overhead and Profit						10%	136	189	325
Subtotals							1,499	2,078	3,577

Grand Total

Grand Total   **$3,577**

Note: Estimate is based on typical project materials available at home centers and may not include all elements in photo. Costs are national averages; see the Location Factors at the back of the book to adjust them to your area.

Cost per Square Foot   **$13**

Alternates (Installed Costs)

	Unit	Total Cost
Skylights		
46" x 21-1/2" venting	Ea.	$425
Flashing set for above	Ea.	$106
46" x 28" venting	Ea.	$410
Flashing set for above	Ea.	$107
57" x 44" venting	Ea.	$585
Flashing set for above	Ea.	$114
Electrical		
Paddle fan	Ea.	$440
Fluorescent light fixture	Ea.	$105
Ceiling canopy-style light fixture	Ea.	$62
Chandelier	Ea.	$272
Wall-mounted incandescent fixture	Ea.	$90
8' track lighting section	Ea.	$145
White cylinder light fixtures for track lighting	Ea.	$79

Loft

Lofts can range from a small platform for a bed to free up space below, to garage storage areas over vehicles, to new living space in one of the main rooms of a house. A large family or great room with a vaulted ceiling is often a good candidate for a home office, sitting, or study area loft above. These are spaces set apart, with the advantage that users can be aware of what's going on below. These interior remodeling projects can be economical, provided there aren't too many major new features or extensive structural changes.

Because the project estimated here may have such a big visual impact on one of the house's most-used spaces, some homeowners may want an architect to devise a plan. An architect or engineer may also be required to address structural issues, including the effect of the new construction on load-bearing walls, the need to strengthen the floor below, and adequate support for the new living space. Other considerations include:

- Fire safety: including smoke detectors and an acceptable fire escape route.

- Stairs: enough space for a code-compliant staircase. Spiral stairs are good space-savers for lofts as long as the homeowners are comfortable with their limitations. *See also the New Set of Stairs project.*

- Sound insulation: a good idea for the floor of the new space, making it more useful for reading or studying.

- Windows: may need to be added to the new space – for both ventilation and light.

- A fan: may be necessary to recirculate rising hot air and keep the space comfortable.

- Electrical requirements: will depend on code and the homeowner's particular use of the space.

The project estimated here is a 24' x 12' loft constructed over part of a great room. It includes removal of finish materials as needed for the new framing, and installation of partitions, stairs, and finish materials, including a hardwood floor on the upper level. The space under the loft requires a bearing partition and door for access.

Project Estimate

Description	Quantity	Unit	Labor Hrs Per Unit	Labor Hrs Total	Material Per Unit	Installation Per Unit	Material Total	Installation Total	Total
Self-Performed									
Dust partition	432	S.F.	0.01	4.32	0.35	0.34	151	147	298
Remove ceiling gypsum wallboard for deck framing	432	S.F.	0.02	8.64		0.60		259	259
Remove wall gypsum wallbord for framing	720	S.F.	0.01	7.20		0.24		173	173
Remove ceiling insulation for framing	432	C.F.	0.01	4.32		0.17		73	73
Remove wall insulation for framing	240	C.F.	0.01	2.40		0.17		41	41
Remove flooring at new loft area	480	S.F.	0.01	4.80		0.05		24	24
Debris removal	5	C.Y.	0.97	4.85		29.50		148	148
Studs for framing connections	36	L.F.	0.03	1.08	0.41	1.35	15	49	64
Load-bearing partition	12	L.F.	0.16	1.92	4.05	6.75	49	81	130
Front wall partition	24	L.F.	0.16	3.84	4.05	6.75	97	162	259
Under-stair partition framing	12	L.F.	0.16	1.92	4.05	6.75	49	81	130
Floor framing	264	L.F.	0.02	5.28	1.42	0.75	375	198	573
Subfloor	304	SF Flr.	0.01	3.04	0.73	0.50	222	152	374
Stair stringers	36	L.F.	0.12	4.32	1.76	5.20	63	187	250
New wall insulation	720	S.F.	0.01	7.20	0.32	0.21	230	151	381
New floor/ceiling insulation	736	S.F.	0.01	7.36	0.78	0.25	574	184	758
New furring	304	L.F.	0.02	6.08	0.31	0.97	94	295	389
Gypsum wallboard on walls	1360	S.F.	0.02	27.20	0.34	0.70	462	952	1,414
Gypsum wallboard on ceiling	432	S.F.	0.02	8.64	0.34	0.88	147	380	527
Pre-hung doors	2	Ea.	0.84	1.68	292	35.50	584	71	655
Door trim	4	Opng.	1.36	5.44	24	57.50	96	230	326
Stair risers	13	L.F.	0.12	1.56	3.36	5.10	44	66	110
Stair skirt board	28	L.F.	0.15	4.20	3.80	6.50	106	182	288
Stair treads	12	Ea.	0.47	5.64	128	19.90	1,536	239	1,775
Stair tread returns	12	L.F.	0.01	0.12	4.29		51		51
Newel posts	5	Ea.	1.14	5.70	42	48.50	210	243	453
Stair and loft railings	36	L.F.	0.13	4.68	35	5.65	1,260	203	1,463
Balusters	95	Ea.	0.30	28.50	11.75	12.50	1,116	1,188	2,304
Baseboard	156	L.F.	0.03	4.68	2.43	1.41	379	220	599
Loft trim at floor/wall	24	L.F.	0.04	0.96	1.38	1.54	33	37	70
Hardwood flooring	304	S.F.	0.09	27.36	4.08	3.76	1,240	1,143	2,383
Sand and finish hardwood flooring	304	S.F.	0.03	9.12	0.78	0.82	237	249	486
Prime and paint, trim	180	L.F.	0.02	3.60	0.09	0.91	16	164	180
Finishing of skirts, treads, and risers	28	L.F.	0.02	0.56	0.17	0.91	5	25	30
Stairway and loft railing finish	108	S.F.	0.02	2.16	0.11	0.91	12	98	110
Priming at walls and ceiling, cut in	400	S.F.	0.01	4	0.06	0.25	24	100	124
Priming at walls and ceiling, roller	400	S.F.	0.01	4	0.06	0.23	24	92	116
Painting at walls and ceiling, cut in	1792	S.F.	0.01	17.92	0.06	0.25	108	448	556
Painting at walls and ceiling, roller	1792	S.F.	0.01	17.92	0.12	0.37	215	663	878
Prime and paint doors and trim	2	Ea.	3.20	6.40	12.05	119	24	238	262
Subcontract									
Dumpster	1	Week	1	1	385	33.50	385	34	419
Subtotals							10,233	9,670	19,903
General Requirements (Site Overhead)						12%	1,228	1,160	2,388
Subtotals							11,461	10,830	22,291
Overhead and Profit						10%	1,146	1,083	2,229
Subtotals							12,607	11,913	24,520

Grand Total $24,520

Note: Estimate is based on typical project materials available at home centers and may not include all elements in photo. Costs are national averages; see the Location Factors at the back of the book to adjust them to your area.

Cost per Square Foot $81

Renovations

Alternates (Installed Costs)

	Unit	Total Cost
Skylights		
46" x 21-1/2" venting	Ea.	$425
Flashing set for above	Ea.	$106
46" x 28" venting	Ea.	$410
Flashing set for above	Ea.	$107
57" x 44" venting	Ea.	$585
Flashing set for above	Ea.	$114
Electrical		
Paddle fan	Ea.	$440
Fluorescent light fixture	Ea.	$105
Ceiling canopy-style light fixture	Ea.	$62
Chandelier	Ea.	$272
Wall-mounted incandescent fixture	Ea.	$90
8' track lighting section	Ea.	$145
White cylinder light fixtures for track lighting	Ea.	$79
Stair Parts		
Simple pine balusters, 30"	Ea.	$16
Ornate pine balusters, 30"	Ea.	$34
Simple birch balusters, 30"	Ea.	$19
Ornate birch balusters, 30"	Ea.	$43
Simple pine balusters, 42"	Ea.	$18
Ornate pine balusters, 42"	Ea.	$44
Simple birch balusters, 42"	Ea.	$25
Ornate birch balusters, 42"	Ea.	$56
Simple starting newel post	Ea.	$91
Ornate starting newel post	Ea.	$405
Simple landing post	Ea.	$182
Ornate landing post	Ea.	$470
Simple oak railing	L.F.	$41
Ornate oak railing	L.F.	$54
Beech risers	L.F.	$12
Fir risers	L.F.	$7
Oak risers	L.F.	$12
Pine risers	L.F.	$8
Pine stairway skirtboard	L.F.	$9
3' long oak stair treads	Ea.	$53
3' long beech stair treads	Ea.	$59
3' long plywood stair treads	Ea.	$29
3' long maple stair treads	Ea.	$59
3' long pine/fir stair treads	Ea.	$36

Lofts can include storage and accent spaces. For example, the half wall that overlooks the area below might be lined with open bookshelves or cupboards.

Project Worksheet

	Unit	Quantity	Price per Unit	Total	Dimensions	Source/Model#/ Specs

Converting a Half Attic

Using part of an attic for a playroom, office, or home theater is a good solution for many homeowners. It leaves some storage space, is out of the way, and can be sound-proofed with insulation, carpeting, and acoustical ceiling and wall coverings. Although these projects are easier than full attic conversions – there's less space to finish and no bath – you still have to deal with most of the framing, access, and code issues outlined in the *Converitng a Full Attic* project.

One of the challenges with all attic conversions is access: getting rubbish out and new building materials in. If stairways are inadequate, you could cut and frame the opening for a new gable-end window early in the project. (Don't forget scaffold and dumpster rentals and disposal fees – a major budget item in any project of this size.)

Heat is a factor when locating skylights and windows. Choose shaded sides of the house if possible. If direct sunlight is unavoidable, "selective glazing" provides a clear appearance and screens out heating rays, while allowing visible light to pass through.

Playrooms should have maximum open floor space. You might suggest kneewall or other built-in cabinets/shelves for toy storage.

Offices and home theaters have specific needs for new circuits and upgraded wiring for devices and speakers, along with phone, Internet, and video cable hook-ups. Your client might consider installing "structured cabling" – a low-voltage power system that links voice, data, audio-video, and security outlets throughout the house to a central distribution source. Hire a custom technology firm or specialized electrical contractor for this. Although it's cheaper to install in new construction or a gutted renovation, it can be retrofitted in finished homes.

This project estimate covers the costs to convert a 24' x 22' half attic into an entertainment area or office. It includes construction and demolition to install new skylights and windows, new insulated and finished walls and ceilings, an interior door and baseboard/trim, carpet, and some upgrades to existing stairs.

Subcontracted work includes new baseboard heat, and wiring for electrical switches/lighting/outlets, and phone, cable TV, and Internet.

Project Estimate

Description	Quantity	Unit	Labor Hrs Per Unit	Labor Hrs Total	Material Per Unit	Installation Per Unit	Material Total	Installation Total	Total
Self-Performed									
Remove sections of roof rafters for new skylights	32	L.F.	0.02	0.64		0.58		19	19
Remove roofing for new skylights	100	S.F.	0.01	1		0.35		35	35
Remove roof sheathing for new skylights	52	S.F.	0.01	0.52		0.35		18	18
Skylight headers	48	L.F.	0.05	2.40	0.94	1.99	45	96	141
Sister rafters for skylight framing	96	L.F.	0.03	2.88	0.94	1.06	90	102	192
Skylights	3	Ea.	1.33	3.99	395	56.50	1,185	170	1,355
Skylight flashing sets	3	Ea.	1.60	4.80	46.50	67.50	140	203	343
Roofing installation at skylights	1	Sq.	1.45	1.45	42	56.50	42	57	99
Roofing underlayment at skylights	1	Sq.	0.36	0.36	50.50	14.10	51	14	65
Floor underlayment in attic	560	SF Flr.	0.01	5.60	1.34	0.48	750	269	1,019
Siding removal for new windows	100	S.F.	0.02	2		0.69		69	69
Framing removal for new windows	18	L.F.	0.01	0.18		0.24		4	4
Framing for new windows	18	L.F.	0.03	0.54	0.41	1.06	7	19	26
Headers for new windows	24	L.F.	0.04	0.96	0.65	1.88	16	45	61
Sheathing removal at new windows	45	S.F.	0.01	0.45		0.43		19	19
New windows	3	Ea.	1.33	3.99	278	56.50	834	170	1,004
Exterior window trim	44	L.F.	0.03	1.32	2.16	1.35	95	59	154
Replace wood siding around new windows		Sq.	4	1	179	169	45	42	87
New ceiling joists	192	L.F.	0.01	1.92	0.65	0.54	125	104	229
Furring at sloped and flat ceiling	480	L.F.	0.02	9.60	0.31	0.97	149	466	615
Interior partitions	32	L.F.	0.16	5.12	4.05	6.75	130	216	346
Wall insulation	640	S.F.	0.01	6.40	0.32	0.21	205	134	339
Ceiling insulation	640	S.F.	0.01	6.40	0.78	0.25	499	160	659
Gypsum wallboard on walls	640	S.F.	0.02	12.80	0.34	0.70	218	448	666
Gypsum wallboard on ceilings	640	S.F.	0.02	12.80	0.34	0.88	218	563	781
Gypsum wallboard around skylights	30	S.F.	0.03	0.90	0.34	1.42	10	43	53
Interior door	1	Ea.	0.84	0.84	292	35.50	292	36	328
Baseboard	76	L.F.	0.03	2.28	2.43	1.41	185	107	292
Door trim	1	Opng.	1.51	1.51	34	64	34	64	98
Window trim	3	Opng.	0.80	2.40	38.50	34	116	102	218
Railing at stairway opening	8	L.F.	0.17	1.36	23	7.05	184	56	240
Prime and paint door	1	Ea.	1.60	1.60	11.80	59.50	12	60	72
Prime and paint interior of windows	3	Ea.	1.33	3.99	2.38	49.50	7	149	156
Prime and paint trim at exterior of windows	3	Ea.	1.33	3.99	2.73	49.50	8	149	157
Prime and paint wood trim	140	L.F.	0.02	2.80	0.09	0.91	13	127	140
Prime and paint stairway railing	24	S.F.	0.02	0.48	0.11	0.91	3	22	25
Paint walls, cut in with primer	252	S.F.	0.01	2.52	0.05	0.26	13	66	79
Paint walls, cut in with paint	252	S.F.	0.01	2.52	0.11	0.44	28	111	139
Paint walls, roll with primer	1280	S.F.	0.01	12.80	0.05	0.22	64	282	346
Paint walls, roll with paint	1280	S.F.	0.01	12.80	0.12	0.37	154	474	628
Carpet	1020	S.F.	0.02	20.40	2.94	0.69	2,999	704	3,703
Carpet pad	1020	S.F.	0.01	10.20	0.82	0.23	836	235	1,071
Subcontract									
Baseboard radiation	20	L.F.	0.28	5.60	7.35	11.60	147	232	379
Thermostat	1	Ea.	1	1	29.50	47	30	47	77
Copper pipe	80	L.F.	0.10	8	2.36	4.76	189	381	570
Copper fittings	12	Ea.	0.42	5.04	1.25	19.55	15	235	250
Electrical switch	2	Ea.	0.47	0.94	9.30	21.50	19	43	62
Duplex outlets	10	Ea.	0.55	5.50	7.50	25	75	250	325
Telephone receptacle	1	Ea.	0.31	0.31	8.70	14.10	9	14	23
Cable TV receptacle	1	Ea.	0.50	0.50	14.50	23	15	23	38
Lighting wiring	4	Ea.	0.25	1	5.20	11.50	21	46	67

Project Estimate (continued)

Description	Quantity		Labor		Cost per Unit		Total Cost		
	Quantity	Unit	Labor Hrs Per Unit	Labor Hrs Total	Material Per Unit	Installation Per Unit	Material Total	Installation Total	Total
Computer receptacle	1	Ea.	0.50	0.50	14.50	23	15	23	38
Recessed lighting	4	Ea.	0.27	1.08	39.50	12.25	158	49	207
Smoke detector	1	Ea.	0.55	0.55	33	25	33	25	58
Sub-panel	1	Ea.	5.71	5.71	171	262	171	262	433
Dumpster	1	Week	1	1	256	33.50	256	34	290
Subtotals							10,955	7,952	18,907
General Requirements (Site Overhead)						12%	1,315	954	2,269
Subtotals							12,270	8,906	21,176
Overhead and Profit						10%	1,227	891	2,118
Subtotals							13,497	9,797	23,294

Grand Total $23,294

Note: Estimate is based on typical project materials available at home centers and may not include all elements in photo. Costs are national averages; see the Location Factors at the back of the book to adjust them to your area.

Cost per Square Foot **$42**

Alternates (Installed Costs)

	Unit	Total Cost
Skylights		
46" x 21-1/2" venting	Ea.	$425
Flashing set for above	Ea.	$106
46" x 28" venting	Ea.	$410
Flashing set for above	Ea.	$107
57" x 44" venting	Ea.	$585
Flashing set for above	Ea.	$114
Electrical		
Paddle fan	Ea.	$440
Fluorescent light fixture	Ea.	$105
Ceiling canopy-style light fixture	Ea.	$62
Chandelier	Ea.	$272
Wall-mounted incandescent fixture	Ea.	$90
8' track lighting section	Ea.	$145
White cylinder light fixtures for track lighting	Ea.	$79
Flooring		
Floating laminate flooring	S.F.	$6
Linoleum flooring	S.F.	$6
12" x 12" ceramic tile flooring	S.F.	$6
Stone flooring	S.F.	$22
Hardwood flooring	S.F.	$8

Fiberglass batts are the usual insulation in attics, but a more "green" alternative is cotton – it's skin- and lung-friendly, with an R-rating that compares favorably to fiberglass. The downside is cost; it's special-order and premium-priced from most building suppliers. Many clients will pay more for healthy materials, however, and appreciate your environmental awareness.

New windows, skylights, and a cathedral ceiling transform an attic into a bright, open living space.

Renovations

Project Worksheet

	Unit	Quantity	Price per Unit	Total	Dimensions	Source/Model#/ Specs

Converting a Full Attic

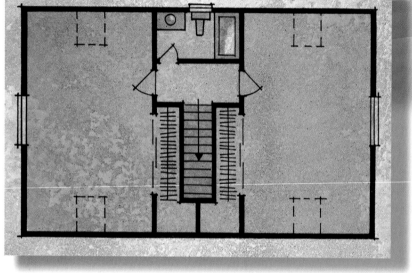

T<i>hese projects vary</i> widely in complexity depending on the features the homeowner wants to include and the existing conditions in the attic. Among the major items to consider:

- Code requirements, including headroom, rafter spacing, and egress/ingress elements like stairs and windows.

- Additional structural/framing issues, such as the need to:
  - Add larger joists to support the new materials and the live load.
  - Assess the existing roof slope and height vs. needed headroom.
  - Add windows, dormers, and/or skylights.
  - Build new stairs.

- Plumbing and electrical, such as the need to:
  - Upgrade electrical service to handle additional circuits.
  - Add lighting or ceiling/bathroom exhaust fans.
  - Build a chase to convey plumbing and heating.
  - Add heating/AC capacity or new units for the new space.
  - Relocate ductwork, piping, and wiring without losing essential headroom or excessively notching structural framing members.

Among the biggest challenges can be figuring out where to locate a new set of stairs if the existing ones are inadequate. For a 13-step set of stairs (with 7-1/2" risers and 10" runs and 8' floor to floor), you'll need a space 10'-10" long by 3' wide (code minimum) from the floor below. If the stairs can't fit in an existing hallway or other space, the only option is building them outside, if that suits the homeowner's needs, and if it can be done within setback, zoning, and other restrictions. Spiral staircases are popular in attic conversions because of their space savings, but may not work for every homeowner. *See also the New Set of Stairs project.*

Project costs can be cut by using skylights instead of dormers with windows, provided there is adequate headroom, and the sky windows meet code requirements. These are a good option with vaulted ceilings.

Don't forget to include protection in your estimate for stair and hallway finishes as well as dust protection.

The project estimated here is the conversion of a 24' x 36' unfinished full attic to two bedrooms and a bath. It involves framing for four new skylights and new wall partitions; roof demolition, flashing, etc. for the skylights; insulation and wallboard; baseboard and trim; and painting and carpeting. The subcontracted items include piping for the bath fixtures, baseboard radiation, and installation of wiring for 20 duplex outlets and one GFCI receptacle, eight recessed lights, and a smoke detector, as well as phone, computer, and cable TV jacks. It's assumed that the attic is weathertight, and the floor framing is adequate to support the new use of this space.

See the Converting a Half Attic project for more on attic renovations.

Project Estimate

Description	Quantity	Unit	Labor Hrs Per Unit	Labor Hrs Total	Material Per Unit	Installation Per Unit	Material Total	Installation Total	Total
Self-Performed									
Remove sections of roof rafters for new skylights	42	L.F.	0.02	0.84		0.58		24	24
Remove roofing for new skylights	135	S.F.	0.01	1.35		0.35		47	47
Remove roof sheathing for new skylights	70	S.F.	0.01	0.70		0.35		25	25
Skylight headers	64	L.F.	0.05	3.20	0.94	1.99	60	127	187
Sister rafters for skylight framing	128	L.F.	0.03	3.84	0.94	1.06	120	136	256
Skylight	4	Ea.	1.33	5.32	395	56.50	1,580	226	1,806
Skylight flashing set	4	Ea.	1.60	6.40	46.50	67.50	186	270	456
Roofing installation at skylights	2	Sq.	1.45	2.90	42	56.50	84	113	197
Roofing underlayment at skylights	1	Sq.	0.36	0.36	50.50	14.10	51	14	65
Floor underlayment in attic	864	SF Flr.	0.01	8.64	1.34	0.48	1,158	415	1,573
New ceiling joists	392	L.F.	0.01	3.92	0.65	0.54	255	212	467
Furring	792	L.F.	0.02	15.84	0.31	0.97	246	768	1,014
Interior partitions	122	L.F.	0.16	19.52	3.68	6.75	449	824	1,273
Wall insulation	360	S.F.	0.01	3.60	0.32	0.21	115	76	191
Ceiling insulation	756	S.F.	0.01	7.56	0.78	0.25	590	189	779
Gysum wallboard on walls	2920	S.F.	0.02	58.40	0.34	0.70	993	2,044	3,037
Gypsum wallboard on ceilings	504	S.F.	0.02	10.08	0.34	0.88	171	444	615
Interior doors	3	Ea.	0.84	2.52	292	35.50	876	107	983
Door trim sets	6	Opng.	1.36	8.16	24	57.50	144	345	489
Locksets	3	Ea.	0.67	2.01	58.50	28	176	84	260
Closet door slabs	6	Ea.	0.89	5.34	158	37.50	948	225	1,173
Closet door frame	44	L.F.	0.04	1.76	6.40	1.80	282	79	361
Closet door trim	4	Ea.	0.67	2.68	48	28	192	112	304
Closet shelf and pole	16	L.F.	0.13	2.08	2.40	5.65	38	90	128
Baseboard	274	L.F.	0.03	8.22	2.43	1.41	666	386	1,052
Window trim	2	Opng.	0.80	1.60	38.50	34	77	68	145
Stair railing	16	L.F.	0.17	2.72	23	7.05	368	113	481
Prime and paint interior of windows	2	Ea.	1.33	2.66	2.38	49.50	5	99	104
Prime and paint wood trim	490	L.F.	0.02	9.80	0.09	0.91	44	446	490
Prime and paint interior doors, frame, and trim	9	Ea.	1.60	14.40	11.80	59.50	106	536	642
Prime and paint stairway railing	16	S.F.	0.02	0.32	0.11	0.91	2	15	17
Paint walls, cut in with primer	490	S.F.	0.01	4.90	0.05	0.26	25	127	152
Paint walls, cut in with paint	490	S.F.	0.01	4.90	0.11	0.44	54	216	270
Paint walls, prime with roller	3424	S.F.	0.01	34.24	0.05	0.22	171	753	924
Paint walls, paint with roller	3424	S.F.	0.01	34.24	0.12	0.37	411	1,267	1,678
Carpet pad	820	S.F.	0.01	8.20	0.82	0.23	672	189	861
Carpet	820	S.F.	0.02	16.40	2.94	0.69	2,411	566	2,977
Vanity top	3	L.F.	0.27	0.81	24.50	11.25	74	34	108
Vanity base	1	Ea.	1	1	232	42.50	232	43	275
Subcontract									
Baseboard radiation	40	L.F.	0.28	11.20	7.35	11.60	294	464	758
Thermostat	1	Ea.	1	1	29.50	47	30	47	77
Copper pipe for hot water supply	120	L.F.	0.10	12	2.36	4.76	283	571	854
Fittings for copper pipe	12	Ea.	0.42	5.04	1.25	19.55	15	235	250

Project Estimate (continued)

Description	Quantity		Labor		Cost per Unit		Total Cost		
	Quantity	Unit	Labor Hrs Per Unit	Labor Hrs Total	Material Per Unit	Installation Per Unit	Material Total	Installation Total	Total
Lavatory	1	Ea.	2.50	2.50	234	104	234	104	338
Rough plumbing for lavatory	1	Ea.	6.96	6.96	124	290	124	290	414
Tub/shower	1	Ea.	3.20	3.20	380	134	380	134	514
Rough plumbing for tub/shower	1	Ea.	7.73	7.73	182	325	182	325	507
Toilet	1	Ea.	3.02	3.02	186	126	186	126	312
Rough plumbing for toilet	1	Ea.	5.86	5.86	485	245	485	245	730
Electrical switches	3	Ea.	0.47	1.41	9.30	21.50	28	65	93
Duplex outlets	20	Ea.	0.55	11	7.50	25	150	500	650
Telephone jack	2	Ea.	0.31	0.62	8.70	14.10	17	28	45
Cable TV jack	2	Ea.	0.50	1	14.50	23	29	46	75
Lighting wiring	8	Ea.	0.25	2	5.20	11.50	42	92	134
Computer cable jack	2	Ea.	0.50	1	14.50	23	29	46	75
GFCI receptacle	1	Ea.	0.65	0.65	39	30	39	30	69
Recessed lighting	8	Ea.	0.27	2.16	39.50	12.25	316	98	414
Smoke detector	1	Ea.	0.55	0.55	33	25	33	25	58
Sub-panel	1	Ea.	5.71	5.71	171	262	171	262	433
Dumpster	1	Week	1	1	385	33.50	385	34	419
Subtotals							17,484	15,621	33,105
General Requirements (Site Overhead)						12%	2,098	1,875	3,973
Subtotals							19,582	17,496	37,078
Overhead and Profit						10%	1,958	1,750	3,708
Subtotals							21,540	19,246	40,786

Grand Total $40,786

Note: Estimate is based on typical project materials available at home centers and may not include all elements in photo. Costs are national averages; see the Location Factors at the back of the book to adjust them to your area.

Cost per Square Foot $47

Alternates (Installed Costs)

	Unit	Total Cost
Flooring		
Floating laminate	S.F.	$6
Sheet vinyl	S.F.	$5
Linoleum	S.F.	$6
12″ x 12″ ceramic tile	S.F.	$6
Stone	S.F.	$22
Lavatory faucets		
Cross-handle polished chrome faucet and pop-up drain	Ea.	$177
Cross-handle polished brass faucet and pop-up drain	Ea.	$238
Single-lever black nickel faucet and pop-up drain	Ea.	$289
Single-lever polished brass faucet and pop-up drain	Ea.	$289
Single-lever polished chrome faucet and pop-up drain	Ea.	$211
Vanity Cabinets		
Vanity bases, 2 doors, 30″ high, 21″ deep, 24″ wide, average	Ea.	$236
Vanity bases, 2 doors, 30″ high, 21″ deep, 24″ wide, custom	Ea.	$335
Vanity bases, 2 doors, 30″ high, 21″ deep, 36″ wide, average	Ea.	$360
Vanity bases, 2 doors, 30″ high, 21″ deep, 36″ wide, custom	Ea.	$545
Vanity Countertops/Sinks		
Solid surface top/lavatory, 25″ wide	Ea.	$270
Solid surface top/lavatory, 31″ wide	Ea.	$320
Granite top	L.F.	$148
Vitreous china lavatory	Ea.	$284
Porcelain enamel on cast iron lavatory	Ea.	$350

If floor space is limited, built-in kneewall cabinets, bookcases, or dresser units will leave more room for free-standing furniture.

If you're installing new floor joists, you can prevent excessive movement (and cracks or nail pops in the ceiling below) by the use of bridging, and installing a ledger strip or standard joist hangers.

Renovations

Project Worksheet

	Unit	Quantity	Price per Unit	Total	Dimensions	Source/Model#/ Specs

Converting an Attached Garage

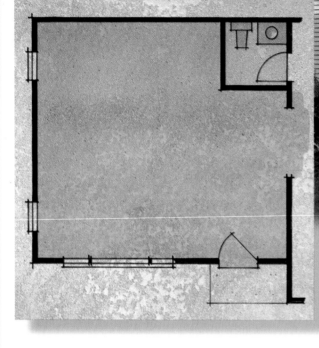

A *typical attached* two-car garage provides at least 440 square feet. This space could become a family room, home theater, in-law or guest apartment, studio, or professional office. There's space to include features like closets, a bath and/or laundry area, a mudroom, built-in bookcases and cabinets, or a fireplace or wood stove.

Garage floors are often at or below grade level, and drainage slopes need to be dealt with. Surface water run-off must be diverted via drains or berms. This can be tricky; expert advice might be needed to avoid future problems. Floors are typically framed with 2 x 6 or 2 x 8 sleepers to create space for the vapor barrier, insulation, plumbing, and electrical/media wiring.

Be sure to factor in roof ventilation – soffit, ridge, and/or gable vents may be used.

Local codes may consider this conversion a bedroom based on criteria such as an opaque "privacy" door and/or a closet. Talk to the building inspector before you go too far with planning to be clear on this and other code issues.

To keep the exterior of this conversion from looking like an ex-garage:

- Carefully match and weave the new siding into the old, and duplicate the existing molding and trimwork.

- Upgrade the outside door (formerly the side door, if there was one).

- Make sure windows duplicate or complement those on the house; consider a floor-to-ceiling bay window to break up the "flat" façade.

- Provide landscaping, including re-routing the driveway; creating a buffer space for plantings between the driveway and the converted garage; and dressing up the approach to the outside door with a walkway, garden, or a small patio/deck.

This project estimate covers the costs to convert an attached two-car garage to a family room with a half bath. It includes demolition to remove the garage doors and some siding, and installation of a picture window and glazed door, insulating, and some re-siding. Finish work includes vinyl flooring installation and painting. Subcontracted items are the half bath piping and fixtures, along with electric baseboard heat, a switch, and receptacles.

Project Estimate

Description	Quantity		Labor		Cost per Unit		Total Cost		
	Quantity	Unit	Labor Hrs Per Unit	Labor Hrs Total	Material Per Unit	Installation Per Unit	Material Total	Installation Total	Total
Self-Performed									
Demolish slab for plumbing	1	Job	20	20		701		701	701
Patch slab at plumbing	1	Job	16	16		675		675	675
Sleeper joists	525	L.F.	0.01	5.25	0.41	0.54	215	284	499
Plywood subfloor	704	S.F.	0.02	14.08	0.73	0.64	514	451	965
Garage door infill, top plates	27	L.F.	0.02	0.54	0.41	0.85	11	23	34
Garage door infill, bottom plate	13	L.F.	0.03	0.39	0.53	1.23	7	16	23
Garage door infill, studs	192	L.F.	0.01	1.92	0.41	0.61	79	117	196
Headers	28	L.F.	0.04	1.12	0.65	1.88	18	53	71
Garage door infill, sheathing	112	S.F.	0.01	1.12	0.68	0.60	76	67	143
Cedar siding	155	S.F.	0.03	4.65	3.52	1.35	546	209	755
Floor and wall insulation	1000	S.F.	0.01	10	0.40	0.48	400	480	880
Ceiling insulation	500	S.F.	0.01	5	0.54	0.56	270	280	550
Picture window	1	Ea.	1.45	1.45	740	61.50	740	62	802
Glazed door	1	Ea.	2.29	2.29	1175	96.50	1,175	97	1,272
Gypsum wallboard for walls and ceiling	1216	S.F.	0.02	24.32	0.37	0.70	450	851	1,301
Window and door trim	50	L.F.	0.03	1.50	1.41	1.41	71	71	142
Interior door	1	Ea.	0.84	0.84	292	35.50	292	36	328
Interior door trim	2	Opng.	1.36	2.72	24	57.50	48	115	163
Interior door lockset	1	Ea.	0.67	0.67	58.50	28	59	28	87
Baseboard	90	L.F.	0.03	2.70	2.43	1.41	219	127	346
Bath vanity	1	Ea.	0.80	0.80	240	34	240	34	274
Vanity top	1	Ea.	1	1	475	42.50	475	43	518
Sheet vinyl flooring	500	S.F.	0.03	15	2.96	1.34	1,480	670	2,150
Paint wall, ceiling, and trim, primer	1200	S.F.	0.01	12	0.05	0.22	60	264	324
Paint wall, ceiling, and trim, 1 coat	1200	S.F.	0.01	12	0.06	0.23	72	276	348
Paint exterior siding, oil-base, primer	185	S.F.	0.01	1.85	0.10	0.46	19	85	104
Paint exterior siding, oil-base, 2 coats, brushwork	185	S.F.	0.02	3.70	0.15	0.73	28	135	163
Prime and paint interior door	1	Ea.	1.60	1.60	11.80	59.50	12	60	72
Subcontract									
Toilet	1	Ea.	3.02	3.02	545	126	545	126	671
Rough plumbing for toilet	1	Ea.	5.25	5.25	210	219	210	219	429
Rough plumbing for vanity	1	Ea.	7.92	7.92	141	330	141	330	471
Vanity faucet and trim	1	Ea.	0.80	0.80	183	37	183	37	220
Duplex receptacles	8	Ea.	1.50	12	29	69	232	552	784
GFCI receptacle	1	Ea.	0.65	0.65	39	30	39	30	69
Switch	1	Ea.	1.40	1.40	31	64.50	31	65	96
Baseboard heaters, 10' long	4	Ea.	2.42	9.68	105	111	420	444	864
Dumpster	1	Week	1	1	385	33.50	385	34	419
Subtotals							9,762	8,147	17,909
General Requirements (Site Overhead)						12%	1,171	978	2,149
Subtotals							10,933	9,125	20,058
Overhead and Profit						10%	1,093	913	2,006
Subtotals							12,026	10,038	22,064

Grand Total $22,064

Note: Estimate is based on typical project materials available at home centers and may not include all elements in photo. Costs are national averages; see the Location Factors at the back of the book to adjust them to your area.

Cost per Square Foot $31

Alternates (Installed Costs)

	Unit	Total Cost
Flooring		
Floating laminate	S.F.	$6
Sheet vinyl	S.F.	$5
Linoleum	S.F.	$6
12" x 12" ceramic tile	S.F.	$6
Stone	S.F.	$22
Lavatory faucets		
Cross-handle polished chrome faucet and pop-up drain	Ea.	$177
Cross-handle polished brass faucet and pop-up drain	Ea.	$238
Single-lever black nickel faucet and pop-up drain	Ea.	$289
Single-lever polished brass faucet and pop-up drain	Ea.	$289
Single-lever polished chrome faucet and pop-up drain	Ea.	$211
Vanity Cabinets		
Vanity bases, 2 doors, 30" high, 21" deep, 24" wide, average	Ea.	$236
Vanity bases, 2 doors, 30" high, 21" deep, 24" wide, custom	Ea.	$335
Vanity bases, 2 doors, 30" high, 21" deep, 30" wide, average	Ea.	$275
Vanity bases, 2 doors, 30" high, 21" deep, 30" wide, custom	Ea.	$385
Vanity bases, 2 doors, 30" high, 21" deep, 36" wide, average	Ea.	$360
Vanity bases, 2 doors, 30" high, 21" deep, 36" wide, custom	Ea.	$545
Vanity bases, 2 doors, 30" high, 21" deep, 48" wide, average	Ea.	$430
Vanity bases, 2 doors, 30" high, 21" deep, 48" wide, custom	Ea.	$625
Vanity Countertops/Sinks		
Solid surface top/lavatory, 25" wide	Ea.	$270
Solid surface top/lavatory, 31" wide	Ea.	$320
Solid surface top/lavatory, 37" wide	Ea.	$370
Solid surface top/lavatory, 49" wide	Ea.	$400
Plastic laminate top	L.F.	$34
Granite top	L.F.	$148
Enameled steel lavatory	Ea.	$239
Vitreous china lavatory	Ea.	$284
Porcelain enamel on cast iron lavatory	Ea.	$350
Specialties		
Medicine cabinet	Ea.	$105
Electrical		
Exhaust fan	Ea.	$112

Garage door openings are often framed-in to accommodate windows. If there's no architect involved in the project, you may need to find a creative way to get the homeowners' agreement on window style and location. One is to tack up plywood to temporarily fill the openings, then cut out and staple up rectangles of different shapes and sizes from roofing felt. If they step back a distance, they can get a sense of proportions and see how the new windows will blend with the features of the main house.

Renovations

Project Worksheet

	Unit	Quantity	Price per Unit	Total	Dimensions	Source/Model#/ Specs

Guest Apartment Above Garage

M*any garages have* unfinished second-story space with adequate headroom that can be converted to an apartment, home office, or studio. New garages are often built with this kind of future expansion in mind. In fact, judging by the number of currently marketed garage plans that include apartments above, this is a very popular feature.

For homeowners, the advantages include:

- Economical new living area in an existing structure
- Separate housing for guests
- Rental income from an apartment
- Housing for an elderly parent or au pair

Among the planning issues:

- Zoning restrictions on added apartments
- Code requirements for living space above vehicles
- Access to and separate metering for utilities (in the case of a rental unit)
- Stair location. (Is space available and appropriate inside the downstairs garage? If intended for an elderly person, will their current and future mobility become a problem?)

Design and construction issues are similar to those of the *Converting a Full Attic* project, including headroom; rafter spacing; egress/ingress; framing support; windows, dormers, and/or skylights; and location of stairs.

Plumbing and electrical needs involve upgrade to service for additional circuits; installing lighting and a bathroom exhaust fan; and adding heating/AC units.

Possible extras include a balcony, fireplace, and kitchen.

The project estimated here includes insulating walls and ceilings, constructing new partitions, and installing new doors and window trim. Finish materials are drywall, ceramic tile in the bath, and carpet. Plumbing costs cover a full bath with shower, and electrical items are a new sub-panel, receptacles, switches, light fixtures, and baseboard heat.

See also the New Set of Stairs and Converting a Full Attic projects.

Project Estimate

Description	Quantity		Labor		Cost per Unit		Total Cost		
	Quantity	Unit	Labor Hrs Per Unit	Labor Hrs Total	Material Per Unit	Installation Per Unit	Material Total	Installation Total	Total
Self-Performed									
Interior partitions	52	L.F.	0.16	8.32	3.68	6.75	191	351	542
Wall insulation	704	S.F.	0.01	7.04	0.40	0.48	282	338	620
Ceiling insulation	484	S.F.	0.01	4.84	0.54	0.56	261	271	532
Gypsum wallboard for walls	1536	S.F.	0.02	30.72	0.37	0.70	568	1,075	1,643
Gypsum wallboard ceilings	484	S.F.	0.02	9.68	0.34	0.88	165	426	591
Gypsum wallboard around existing skylights	40	S.F.	0.03	1.20	0.34	1.42	14	57	71
Entry door	1	Ea.	1.07	1.07	570	45	570	45	615
Bath and closet doors	2	Ea.	0.80	1.60	170	34	340	68	408
Door locksets	3	Ea.	0.67	2.01	58.50	28	176	84	260
Door trim	3	Opng.	1.36	4.08	24	57.50	72	173	245
Picture window trim set	1	Ea.	1	1	52.50	42.50	53	43	96
Window trim sets	3	Opng.	0.62	1.86	32.50	26	98	78	176
Closet shelf and pole	2	Ea.	0.40	0.80	9.55	16.90	19	34	53
Ceramic tile floor in bathroom	60	S.F.	0.09	5.40	4.06	2.99	244	179	423
Baseboard	192	L.F.	0.03	5.76	2.43	1.41	467	271	738
Carpet	425	S.F.	0.02	8.50	3.04	0.69	1,292	293	1,585
Carpet pad	425	S.F.	0.01	4.25	0.64	0.20	272	85	357
Paint wall, ceiling, and trim, primer	1960	S.F.	0.01	19.60	0.05	0.22	98	431	529
Paint wall, ceiling, and trim, 1 coat	1960	S.F.	0.01	19.60	0.06	0.23	118	451	569
Subcontract									
Toilet	1	Ea.	3.02	3.02	186	126	186	126	312
Rough plumbing for toilet	1	Ea.	5.25	5.25	210	219	210	219	429
Pedestal lavatory	1	Ea.	2.50	2.50	455	104	455	104	559
Rough plumbing for lavatory	1	Ea.	6.96	6.96	124	290	124	290	414
Shower	1	Ea.	3.20	3.20	500	134	500	134	634
Rough plumbing for shower	1	Ea.	7.80	7.80	268	325	268	325	593
Electrical sub panel	1	Ea.	5.71	5.71	171	262	171	262	433
Electrical, duplex receptacles	8	Ea.	1.50	12	29	69	232	552	784
GFCI receptacle	1	Ea.	0.65	0.65	39	30	39	30	69
Electrical, switch	1	Ea.	1.40	1.40	31	64.50	31	65	96
Electrical, baseboard heaters, 10' long	4	Ea.	2.42	9.68	105	111	420	444	864
Dumpster	1	Week	1	1	385	33.50	385	34	419
Subtotals							8,321	7,338	15,659
General Requirements (Site Overhead)						12%	999	881	1,879
Subtotals							9,320	8,219	17,538
Overhead and Profit						10%	932	822	1,754
Subtotals							10,252	9,041	19,292

Grand Total   **$19,292**

Note: Estimate is based on typical project materials available at home centers and may not include all elements in photo. Costs are national averages; see the Location Factors at the back of the book to adjust them to your area.

Cost per Square Foot   **$40**

Alternates (Installed Costs)

	Unit	Total Cost
Unit Kitchens		
30" unit kitchen (range, refrigerator, sink)	Ea.	$1,475
60" unit kitchen (range, refrigerator, sink)	Ea.	$3,975
72" unit kitchen (range, refrigerator, sink)	Ea.	$4,500

Converting a Standard Basement

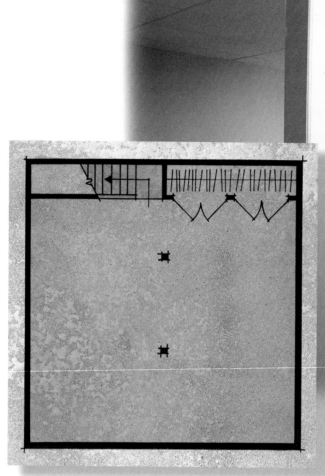

*B*asements are one of the most economical sources of new living space. Except for old dirt-floor, low-headroom types, most unfinished basements can be converted to offices, playrooms, and home theaters.

The first issue to deal with is water in any form – leaks, moisture, or dampness. Wet conditions must be eliminated before building begins. Moderate, intermittent dampness can often be treated with patches (hydraulic cement) and sealants. More extreme wetness may require drain tiles – possibly both outside and inside the foundation – and a sump pump. Don't put the finished project at risk – when in doubt about the moisture source or best method to cure it, consult an expert.

Because basement walls may be rough, uneven, or out-of-plumb, stud framing is generally preferable to furring. It allows more behind-the-wall space for wiring, ductwork, plumbing, and insulation. If the space will house a home theater, you may need to contract a specialist to run the wiring. If an office, consider computer and phone cabling needs.

Many contractors frame partition and non-loadbearing walls with lightweight, 25-ga. metal studs. They cost less than wood; are stable, straight, and uniform; and are easily cut with tin snips, then fastened with 7/16" type-S self-drilling, pan-head framing screws.

Standard 1/2" wallboard is attached with 1-1/8" type-S drywall screws. Metal studs have pre-punched holes for plumbing and wiring, and can be lined with wood studs

to create nailable rough openings for doors and windows.

Code-compliant ceiling height is a big factor in basement conversions. Some height will be lost to furring and finishing, and to boxing-in of pipes. In some cases, piping may have to be re-routed, a significant expense that should be evaluated with your plumbing contractor up-front.

Light-colored finishes are recommended for basement rooms, with wall washers or other lights to supplement task lighting. Suspended ceiling systems allow future access to any pipes in this area.

Fresh, filtered air can be circulated through a central air system or with fans. All basements should be tested for radon and carbon monoxide, and equipped with alarms for these gases.

This project estimate lists the items and costs involved in converting an unfinished basement to general purpose living space. It includes new partitions, insulation, and drywall; building new closets and a set of stairs; and installing carpet along with the other finish work (trim and paint). Electrical costs include 12 recessed light fixtures, 6 baseboard heating units, and switches and outlets.

See also the Walk-out Basement Apartment project.

Project Estimate

Description	Quantity	Unit	Labor Hrs Per Unit	Labor Hrs Total	Material Per Unit	Installation Per Unit	Material Total	Installation Total	Total
Self-Performed									
Partitions	155	L.F.	0.16	24.80	3.68	6.75	570	1,046	1,616
Insulation	976	S.F.	0.01	9.76	0.32	0.21	312	205	517
Gypsum wallboard	1504	S.F.	0.02	30.08	0.34	0.70	511	1,053	1,564
Suspended ceiling	930	S.F.	0.02	18.60	1.88	0.89	1,748	828	2,576
Stairway skirt board	28	L.F.	0.15	4.20	3.19	6.15	89	172	261
Stair risers	14	Ea.	0.36	5.04	10.05	11	141	154	295
Stair treads, oak	13	Ea.	0.44	5.72	32	18.80	416	244	660
Stair railing	28	L.F.	0.13	3.64	35	5.65	980	158	1,138
Closet doors and frames	4	Ea.	0.84	3.36	292	35.50	1,168	142	1,310
Baseboard trim	140	L.F.	0.03	4.20	2.43	1.41	340	197	537
Closet door casing	84	L.F.	0.03	2.52	1.41	1.41	118	118	236
Closet shelf and pole	14	L.F.	0.13	1.82	2.40	5.65	34	79	113
Prime trim	224	L.F.	0.01	2.24	0.03	0.46	7	103	110
Paint trim	224	L.F.	0.01	2.24	0.03	0.46	7	103	110
Prime gypsum wallboard	1504	S.F.	0.01	15.04	0.05	0.22	75	331	406
Finish paint, 2 coats	1504	S.F.	0.01	15.04	0.12	0.37	180	556	736
Carpet pad	124	S.Y.	0.05	6.20	7.40	2.06	918	255	1,173
Carpet	124	S.Y.	0.11	13.64	20	4.12	2,480	511	2,991
Subcontract									
Duplex receptacles	8	Ea.	1.50	12	29	69	232	552	784
Recessed light fixtures	12	Ea.	0.27	3.24	39.50	12.25	474	147	621
Switches	3	Ea.	1.40	4.20	31	64.50	93	194	287
Electric baseboard heat	6	Ea.	2.42	14.52	105	111	630	666	1,296
Dumpster	1	Week	1	1	256	33.50	256	34	290
Subtotals							11,779	7,848	19,627
General Requirements (Site Overhead)						12%	1,413	942	2,355
Subtotals							13,192	8,790	21,982
Overhead and Profit						10%	1,319	879	2,198
Subtotals							14,511	9,669	24,180

Grand Total $24,180

Note: Estimate is based on typical project materials available at home centers and may not include all elements in photo. Costs are national averages; see the Location Factors at the back of the book to adjust them to your area.

Cost per Square Foot $26

Alternates (Installed Costs)

	Unit	Total Cost
Lighting		
Ceiling canopy-style light fixture	Ea.	$62
Chandelier	Ea.	$272
Wall-mounted incandescent fixture	Ea.	$90
8' track lighting section	Ea.	$145
White cylinder light fixtures for track lighting	Ea.	$79
Flooring		
Sheet vinyl	S.F.	$5
Linoleum	S.F.	$6
12" x 12" ceramic tile	S.F.	$6
Stone	S.F.	$22

Walk-out Basement Apartment

*T**his project includes** a full bath, kitchen, living area, and closets, along with new lighting, ventilation, and access. Local zoning laws strictly regulate apartments, and building and safety codes are more stringent when renovated space includes a bedroom and kitchen.

In many communities, a proposed bedroom addition automatically calls for certification of the septic or sewerage system capacity, and fire codes have egress requirements for windows, doors, and stairways. (If the apartment is for an elderly or infirm person, consult building codes as well as standards such as the Americans with Disabilities Act.)

Most contractors agree that the plumbing can be the most critical part of this project. Include your plumber in the planning phase to locate and assess existing drains, vents, and hot and cold water pipes; determine the possible need for a sewage ejector and sump basin; and assist with fixture placement. Space restrictions may require undersized appliances and fixtures, often special order/higher cost, which should be factored into your estimate and schedule.

If the bathroom doesn't have a window, an exhaust fan will need to be ducted to the outside. Two-way (draw/exhaust) portable window fans and floor fans can provide adequate circulation in basements, since they tend to be cool in summer.

This project estimate lists the costs to convert an unfinished walk-out basement to an apartment with a small kitchen and bath. It includes new insulated, finished walls; a new set of stairs and closets; electrical baseboard heat, light fixtures, and switches/outlets; and piping and fixtures for the kitchen and bath. The bath has a solid surface lavatory with vanity, shower, and toilet. The kitchen costs include solid surface countertops, but no appliances. Flooring for the kitchen and bath are ceramic tile, with carpet for the remaining living area.

See also the Converting a Standard Basement project for tips for finishing walls.

Project Estimate

Description	Quantity		Labor		Cost per Unit		Total Cost		
	Quantity	Unit	Labor Hrs Per Unit	Labor Hrs Total	Material Per Unit	Installation Per Unit	Material Total	Installation Total	Total
Self-Performed									
Partitions	155	L.F.	0.16	24.80	3.68	6.75	570	1,046	1,616
Insulation	976	S.F.	0.01	9.76	0.32	0.21	312	205	517
Demolish slab for plumbing	1	Job	20	20		701		701	701
Gypsum wallboard	1504	S.F.	0.02	30.08	0.34	0.70	511	1,053	1,564
Suspended ceiling	930	S.F.	0.02	18.60	1.88	0.89	1,748	828	2,576
Stairway skirt board	28	L.F.	0.15	4.20	3.19	6.15	89	172	261
Stair risers	14	Ea.	0.36	5.04	10.05	11	141	154	295
Stair treads, oak	13	Ea.	0.44	5.72	32	18.80	416	244	660
Stair railing	28	L.F.	0.13	3.64	35	5.65	980	158	1,138
Closet doors and frames	4	Ea.	0.84	3.36	292	35.50	1,168	142	1,310
Kitchenette cabinets	12	L.F.	0.53	6.36	105	22.50	1,260	270	1,530
Bath vanities	2	Ea.	0.80	1.60	240	34	480	68	548
Solid surface kitchen counter	12	L.F.	0.80	9.60	104	34	1,248	408	1,656
Solid surface vanity top w/center bowl	1	Ea.	1	1	475	42.50	475	43	518
Baseboard trim	140	L.F.	0.03	4.20	2.43	1.41	340	197	537
Closet door casing	84	L.F.	0.03	2.52	1.41	1.41	118	118	236
Closet shelf and pole	8	L.F.	0.13	1.04	2.40	5.65	19	45	64
Prime trim	224	L.F.	0.01	2.24	0.03	0.46	7	103	110
Paint trim	224	L.F.	0.01	2.24	0.03	0.46	7	103	110
Prime gypsum wallboard	1504	S.F.	0.01	15.04	0.05	0.22	75	331	406
Finish paint, 2 coats	1504	S.F.	0.01	15.04	0.12	0.37	180	556	736
Patch slab at plumbing	1	Job	16	16		675		675	675
Carpet pad	124	S.Y.	0.05	6.20	7.40	2.06	918	255	1,173
Carpet	124	S.Y.	0.11	13.64	20	4.12	2,480	511	2,991
Ceramic tile flooring	50	S.F.	0.06	3	3.45	2.19	173	110	283
Subcontract									
Kitchen sink	1	Ea.	0.01	0.01	185		185		185
Kitchen sink rough plumbing	1	Ea.	7.48	7.48	143	310	143	310	453
Shower	1	Ea.	4	4	625	167	625	167	792
Shower rough plumbing	1	Ea.	7.80	7.80	268	325	268	325	593
Toilet	1	Ea.	3.02	3.02	545	126	545	126	671
Toilet rough plumbing	1	Ea.	5.25	5.25	210	219	210	219	429
Vanity rough plumbing	1	Ea.	7.92	7.92	141	330	141	330	471
Vanity faucet	1	Ea.	0.80	0.80	183	37	183	37	220
Duplex receptacles	8	Ea.	1.50	12	29	69	232	552	784
Recessed light fixtures	12	Ea.	0.27	3.24	39.50	12.25	474	147	621
Switches	3	Ea.	1.40	4.20	31	64.50	93	194	287
Electrical, baseboard heaters, 10' long	6	Ea.	2.42	14.52	105	111	630	666	1,296
GFCI receptacles	3	Ea.	0.65	1.95	39	30	117	90	207
Dumpster	1	Week	1	1	256	33.50	256	34	290
Subtotals							17,817	11,693	29,510
General Requirements (Site Overhead)						12%	2,138	1,403	3,541
Subtotals							19,955	13,096	33,051
Overhead and Profit						10%	1,996	1,310	3,305
Subtotals							21,951	14,406	36,356

Grand Total

Grand Total   **$36,356**

Note: Estimate is based on typical project materials available at home centers and may not include all elements in photo.
Costs are national averages; see the Location Factors at the back of the book to adjust them to your area.

Cost per Square Foot   **$39**

Renovations

Alternates (Installed Costs)

	Unit	Total Cost
Partitions for Separate Bedroom:		
Wood stud and gypsum wallboard partition	S.F.	$3
Electrical for Separate Bedroom:		
Switch device	Ea.	$31
Duplex receptacle	Ea.	$33
Telephone jack	Ea.	$23
Alternate Doors and Frames		
Pine door jamb	Ea.	$170
Lauan mahogany flush door slab	Ea.	$83
Birch face flush door slab	Ea.	$95
Oak face flush door slab	Ea.	$131
Walnut face flush door slab	Ea.	$211
Molded hardbord paneled door slab	Ea.	$102
Six-panel pine door slab	Ea.	$228
Two-panel pine door slab	Ea.	$425
Hand-carved fir door slab	Ea.	$585
Hand-carved mahogany door slab	Ea.	$860

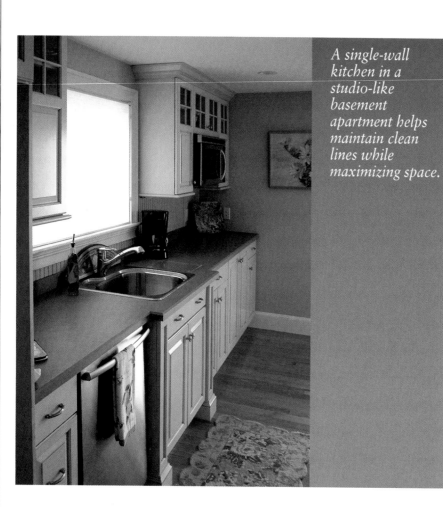

A single-wall kitchen in a studio-like basement apartment helps maintain clean lines while maximizing space.

Whether or not the apartment will be occupied by someone with respiratory problems, consider "green" materials, such as low- or no-VOC paint and low-odor, no-solvent tile adhesives.

For the healthiest air, also avoid pressed-wood products (particle board, plywood paneling, and medium-density fiberboard) made with adhesives and binders that contain urea-formaldehyde (UF) resins that release formaldehyde gas.

Wall-to-wall carpeting can "off-gas" after installation, as well as accumulate dust, mold, dander, and pollen, which can trigger allergic reactions. A greener choice is area rugs – which can be removed for frequent cleaning – over a tile, linoleum, or floating wood floor.

Project Worksheet

	Unit	Quantity	Price per Unit	Total	Dimensions	Source/Model#/ Specs

Enclosing a Breezeway

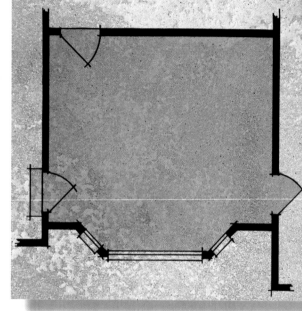

This project is a relatively low-cost way to gain more living space and add value to a home. Common uses for converted breezeways include sunrooms, kitchen expansions (such as adding a breakfast room/pantry), and family rooms.

Whenever new features are added to a house's façade, it's important to blend the style of trim, windows, and siding with the rest of the structure. An interesting window, such as a bay or other style in keeping with the home's architecture, can become a new focal point on the front of the house.

The basic steps involved in this project include framing the open sides of the breezeway, installing one or more doors and windows, and the exterior and interior finish work, including new flooring. Don't forget demolition – stripping the exterior siding from the two outside walls that will become inside walls – and insulation. You may also need to replace the existing door to the garage with an upgrade, and possibly build a step up (or down) to it.

Electrical work includes new outlets as required by code and any extras needed by the homeowner, including special locations and types of light switches and overhead light/fan fixtures.

This project could be combined with a new deck off the back of the new living space, or a porch on the front. French or sliding glass doors are a natural feature on the back wall. *See the Sunroom project in Part Two of this book for more ideas.*

The project estimated here is a 12' x 16' conversion from a breezeway to finished living space with a bow window. It involves some demolition, as well as framing, sheathing, insulation, siding, and interior finishes – in this case a ceramic tile floor and painted drywall. Electrical work includes baseboard heating, four outlets, four recessed lights, and switches.

Project Estimate

Description	Quantity	Unit	Labor Hrs Per Unit	Labor Hrs Total	Material Per Unit	Installation Per Unit	Material Total	Installation Total	Total
Self-Performed									
Remove sidewall shingles	222	L.F.	0.02	4.44		0.56		124	124
Treated wall framing plates	32	L.F.	0.02	0.64	0.53	0.85	17	27	44
Wall framing top plates	64	L.F.	0.02	1.28	0.41	0.85	26	54	80
Wall framing studs	256	L.F.	0.01	2.56	0.41	0.61	105	156	261
Framing for door	1	Ea.	0.25	0.25	17.35	10.55	17	11	28
Framing for window	1	Ea.	0.33	0.33	28	14.10	28	14	42
Wall sheathing	256	S.F.	0.01	2.56	0.68	0.48	174	123	297
Housewrap	256	S.F.	0.01	2.56	0.20	0.09	51	23	74
New exterior door	1	Ea.	1	1	570	42.50	570	43	613
New bow window	1	Ea.	1.60	1.60	1325	67.50	1,325	68	1,393
Cedar shingles	3	Sq.	4	12	179	169	537	507	1,044
Frieze trim	32	L.F.	0.02	0.64	0.40	1.02	13	33	46
Furring on existing ceiling framing	144	L.F.	0.02	2.88	0.31	0.97	45	140	185
Ceiling insulation	192	S.F.	0.01	1.92	0.78	0.29	150	56	206
Wall insulation	478	S.F.	0.01	4.78	0.32	0.21	153	100	253
Gypsum wallboard for ceilings	192	S.F.	0.02	3.84	0.34	0.88	65	169	234
Gypsum wallboard for walls	478	S.F.	0.02	9.56	0.34	0.70	163	335	498
Door trim	1	Opng.	1.36	1.36	24	57.50	24	58	82
Window trim	1	Ea.	1	1	52.50	42.50	53	43	96
Baseboard	56	L.F.	0.03	1.68	2.43	1.41	136	79	215
Ceramic tile floor	192	S.F.	0.06	11.52	3.45	2.19	662	420	1,082
Cut in painting with primer	152	S.F.	0.01	1.52	0.05	0.26	8	40	48
Prime gypsum wallboard	478	S.F.	0.01	4.78	0.05	0.22	24	105	129
Cut in painting, 2 coats finish	152	S.F.	0.01	1.52	0.11	0.44	17	67	84
Paint gypsum wallboard, 2 coats finish	152	S.F.	0.01	1.52	0.12	0.37	18	56	74
Prime and paint doors	3	Ea.	3.20	9.60	12.05	119	36	357	393
Prime and paint window	1	Ea.	1.60	1.60	2.38	59.50	2	60	62
Subcontract									
Baseboard radiation	20	L.F.	0.27	5.40	6.85	11.20	137	224	361
Connection to boiler	1	Job	5	5		210		210	210
Lighting switches	2	Ea.	0.38	0.76	5.25	17.50	11	35	46
Duplex outlets	4	Ea.	0.55	2.20	7.50	25	30	100	130
Recessed lighting	4	Ea.	0.29	1.16	59.50	13.10	238	52	290
Dumpster	1	Week	1	1	256	33.50	256	34	290
Subtotals							5,091	3,923	9,014
General Requirements (Site Overhead)						12%	611	471	1,082
Subtotals							5,702	4,394	10,096
Overhead and Profit						10%	570	439	1,010
Subtotals							6,272	4,833	11,106

Grand Total $11,106

Note: Estimate is based on typical project materials available at home centers and may not include all elements in photo. Costs are national averages; see the Location Factors at the back of the book to adjust them to your area.

Cost per Square Foot $58

Alternates (Installed Costs)

	Unit	Total Cost
Flooring		
Linoleum	S.F.	$6
Stone	S.F.	$22
Shelving/Storage		
Built-in unit	S.F.	$11
12″ wide shelves with mounting cleats	L.F.	$3
Coat hooks on 18″ wood board	Ea.	$64

Enclosing a Front Porch

When a driveway leads to or passes by the front door, this entrance tends to be truly functional – versus those that are more decorative. Unfortunately, front doors often open directly into living space or have only a small foyer scarcely larger than a stairway landing. A more spacious entryway can sometimes be created by enclosing all or part of an existing front porch.

Creating a visual and thermal buffer zone may be the primary motive for this project, but design is also a top priority, since you'll be altering the focal point of a house's façade. A poorly designed enclosure detracts from the home's curb appeal and resale value. If the house is antique, check for deeded covenants or historic restrictions.

Entryways created by enclosing a small portico sometimes end up looking like a tacked-on box. Some ways to avoid this:

- Install a top-grade door with narrow casement windows, fixed side lites, and/or a transom.
- Expand the plan to include a porch off one or both sides of the entryway.
- Top a flat roof with a decorative balcony-like railing.
- If appropriate, add built-up moldings, dentil bands, framed panels, pilasters, and other trim elements that can make the renovation a truly elegant upgrade.

Deciding which elements of the porch to retain depends on their condition and appropriateness to the new design. Usually, the more demolition you can avoid, the faster the job will be – allowing, of course, for the extra time to work with a structure that may have settled and is not likely to be perfectly level and plumb.

The old front door can remain where it is, and a new door added on the outside of the new enclosure, cutting down on material and labor cost. Another option is moving an old front door to the outside of the enclosure and purchasing a mostly glass exterior door for the inside, thereby opening the space up visually. Carefully removing and reinstalling the old door can be time-consuming.

An existing screened porch may have a fully usable concrete or framed wood floor, but open porches and porticos usually have water-shedding sloped floors, typically with a drop of about 1/4" per horizontal foot. When fully enclosed, that 2-1/2" slope in a 10' wide entryway serves no purpose and will just look like poor construction. There's no choice but to remove the decking and level the joists with tapered shims. Leveling a concrete deck is simpler.

Stone or ceramic tiles provide a long-lasting, low-maintenance floor, in a wide variety of colors and styles.

The project estimated here is the conversion of an existing 12' x 6' covered porch entryway into an enclosed foyer. It involves preparation of walls, then framing for the new walls, door, and two window openings. The rest of the work includes sheathing and siding, and installing the windows, door, and false columns. Finish treatments are ceramic floor tile, baseboard and trim, and paint. The electrical work includes an overhead light and switch.

Project Estimate

Description	Quantity	Unit	Labor Hrs Per Unit	Labor Hrs Total	Material Per Unit	Installation Per Unit	Material Total	Installation Total	Total
Self-Performed									
Remove siding	240	L.F.	0.02	4.80		0.56		134	134
Interior demolition	2	Job	2	4		60.50		121	121
Treated wall framing plates	16	L.F.	0.02	0.32	0.53	0.85	8	14	22
Wall framing top plates	32	L.F.	0.02	0.64	0.41	0.85	13	27	40
Wall framing studs	80	L.F.	0.01	0.80	0.41	0.61	33	49	82
Framing for door	1	Ea.	0.25	0.25	17.35	10.55	17	11	28
Framing for small windows	2	Ea.	0.33	0.66	18.20	14.10	36	28	64
Wall sheathing	128	S.F.	0.01	1.28	0.68	0.48	87	61	148
Housewrap	128	S.F.	0.01	1.28	0.20	0.09	26	12	38
New exterior door	1	Ea.	1	1	271	42.50	271	43	314
Exterior door lockset	1	Ea.	1	1	71.50	42.50	72	43	115
New casement windows at entry	2	Ea.	0.84	1.68	340	35.50	680	71	751
Clapboard siding	192	S.F.	0.03	5.76	3.52	1.35	676	259	935
False column	16	L.F.	0.04	0.64	2.08	1.88	33	30	63
Base of false column	5	L.F.	0.04	0.20	2.08	1.88	10	9	19
Trim at false column	10	L.F.	0.12	1.20	5.50	5.20	55	52	107
Furring on existing ceiling framing	30	L.F.	0.02	0.60	0.31	0.97	9	29	38
Wall insulation	128	S.F.	0.01	1.28	0.32	0.21	41	27	68
Gypsum wallboard for ceilings	20	S.F.	0.02	0.40	0.34	0.88	7	18	25
Gypsum wallboard for walls	128	S.F.	0.02	2.56	0.34	0.70	44	90	134
Door trim	1	Opng.	1.36	1.36	24	57.50	24	58	82
Window trim	2	Ea.	1	2	52.50	42.50	105	85	190
Baseboard	16	L.F.	0.03	0.48	2.43	1.41	39	23	62
Ceramic tile floor	20	S.F.	0.06	1.20	3.45	2.19	69	44	113
Exterior painting	3	Gal.	1.38	4.14	29.50	51	89	153	242
Cut in painting with primer	52	S.F.	0.01	0.52	0.05	0.26	3	14	17
Prime gypsum wallboard	148	S.F.	0.01	1.48	0.05	0.22	7	33	40
Cut in painting, 2 coats finish	52	S.F.	0.01	0.52	0.11	0.44	6	23	29
Paint gypsum wallboard, 2 coats finish	148	S.F.	0.01	1.48	0.12	0.37	18	55	73
Prime and paint doors	1	Ea.	3.20	3.20	12.05	119	12	119	131
Prime and paint window	2	Ea.	1.60	3.20	2.38	59.50	5	119	124
Subcontract									
Lighting switches	2	Ea.	0.38	0.76	5.25	17.50	11	35	46
Electrician minimum	1	Job	4	4		184		184	184
Overhead light	3	Ea.	0.29	0.87	59.50	13.10	179	39	218
Dumpster	1	Week	1	1	256	33.50	256	34	290
Subtotals							2,941	2,146	5,087
General Requirements (Site Overhead)						12%	353	258	610
Subtotals							3,294	2,404	5,697
Overhead and Profit						10%	329	240	570
Subtotals							3,623	2,644	6,267

Grand Total $6,267

Note: Estimate is based on typical project materials available at home centers and may not include all elements in photo. Costs are national averages; see the Location Factors at the back of the book to adjust them to your area.

Cost per Square Foot $313

Alternates (Installed Costs)

	Unit	Total Cost
Flooring		
Floating laminate	S.F.	$6
Sheet vinyl	S.F.	$5
Linoleum	S.F.	$6
12″ x 12″ ceramic tile	S.F.	$6
Stone	S.F.	$22
Storage Items		
Hardwood bench	L.F.	$37
Coat hooks on 18″ wood board	Ea.	$64

This simple enclosed porch provides a more formal entryway and adds interest to a flat façade.

An enclosed foyer, with an inside and an outside door, serves as an effective thermal barrier between heated living space and the weather.

Although insulation is recommended, the entryway itself doesn't have to be heated, as long as it's no more than a foyer and a closet. If a half bath is planned, heat is a must, and the project should be treated as a bump-out addition, subject to codes governing living space.

Project Worksheet

	Unit	Quantity	Price per Unit	Total	Dimensions	Source/Model#/Specs

Enclosing a Side Porch

Side or back doors often open into a small hallway or directly into the kitchen. If the door faces the driveway, it's probably the most-used entrance and a prime candidate for a mudroom. If the porch's layout and size offer enough space, a coat closet, pantry, laundry, or half bath are all possibilities – and good investments in the home's function and resale value.

Typical mudroom dimensions are anywhere between 36 S.F. and 60 S.F. To act as a thermal buffer, mudrooms should have both an exterior and interior door. In an unheated mudroom, you could insulate just the walls and ceiling/roof, and avoid the cost and difficulty of insulating the floor.

Basic mudroom features include a closet or cupboard, hooks, a durable floor, and electrical outlets. If you're building a pantry, find out what your client wants to store there so you can customize the depth and heights of shelves, add hooks, etc., to meet their needs. For a half bath, consider a pocket door and smaller fixtures if space is tight.

An unheated pantry (provided it doesn't freeze) serves as the "cool, dry place" often recommended for food storage. There must be adequate ventilation though, to prevent excess humidity. Heat is nice, but not essential. If a half bath is planned, heat and full insulation are required. Insulating the floor joist bays via a crawl space may be necessary in the case of an enclosed or screened porch with a usable floor. Open porch decking is likely to be too weathered or sloped to be usable, even as a subfloor, so should be replaced. In a half bath partitioned from the mudroom and opening into the house, costs can be reduced by heating only the bathroom.

A mudroom floor should be water-, stain-, and slip-resistant; durable; and low-maintenance. The best choices are stone, non-slip ceramic tiles, vinyl tiles, sheet vinyl, or linoleum. (Be sure to include a moisture-proof substrate.) If nothing will do but wood, go with solid or engineered hardwood, and three coats of high-gloss polyurethane. Engineered wood flooring typically comes factory-finished (urethane with an aluminum oxide layer is best), but make sure it can be refinished. Some products can be sanded up to three times, and some not at all.

This project estimate is for the enclosure of a 12' x 12' side porch, which will be divided into a mudroom and half bath. The work starts with framing the walls, closet door, and windows (including a round top window). The next steps are siding, sheathing, insulating, and then installing the doors (interior and exterior), windows, and trim. Finishes are tile flooring and paint. Electrical work includes new outlets, recessed light fixtures, and switches. Plumbing includes piping, a toilet, and a vanity for a half bath. *See also the Enclosing a Front Porch project.*

Project Estimate

Description	Quantity	Unit	Labor Hrs Per Unit	Labor Hrs Total	Material Per Unit	Installation Per Unit	Material Total	Installation Total	Total
Self-Performed									
Remove sidewall shingles	132	L.F.	0.02	2.64		0.56		74	74
Demolish slab for plumbing	1	Job	20	20		701		701	701
Treated wall framing plates	34	L.F.	0.02	0.68	0.53	0.85	18	29	47
Wall framing top plates	68	L.F.	0.02	1.36	0.41	0.85	28	58	86
Wall framing studs	272	L.F.	0.01	2.72	0.41	0.61	112	166	278
Framing for door	1	Ea.	0.25	0.25	17.35	10.55	17	11	28
Framing for small windows	2	Ea.	0.33	0.66	18.20	14.10	36	28	64
Framing for round top window	1	Ea.	0.33	0.33	23.50	14.10	24	14	38
Wall sheathing	300	S.F.	0.01	3	0.68	0.48	204	144	348
Housewrap	300	S.F.	0.01	3	0.20	0.09	60	27	87
New exterior door	2	Ea.	1	2	570	42.50	1,140	85	1,225
Exterior door lockset	1	Ea.	1	1	71.50	42.50	72	43	115
New casement windows at entry	2	Ea.	0.84	1.68	340	35.50	680	71	751
New window	1	Ea.	0.89	0.89	560	37.50	560	38	598
Round top for window	1	Ea.	1.33	1.33	495	56.50	495	57	552
Cedar shingles	2	Sq.	4	8	179	169	358	338	696
Clapboard siding	100	S.F.	0.03	3	3.52	1.35	352	135	487
Frieze trim	24	L.F.	0.02	0.48	0.40	1.02	10	24	34
Furring on existing ceiling framing	108	L.F.	0.02	2.16	0.31	0.97	33	105	138
Entry soffit plywood	36	S.F.	0.04	1.44	0.86	1.61	31	58	89
Interior partitions	12	L.F.	0.16	1.92	3.68	6.75	44	81	125
Ceiling insulation	108	S.F.	0.01	1.08	0.78	0.29	84	31	115
Wall insulation	300	S.F.	0.01	3	0.32	0.21	96	63	159
Gypsum wallboard for ceilings	192	S.F.	0.02	3.84	0.34	0.88	65	169	234
Gypsum wallboard for walls	456	S.F.	0.02	9.12	0.34	0.70	155	319	474
Interior doors	1	Ea.	0.84	0.84	292	35.50	292	36	328
Closet doors	1	Opng.	1.60	1.60	540	67.50	540	68	608
Closet shelf and pole	6	L.F.	0.13	0.78	2.40	5.65	14	34	48
Door trim	3	Opng.	1.36	4.08	24	57.50	72	173	245
Window trim	3	Ea.	1	3	52.50	42.50	158	128	286
Patch slab at plumbing	1	Job	16	16		675		675	675
Baseboard	57	L.F.	0.03	1.71	2.43	1.41	139	80	219
Vanity cabinet	1	Ea.	0.80	0.80	240	34	240	34	274
Solid surface vanity top and bowl	1	Ea.	1	1	475	42.50	475	43	518
Ceramic tile floor	108	S.F.	0.06	6.48	3.45	2.19	373	237	610
Cut in painting with primer	174	S.F.	0.01	1.74	0.05	0.26	9	45	54
Prime gypsum wallboard	456	S.F.	0.01	4.56	0.05	0.22	23	100	123
Cut in painting, 2 coats finish	174	S.F.	0.01	1.74	0.11	0.44	19	77	96
Paint gypsum wallboard, 2 coats finish	456	S.F.	0.01	4.56	0.12	0.37	55	169	224
Prime and paint doors	3	Ea.	3.20	9.60	12.05	119	36	357	393
Prime and paint window	3	Ea.	1.60	4.80	2.38	59.50	7	179	186
Subcontract									
Toilet	1	Ea.	3.02	3.02	545	126	545	126	671
Rough plumbing for toilet	1	Ea.	5.25	5.25	210	219	210	219	429
Rough plumbing for vanity	1	Ea.	7.92	7.92	141	330	141	330	471

Project Estimate (continued)

Description	Quantity	Unit	Labor Hrs Per Unit	Labor Hrs Total	Material Per Unit	Installation Per Unit	Material Total	Installation Total	Total
Vanity faucet	1	Ea.	0.80	0.80	183	37	183	37	220
Electric baseboard radiation	20	L.F.	0.33	6.60	14.35	15.30	287	306	593
Lighting switches	2	Ea.	0.38	0.76	5.25	17.50	11	35	46
Electrician minimum	1	Job	4	4		184		184	184
GFCI receptacle	1	Ea.	0.65	0.65	39	30	39	30	69
Duplex outlets	2	Ea.	0.55	1.10	7.50	25	15	50	65
Recessed lighting	3	Ea.	0.29	0.87	59.50	13.10	179	39	218
Dumpster	1	Week	1	1	256	33.50	256	34	290
Subtotals							8,992	6,694	15,686
General Requirements (Site Overhead)						12%	1,079	803	1,882
Subtotals							10,071	7,497	17,568
Overhead and Profit						10%	1,007	750	1,757
Subtotals							11,078	8,247	19,325

Grand Total $19,325

Note: Estimate is based on typical project materials available at home centers and may not include all elements in photo. Costs are national averages; see the Location Factors at the back of the book to adjust them to your area.

Cost per Square Foot $101

Alternates (Installed Costs)

	Unit	Total Cost
Flooring		
Floating laminate	S.F.	$6
Sheet vinyl	S.F.	$5
Linoleum	S.F.	$6
12" x 12" ceramic tile	S.F.	$6
Stone	S.F.	$22
Storage Items		
Hardwood bench	L.F.	$37
Coat hooks on 18" wood board	Ea.	$64

Renovations

Project Worksheet

	Unit	Quantity	Price per Unit	Total	Dimensions	Source/Model#/ Specs

Converting Small Rooms to a Large Living Area

oday's residential architecture favors open floor plans, high ceilings, and plenty of windows. Introducing some of these elements into an older home can bring it up to date and enhance its resale value. This is a popular project with empty-nesters who have small rooms that no longer fit their lifestyles.

If you're combining two small bedrooms to create a master suite, consider a bath with separate tub or whirlpool and shower, walk-in closets, fireplace, skylights, and/or French doors with a balcony.

If combining the kitchen and dining room into a large eat-in kitchen, the homeowner may want to upgrade with a cooktop with separate wall oven(s), an extra sink, stone countertops, solid wood cabinetry, an island, or a pantry.

If combining rooms to create a family or great room, consider all-media wiring for data and entertainment electronics, French doors opening onto a deck or patio, a fireplace, or built-in bookcases.

Raised or vaulted ceilings with skylights or eyebrow/transom windows help create a light, open look for the new space.

Any time walls are to be removed, wiring and plumbing may have to be relocated. Windows and doors may also have to be moved. And, of course, there's the question of whether walls are load-bearing and require another means of support. If there's any doubt, consult an architect or structural engineer.

This project estimate covers the cost to combine two rooms to create a 16' x 30' family or great room. It includes removal of flooring, trim, drywall, and studs; construction of temporary support walls; framing headers and new openings; and all the finish work. We've included a pine beam, new French doors, and ceramic tile flooring.

See the Opening Up a Wall project for more on the construction process.

Project Estimate

Description	Quantity		Labor		Cost per Unit		Total Cost		
	Quantity	Unit	Labor Hrs Per Unit	Labor Hrs Total	Material Per Unit	Installation Per Unit	Material Total	Installation Total	Total
Self-Performed									
Temporary support walls	42	L.F.	0.16	6.72	3.68	6.75	155	284	439
Remove existing flooring	480	S.F.	0.02	9.60		0.72		346	346
Remove ceiling molding	44	L.F.	0.02	0.88		0.48		21	21
Remove wood baseboard	44	L.F.	0.01	0.44		0.40		18	18
Remove gypsum wallboard	400	S.F.	0.01	4		0.24		96	96
Remove existing studs and sole plate	180	L.F.	0.01	1.80		0.24		43	43
Remove exterior siding	100	S.F.	0.02	2		0.64		64	64
Debris removal	4	C.Y.	0.97	3.88		29.50		118	118
Framing, built-up post for headers	56	L.F.	0.01	0.56	0.41	0.61	23	34	57
Beam hanger	1	Ea.	0.05	0.05	4.15	2.18	4	2	6
Framing, laminated beams	48	L.F.	0.04	1.92	6.15	1.50	295	72	367
Remove temporary support walls	256	S.F.	0.01	2.56		0.40		102	102
Cut out and patch sheathing at new door opening	1	Job	2	2		84.50		85	85
New French door	1	Pr.	2.29	2.29	1300	96.50	1,300	97	1,397
Replace/patch exterior siding	1	Job	2	2		84.50		56	56
Finish pine for beam	48	L.F.	0.03	1.44	1.50	1.41	72	68	140
Paint door frame and trim, brush, primer, and 2 coats	21	L.F.	0.02	0.42	0.06	0.58	1	12	13
Paint doors	2	Ea.	4	8	5.90	148	12	296	308
Paint old baseboard, brush, 2 coats	44	L.F.	0.02	0.88	0.06	0.74	3	33	36
Paint old ceiling molding, brush, 2 coats	44	L.F.	0.02	0.88	0.11	0.74	5	33	38
Paint wall surface, cut in w/ brush, 2 coats	40	S.F.	0.01	0.40	0.11	0.44	4	18	22
Paint entire wall surface, roller, 2 coats	200	S.F.	0.01	2	0.12	0.37	24	74	98
Ceramic tile floor	480	S.F.	0.05	24	4.33	1.69	2,078	811	2,889
Door handles and hardware	2	Ea.	0.80	1.60	145	34	290	68	358
Subcontract									
Dumpster	1	Week	1	1	256	33.50	256	34	290
Subtotals							4,522	2,885	7,407
General Requirements (Site Overhead)						12%	543	346	889
Subtotals							5,065	3,231	8,296
Overhead and Profit						10%	507	323	830
Subtotals							5,572	3,554	9,126

Grand Total $9,126

Note: Estimate is based on typical project materials available at home centers and may not include all elements in photo.
Costs are national averages; see the Location Factors at the back of the book to adjust them to your area.

Alternates (Installed Costs)

	Unit	Total Cost
Flooring		
Floating laminate	S.F.	$6
Sheet vinyl	S.F.	$5
Linoleum	S.F.	$6
Hardwood	S.F.	$8
Stone	S.F.	$22
Finishing Accessories		
Pine crown molding	L.F.	$3
Oak crown molding	L.F.	$6
Chair rail molding	L.F.	$3
Simple 2' high wainscot	S.F.	$16
Ornate 2' high wainscot	S.F.	$27
Economy wallcovering	S.F.	$1
High-end wallcovering	S.F.	$2

Curved ceiling or wall surfaces can be built with precision framing under flexible 1/4" drywall. A top-quality drywall installation – frame to finish – is crucial on spacious, unobstructed areas where light and shadows can show up even tiny surface flaws.

Part Four

Case Studies

Case Study 1

An Illuminating Idea

A Kitchen and Sunroom Project Shines Light on a Change Order Deficiency

Several years ago, Jim and Ann McLaren watched a neighbor's house undergo an extensive renovation that included an addition. They liked what they saw, and when it came time to update their home, the McLarens called Kirkwood, Missouri-based Riggs Design & Construction – the same company that had worked on the neighbor's project.

The McLarens had a large but dark and dated kitchen with an eat-in area. Becky Fisk, Riggs' kitchen and bath designer, helped them devise a plan to turn the space into a bright and modern kitchen.

Fisk changed the overall shape of the kitchen from a rectangle to an L by adding a walk-in pantry to the plan.

A double oven would occupy the space of the previous pantry, and Fisk specified adding a cooktop and prep sink on the new island. Hand-finished cherry cabinets, black granite countertops, and stainless steel appliances completed the kitchen update. In Fisk's design, the new kitchen would open to a separate breakfast room with plenty of windows to let in the view of the patio and backyard along with abundant sunlight. The original plan was to add a sunroom as a connected, but separate, space.

After the initial design, the McLarens came back to Fisk with additions and changes. They elected to open the sunroom so that it flowed from the home's existing family room. To the sunroom addition, they added a coffered ceiling and a wet bar with a granite countertop.

Not long after construction was under way, a few unexpected issues popped up. First, hidden behind the old double oven was a big, round vent for the furnace. Fisk redesigned the area on the spot, re-routing the vent so that the kitchen design did not need to change in a major way.

Then, as the cabinets were going in, the McLarens made another change. Although the option to add a built-in

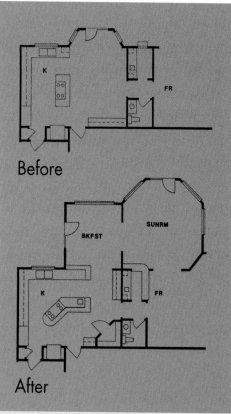

Before

After

coffeemaker had been addressed during the design phase, the McLarens had declined. Then they fell in love with one that they had to have.

In her many years of designing, Fisk had never had to work around such a large coffeemaker during a change order. Thanks to the company's expert trim carpenters, the appliance fit as if it had been part of the original plan.

An Electrical Shock...

On every Riggs Design & Construction project, there is a walk-through with the electrician.

"We have found that our clients are much better off seeing the real thing as opposed to [just] the plans," says Tom Riggs, president of the company.

As usual, the electrician came to the McLaren job site and did a walk-through with the owners, the designer, and the project manager. At that point, the Riggs team had laid out the cabinets on the floor so the McLarens could see where

The original kitchen had a breakfast nook that was eating up valuable square footage.

the island was going to be, why the electrical was there, and picture how they would use it. Though Fisk had gone through the electrical and lighting with the homeowners in the design phase, the McLarens had changes.

While the homeowners were OK with the amount of lighting in the kitchen, they wanted extra switches. The addition of the coffeemaker required extra electrical as well. In the breakfast room, the McLarens added two outlets. The electrical plan was tweaked again during the walk-through. And after the wet bar was built, the McLarens changed their minds about where the lighting should go.

It's typical for clients to have this reaction when they have tangibles in front of them rather than one-dimensional blueprints, according to Riggs. "When people see it when it's built, they say, 'Oh I'd like to add a can there. This should be a three-way switch.' So there's always added things. No matter how many plugs they put in the kitchen, they always want a couple more. It used to be that the electrician would have a guy there nailing up boxes as we did the walk-through. We'd get the price back the next day, but the electrician would be halfway done wiring, and it caused a lot of problems because the owner said, 'Wait a minute, I don't want to spend that kind of money.'"

And this was precisely what happened when the McLarens received the bill for their extra electrical.

Dan Kayich, the project manager, explained the costs to the McLarens and talked them through it. In the end, the clients accepted the charges, but they weren't thrilled.

After this, the project managers came to Riggs and requested a system to avoid future problems like those experienced with the estimate for the McClaren's electrical change orders.

Riggs had been looking for a solution to these small, but troubling, change orders

for some time. "It can cost [customers] more [money in the end] to wait for [the change order] to go through all the channels—get estimated, get the official work order from the office, have the homeowner sign it, have them cut a check before work can proceed." But getting a verbal go-ahead from homeowners without firm pricing wasn't working either.

Riggs went to the electrician and worked out a price chart for his project managers. Now as they do walk-throughs and the clients make changes, the project managers can mark the number of extra outlets, switches, and can lights, add them up very quickly and give clients an accurate estimate on the spot. The project managers then write up the estimated price in a field work order, the customer signs it, and the electrician can continue working without interruption. Since the McLaren project, it's automatic. Nothing is done without a field work order signed by the homeowner.

Riggs has expanded the price charts to include other trades. "[The project managers] have in their books more or less our item list and they have the hourly rate, or the footage rate for drywall, or whatever it may be so they have a real good picture."

The new kitchen features stainless steel appliances and modern conveniences like a handy prep sink and state-of-the-art, built-in coffeemaker.

The coffered ceiling in the sunroom lends to the bright and airy feel of the addition.

Though the work orders state, "This is an estimated price; the official work order may vary from this price," the project managers have the tools on the job to work out the figures and come in very close. "They're usually within one percent," says Riggs. "We very rarely change what they come up with."

– Alicia Garceau, Contributing Editor, *Professional Remodeler Magazine*

Room for Change

Flexibility is the Key to Success for this Garage Conversion Project

The owners of this Cape Cod style home began their project with the idea of converting the existing 24' x 24' garage to a large family room and building a new, larger garage elsewhere on their property. Bert deMartin of Abode Design/Build worked with the homeowners to finalize their ideas, plans were drawn up, and construction began. But the fairly straightforward family room conversion soon became a more involved renovation. Last-minute decisions changed the design and the cost of the project, requiring patience from both the builder and his clients. While the process was challenging at times, it paid off in the end, with a multi-purpose space that added value and beauty to the home.

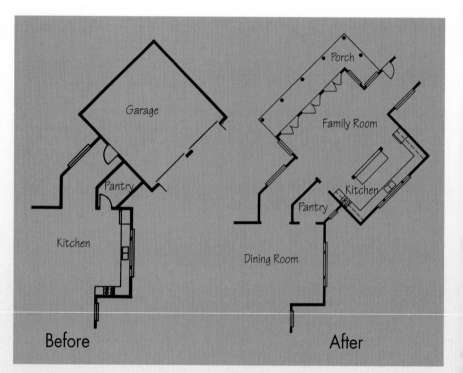

Before   After

The plan first changed when the homeowners decided to add a low deck outside the new family room that would overlook their pool. When the deck was being constructed, they concluded that it needed a roof to offer sun protection for bathers. The problem was that if they used the same asphalt shingles as on the rest of the house, the roof would look vast and uninteresting – like an unsightly addition rather than a natural part of the structure. Also, the new roof's shallow slope would require more upkeep since the shingles would be in danger of rot from collected moisture. The solution was to use metal roofing, which added visual interest, making the new roof lines more attractive. This material also allowed for easier run-off of snow and rain, which would protect the structure for years to come.

As the project progressed, it became clear to the construction team that more changes were in store. The homeowners decided they wanted to build a new kitchen and convert the original kitchen to a formal dining room. Unfortunately,

The remodel was carefully designed to blend with the home's façade.

at this point, construction was well under way, and the clients did not want to rework the entire design to accommodate the new kitchen.

After brainstorming sessions with their architect and builder, the solution became clear: an addition on the former garage structure to house the new kitchen. Construction could continue with the family room (close to the original plan), and a 6' extension would be built, adding 144 square feet.

The old kitchen would also have to be gutted and renovated for its new use as a dining room, which added still more time and expense to the project. The builder was clear about the estimated additional costs, and worked with the homeowners to agree on a changed design and price tag.

Among the other challenges were the structural steel support beams needed in the old garage/future family room walls. These would go between the family room and the new kitchen. The design had to fit the island around these supports, while making them visually appealing. The solution was to enclose the unsightly steel supports in wood to create decorative columns on either side of the new kitchen island.

Support beams in the ceiling were also a problem. These had to be hidden somehow, but the homeowners wanted to avoid a low ceiling with a cramped feeling. The builder suggested disguising the beams with decorative crown molding and adding additional moldings as accents, breaking the ceiling into panels. This solution adds interest to the room and hides the unattractive, but necessary supports.

While firm, final designs are always ideal, this room conversion proves that in residential remodeling, projects rarely go exactly according to plan. Ultimately, homeowner desires must be accommodated. Patience; careful consideration of cost, construction, and schedule issues; and creative solutions help keep the job moving and all parties satisfied. In this case, the builder's flexibility and creativity led to an attractive result and very happy customers.

It's difficult to imagine that this inspired family room/kitchen was once a garage.

The new porch provides a spacious outdoor living area. The metal roof gives it architectural interest.

163

Case Study 3

Down Under

Making the Best Use of Existing Space

The story is typical: The owners of this 1,500-square-foot English Tudor needed to expand their living space, but setbacks and architectural controls in their Denver historic district restricted what could be done with an addition. So they turned to the 1,280-square-foot basement as the likeliest candidate.

"It was dark and restricted, not a place where you would want to spend much time," says remodeler Bill Kennedy of Basements and Beyond.

The homeowners wanted to transform the claustrophobic cellar into an appealing living area that included a family room, bedroom, laundry facility, and wine room. The challenges: code violations such as insulation with asbestos, the lack of an egress window, and a ceiling clearance of only 76".

The first step required roughing in an opening for a 4x4-foot egress window at the rear of the house. The window

Before

became Basements and Beyond's primary access for demolition and reconstruction.

"We couldn't bring in mechanical equipment due to a new driveway and no alley access," says Kennedy. "Everything had to come in and out of a 4 by 4 hole."

He hired a specialist to remove asbestos insulation around the old furnace and ductwork. Then demolition began in earnest. "Down to the bones," Kennedy says.

To increase ceiling height, Basements and Beyond began by digging out enough of

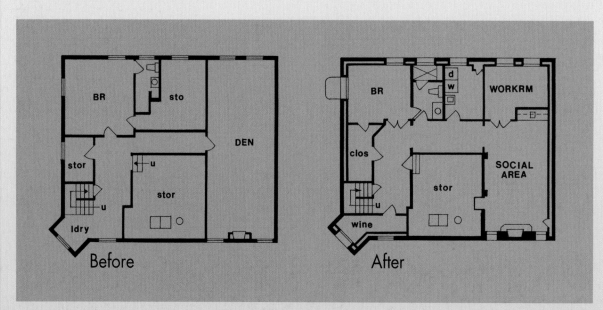

Before

After

the old concrete flooring to pour new footings for steel posts to support four new steel I-beams. Once the I-beams were in place, workers removed old brick support walls to open up the space. Then they removed the remainder of the concrete floor and hand-dug the dirt underneath: 8" down across the entire 1,280 square feet. They wheel-barrowed the dirt out to the street.

In the process, they removed the existing underground plumbing, then lowered it. The crew also had to install an ejector system for sewage because of the change in fall from the sewer line to the street. Finally, they pumped concrete for the new floor through a small window in the front of the house.

Kennedy carefully monitored feasibility on the project. "A lot of engineering was done first," he says. "No surprises."

– Karen Wells, *Professional Remodeler Magazine*

Canned lights throughout the basement brighten up the space, as do new replacement windows, glass block windows, and a new fireplace.

To make the new space feel less like a basement, Basements and Beyond installed a recessed ceiling, hiding ductwork between joists and using soffits when necessary.

Appendix
& Index

Location Factors

Adjusting Project Costs to Your Location

STATE	CITY	Residential		STATE	CITY	Residential
324	Panama City	.67		463-464	Gary	1.03
325	Pensacola	.75		465-466	South Bend	.94
326,344	Gainesville	.77		467-468	Fort Wayne	.92
327-328,347	Orlando	.85		469	Kokomo	.94
329	Melbourne	.87		470	Lawrenceburg	.88
330-332,340	Miami	.83		471	New Albany	.87
333	Fort Lauderdale	.83		472	Columbus	.93
334,349	West Palm Beach	.83		473	Muncie	.92
335-336,346	Tampa	.86		474	Bloomington	.96
337	St. Petersburg	.76		475	Washington	.92
338	Lakeland	.82		476-477	Evansville	.92
339,341	Fort Myers	.80		478	Terre Haute	.92
342	Sarasota	.84		479	Lafayette	.93
GEORGIA				**IOWA**		
300-303,399	Atlanta	.88		500-503,509	Des Moines	.93
304	Statesboro	.66		504	Mason City	.77
305	Gainesville	.74		505	Fort Dodge	.75
306	Athens	.74		506-507	Waterloo	.80
307	Dalton	.70		508	Creston	.82
308-309	Augusta	.76		510-511	Sioux City	.88
310-312	Macon	.77		512	Sibley	.73
313-314	Savannah	.79		513	Spencer	.75
315	Waycross	.71		514	Carroll	.74
316	Valdosta	.70		515	Council Bluffs	.81
317,398	Albany	.75		516	Shenandoah	.75
318-319	Columbus	.79		520	Dubuque	.84
				521	Decorah	.76
HAWAII				522-524	Cedar Rapids	.94
967	Hilo	1.22		525	Ottumwa	.84
968	Honolulu	1.23		526	Burlington	.88
				527-528	Davenport	.98
STATES & POSS.						
969	Guam	1.73		**KANSAS**		
				660-662	Kansas City	.97
IDAHO				664-666	Topeka	.79
832	Pocatello	.87		667	Fort Scott	.86
833	Twin Falls	.74		668	Emporia	.72
834	Idaho Falls	.72		669	Belleville	.78
835	Lewiston	.98		670-672	Wichita	.81
836-837	Boise	.89		673	Independence	.86
838	Coeur d'Alene	.94		674	Salina	.76
				675	Hutchinson	.68
ILLINOIS				676	Hays	.83
600-603	North Suburban	1.13		677	Colby	.76
604	Joliet	1.13		678	Dodge City	.82
605	South Suburban	1.13		679	Liberal	.68
606-608	Chicago	1.14				
609	Kankakee	.99		**KENTUCKY**		
610-611	Rockford	1.04		400-402	Louisville	.92
612	Rock Island	.97		403-405	Lexington	.84
613	La Salle	1.03		406	Frankfort	.81
614	Galesburg	.98		407-409	Corbin	.66
615-616	Peoria	1.00		410	Covington	.92
617	Bloomington	.96		411-412	Ashland	.93
618-619	Champaign	.98		413-414	Campton	.68
620-622	East St. Louis	1.00		415-416	Pikeville	.76
623	Quincy	.97		417-418	Hazard	.66
624	Effingham	.98		420	Paducah	.89
625	Decatur	.99		421-422	Bowling Green	.89
626-627	Springfield	.99		423	Owensboro	.81
628	Centralia	1.01		424	Henderson	.92
629	Carbondale	.96		425-426	Somerset	.66
				427	Elizabethtown	.87
INDIANA						
460	Anderson	.93		**LOUISIANA**		
461-462	Indianapolis	.95		700-701	New Orleans	.85

Location Factors

Adjusting Project Costs to Your Location

STATE	CITY	Residential
703	Thibodaux	.83
704	Hammond	.78
705	Lafayette	.81
706	Lake Charles	.82
707-708	Baton Rouge	.83
710-711	Shreveport	.78
712	Monroe	.73
713-714	Alexandria	.74
MAINE		
039	Kittery	.80
040-041	Portland	.91
042	Lewiston	.91
043	Augusta	.83
044	Bangor	.89
045	Bath	.81
046	Machias	.82
047	Houlton	.86
048	Rockland	.82
049	Waterville	.81
MARYLAND		
206	Waldorf	.84
207-208	College Park	.86
209	Silver Spring	.85
210-212	Baltimore	.90
214	Annapolis	.86
215	Cumberland	.87
216	Easton	.68
217	Hagerstown	.86
218	Salisbury	.75
219	Elkton	.82
MASSACHUSETTS		
010-011	Springfield	1.05
012	Pittsfield	1.03
013	Greenfield	1.02
014	Fitchburg	1.11
015-016	Worcester	1.12
017	Framingham	1.13
018	Lowell	1.14
019	Lawrence	1.14
020-022, 024	Boston	1.20
023	Brockton	1.13
025	Buzzards Bay	1.11
026	Hyannis	1.10
027	New Bedford	1.13
MICHIGAN		
480,483	Royal Oak	1.03
481	Ann Arbor	1.04
482	Detroit	1.10
484-485	Flint	.97
486	Saginaw	.94
487	Bay City	.95
488-489	Lansing	.97
490	Battle Creek	.92
491	Kalamazoo	.91
492	Jackson	.92
493,495	Grand Rapids	.82
494	Muskegon	.88
496	Traverse City	.80
497	Gaylord	.83
498-499	Iron Mountain	.90
MINNESOTA		
550-551	Saint Paul	1.14

STATE	CITY	Residential
553-555	Minneapolis	1.17
556-558	Duluth	1.11
559	Rochester	1.06
560	Mankato	1.02
561	Windom	.83
562	Willmar	.85
563	St. Cloud	1.09
564	Brainerd	.99
565	Detroit Lakes	.97
566	Bemidji	.97
567	Thief River Falls	.95
MISSISSIPPI		
386	Clarksdale	.61
387	Greenville	.68
388	Tupelo	.63
389	Greenwood	.65
390-392	Jackson	.73
393	Meridian	.66
394	Laurel	.62
395	Biloxi	.75
396	McComb	.73
397	Columbus	.64
MISSOURI		
630-631	St. Louis	1.01
633	Bowling Green	.95
634	Hannibal	.87
635	Kirksville	.80
636	Flat River	.95
637	Cape Girardeau	.87
638	Sikeston	.82
639	Poplar Bluff	.83
640-641	Kansas City	1.04
644-645	St. Joseph	.95
646	Chillicothe	.86
647	Harrisonville	.96
648	Joplin	.85
650-651	Jefferson City	.89
652	Columbia	.88
653	Sedalia	.85
654-655	Rolla	.89
656-658	Springfield	.87
MONTANA		
590-591	Billings	.87
592	Wolf Point	.83
593	Miles City	.86
594	Great Falls	.88
595	Havre	.80
596	Helena	.87
597	Butte	.82
598	Missoula	.83
599	Kalispell	.82
NEBRASKA		
680-681	Omaha	.90
683-685	Lincoln	.78
686	Columbus	.69
687	Norfolk	.77
688	Grand Island	.77
689	Hastings	.76
690	Mccook	.70
691	North Platte	.75
692	Valentine	.66
693	Alliance	.65

Location Factors

Adjusting Project Costs to Your Location

STATE	CITY	Residential
NEVADA		
889-891	Las Vegas	1.01
893	Ely	.89
894-895	Reno	.96
897	Carson City	.96
898	Elko	.95
NEW HAMPSHIRE		
030	Nashua	.90
031	Manchester	.90
032-033	Concord	.86
034	Keene	.73
035	Littleton	.81
036	Charleston	.70
037	Claremont	.72
038	Portsmouth	.84
NEW JERSEY		
070-071	Newark	1.15
072	Elizabeth	1.18
073	Jersey City	1.14
074-075	Paterson	1.15
076	Hackensack	1.14
077	Long Branch	1.15
078	Dover	1.14
079	Summit	1.15
080,083	Vineland	1.09
081	Camden	1.10
082,084	Atlantic City	1.13
085-086	Trenton	1.13
087	Point Pleasant	1.11
088-089	New Brunswick	1.15
NEW MEXICO		
870-872	Albuquerque	.85
873	Gallup	.85
874	Farmington	.85
875	Santa Fe	.85
877	Las Vegas	.85
878	Socorro	.85
879	Truth/Consequences	.84
880	Las Cruces	.82
881	Clovis	.85
882	Roswell	.85
883	Carrizozo	.85
884	Tucumcari	.86
NEW YORK		
100-102	New York	1.36
103	Staten Island	1.28
104	Bronx	1.30
105	Mount Vernon	1.17
106	White Plains	1.20
107	Yonkers	1.22
108	New Rochelle	1.21
109	Suffern	1.14
110	Queens	1.28
111	Long Island City	1.31
112	Brooklyn	1.33
113	Flushing	1.30
114	Jamaica	1.30
115,117,118	Hicksville	1.21
116	Far Rockaway	1.29
119	Riverhead	1.22
120-122	Albany	.96
123	Schenectady	.96
124	Kingston	1.04

STATE	CITY	Residential
125-126	Poughkeepsie	1.06
127	Monticello	1.06
128	Glens Falls	.89
129	Plattsburgh	.94
130-132	Syracuse	.97
133-135	Utica	.94
136	Watertown	.90
137-139	Binghamton	.94
140-142	Buffalo	1.06
143	Niagara Falls	1.02
144-146	Rochester	1.00
147	Jamestown	.89
148-149	Elmira	.86
NORTH CAROLINA		
270,272-274	Greensboro	.74
271	Winston-Salem	.74
275-276	Raleigh	.75
277	Durham	.74
278	Rocky Mount	.64
279	Elizabeth City	.62
280	Gastonia	.75
281-282	Charlotte	.75
283	Fayetteville	.72
284	Wilmington	.73
285	Kinston	.62
286	Hickory	.62
287-288	Asheville	.73
289	Murphy	.66
NORTH DAKOTA		
580-581	Fargo	.80
582	Grand Forks	.76
583	Devils Lake	.79
584	Jamestown	.74
585	Bismarck	.80
586	Dickinson	.76
587	Minot	.80
588	Williston	.77
OHIO		
430-432	Columbus	.95
433	Marion	.93
434-436	Toledo	1.00
437-438	Zanesville	.91
439	Steubenville	.96
440	Lorain	1.00
441	Cleveland	1.01
442-443	Akron	.99
444-445	Youngstown	.95
446-447	Canton	.94
448-449	Mansfield	.95
450	Hamilton	.95
451-452	Cincinnati	.95
453-454	Dayton	.92
455	Springfield	.94
456	Chillicothe	.97
457	Athens	.89
458	Lima	.91
OKLAHOMA		
730-731	Oklahoma City	.80
734	Ardmore	.78
735	Lawton	.81
736	Clinton	.77
737	Enid	.77
738	Woodward	.76

Location Factors

Adjusting Project Costs to Your Location

STATE	CITY	Residential
739	Guymon	.66
740-741	Tulsa	.78
743	Miami	.82
744	Muskogee	.72
745	Mcalester	.74
746	Ponca City	.77
747	Durant	.76
748	Shawnee	.75
749	Poteau	.78
OREGON		
970-972	Portland	1.02
973	Salem	1.02
974	Eugene	1.01
975	Medford	1.00
976	Klamath Falls	1.00
977	Bend	1.03
978	Pendleton	1.00
979	Vale	.99
PENNSYLVANIA		
150-152	Pittsburgh	.99
153	Washington	.94
154	Uniontown	.91
155	Bedford	.88
156	Greensburg	.96
157	Indiana	.92
158	Dubois	.90
159	Johnstown	.91
160	Butler	.93
161	New Castle	.93
162	Kittanning	.94
163	Oil City	.90
164-165	Erie	.96
166	Altoona	.89
167	Bradford	.91
168	State College	.92
169	Wellsboro	.90
170-171	Harrisburg	.95
172	Chambersburg	.89
173-174	York	.92
175-176	Lancaster	.92
177	Williamsport	.85
178	Sunbury	.92
179	Pottsville	.91
180	Lehigh Valley	1.02
181	Allentown	1.04
182	Hazleton	.91
183	Stroudsburg	.92
184-185	Scranton	.96
186-187	Wilkes-Barre	.93
188	Montrose	.90
189	Doylestown	1.06
190-191	Philadelphia	1.15
193	Westchester	1.10
194	Norristown	1.08
195-196	Reading	.97
PUERTO RICO		
009	San Juan	.84
RHODE ISLAND		
028	Newport	1.09
029	Providence	1.09
SOUTH CAROLINA		
290-292	Columbia	.73

STATE	CITY	Residential
293	Spartanburg	.71
294	Charleston	.72
295	Florence	.66
296	Greenville	.70
297	Rock Hill	.65
298	Aiken	.84
299	Beaufort	.67
SOUTH DAKOTA		
570-571	Sioux Falls	.77
572	Watertown	.72
573	Mitchell	.75
574	Aberdeen	.76
575	Pierre	.75
576	Mobridge	.72
577	Rapid City	.76
TENNESSEE		
370-372	Nashville	.84
373-374	Chattanooga	.76
375,380-381	Memphis	.85
376	Johnson City	.71
377-379	Knoxville	.74
382	Mckenzie	.73
383	Jackson	.70
384	Columbia	.71
385	Cookeville	.68
TEXAS		
750	Mckinney	.74
751	Waxahachie	.75
752-753	Dallas	.83
754	Greenville	.68
755	Texarkana	.73
756	Longview	.67
757	Tyler	.74
758	Palestine	.66
759	Lufkin	.71
760-761	Fort Worth	.82
762	Denton	.76
763	Wichita Falls	.79
764	Eastland	.72
765	Temple	.74
766-767	Waco	.77
768	Brownwood	.68
769	San Angelo	.71
770-772	Houston	.85
773	Huntsville	.68
774	Wharton	.70
775	Galveston	.84
776-777	Beaumont	.82
778	Bryan	.73
779	Victoria	.73
780	Laredo	.72
781-782	San Antonio	.80
783-784	Corpus Christi	.76
785	Mc Allen	.75
786-787	Austin	.79
788	Del Rio	.65
789	Giddings	.69
790-791	Amarillo	.77
792	Childress	.75
793-794	Lubbock	.75
795-796	Abilene	.74
797	Midland	.76
798-799,885	El Paso	.75

Location Factors

Adjusting Project Costs to Your Location

STATE	CITY	Residential
UTAH		
840-841	Salt Lake City	.82
842,844	Ogden	.81
843	Logan	.81
845	Price	.72
846-847	Provo	.82
VERMONT		
050	White River Jct.	.73
051	Bellows Falls	.75
052	Bennington	.74
053	Brattleboro	.74
054	Burlington	.79
056	Montpelier	.81
057	Rutland	.81
058	St. Johnsbury	.75
059	Guildhall	.74
VIRGINIA		
220-221	Fairfax	.85
222	Arlington	.87
223	Alexandria	.90
224-225	Fredericksburg	.75
226	Winchester	.70
227	Culpeper	.77
228	Harrisonburg	.67
229	Charlottesville	.73
230-232	Richmond	.81
233-235	Norfolk	.82
236	Newport News	.81
237	Portsmouth	.78
238	Petersburg	.79
239	Farmville	.69
240-241	Roanoke	.72
242	Bristol	.68
243	Pulaski	.66
244	Staunton	.69
245	Lynchburg	.70
246	Grundy	.67
WASHINGTON		
980-981,987	Seattle	1.01
982	Everett	1.04
983-984	Tacoma	1.00
985	Olympia	1.00
986	Vancouver	.97
988	Wenatchee	.92
989	Yakima	.96
990-992	Spokane	1.00
993	Richland	.98
994	Clarkston	.97
WEST VIRGINIA		
247-248	Bluefield	.88
249	Lewisburg	.89
250-253	Charleston	.97
254	Martinsburg	.86
255-257	Huntington	.97
258-259	Beckley	.90
260	Wheeling	.94
261	Parkersburg	.92
262	Buckhannon	.93
263-264	Clarksburg	.92
265	Morgantown	.93
266	Gassaway	.92
267	Romney	.88
268	Petersburg	.90

STATE	CITY	Residential
WISCONSIN		
530,532	Milwaukee	1.07
531	Kenosha	1.06
534	Racine	1.04
535	Beloit	1.01
537	Madison	1.01
538	Lancaster	.99
539	Portage	.98
540	New Richmond	1.01
541-543	Green Bay	1.03
544	Wausau	.96
545	Rhinelander	.96
546	La Crosse	.95
547	Eau Claire	1.00
548	Superior	1.01
549	Oshkosh	.97
WYOMING		
820	Cheyenne	.76
821	Yellowstone Nat. Pk.	.72
822	Wheatland	.73
823	Rawlins	.71
824	Worland	.70
825	Riverton	.71
826	Casper	.75
827	Newcastle	.70
828	Sheridan	.74
829-831	Rock Springs	.75
CANADIAN FACTORS (reflect Canadian Currency)		
ALBERTA		
	Calgary	1.05
	Edmonton	1.04
	Fort McMurray	1.02
	Lethbridge	1.03
	Lloydminster	1.02
	Medicine Hat	1.03
	Red Deer	1.03
BRITISH COLUMBIA		
	Kamloops	1.00
	Prince George	1.00
	Vancouver	1.07
	Victoria	1.00
MANITOBA		
	Brandon	.99
	Portage la Prairie	.99
	Winnipeg	1.00
NEW BRUNSWICK		
	Bathurst	.90
	Dalhousie	.90
	Fredericton	.98
	Moncton	.90
	Newcastle	.90
	Saint John	.99
NEWFOUNDLAND		
	Corner Brook	.92
	St. John's	.92
NORTHWEST TERRITORIES		
	Yellowknife	1.01

Location Factors

Adjusting Project Costs to Your Location

STATE	CITY	Residential
NOVA SCOTIA		
	Dartmouth	.93
	Halifax	.93
	New Glasgow	.92
	Sydney	.91
	Yarmouth	.92
ONTARIO		
	Barrie	1.09
	Brantford	1.11
	Cornwall	1.10
	Hamilton	1.11
	Kingston	1.11
	Kitchener	1.05
	London	1.09
	North Bay	1.08
	Oshawa	1.09
	Ottawa	1.11
	Owen Sound	1.08
	Peterborough	1.08
	Sarnia	1.11
	Sudbury	1.02
	Thunder Bay	1.07
	Toronto	1.14
	Windsor	1.08
PRINCE EDWARD ISLAND		
	Charlottetown	.87
	Summerside	.87
QUEBEC		
	Cap-de-la-Madeleine	1.10
	Charlesbourg	1.10
	Chicoutimi	1.10
	Gatineau	1.09
	Laval	1.09
	Montreal	1.10
	Quebec	1.12
	Sherbrooke	1.09
	Trois Rivieres	1.10
SASKATCHEWAN		
	Moose Jaw	.90
	Prince Albert	.90
	Regina	.92
	Saskatoon	.90
YUKON		
	Whitehorse	.89

Abbreviations

A	Area Square Feet; Ampere
ABS	Acrylonitrile Butadiene Stryrene; Asbestos Bonded Steel
A.C.	Alternating Current; Air-Conditioning; Asbestos Cement; Plywood Grade A & C
A.C.I.	American Concrete Institute
AD	Plywood, Grade A & D
Addit.	Additional
Adj.	Adjustable
af	Audio-frequency
A.G.A.	American Gas Association
Agg.	Aggregate
A.H.	Ampere Hours
A hr.	Ampere-hour
A.H.U.	Air Handling Unit
A.I.A.	American Institute of Architects
AIC	Ampere Interrupting Capacity
Allow.	Allowance
alt.	Altitude
Alum.	Aluminum
a.m.	Ante Meridiem
Amp.	Ampere
Anod.	Anodized
Approx.	Approximate
Apt.	Apartment
Asb.	Asbestos
A.S.B.C.	American Standard Building Code
Asbe.	Asbestos Worker
A.S.H.R.A.E.	American Society of Heating, Refrig. & AC Engineers
A.S.M.E.	American Society of Mechanical Engineers
A.S.T.M.	American Society for Testing and Materials
Attchmt.	Attachment
Avg.	Average
A.W.G.	American Wire Gauge
AWWA	American Water Works Assoc.
Bbl.	Barrel
B&B	Grade B and Better; Balled & Burlapped
B.&S.	Bell and Spigot
B.&W.	Black and White
b.c.c.	Body-centered Cubic
B.C.Y.	Bank Cubic Yards
BE	Bevel End
B.F.	Board Feet
Bg. cem.	Bag of Cement
BHP	Boiler Horsepower; Brake Horsepower
B.I.	Black Iron
Bit.; Bitum.	Bituminous
Bk.	Backed
Bkrs.	Breakers
Bldg.	Building
Blk.	Block
Bm.	Beam
Boil.	Boilermaker
B.P.M.	Blows per Minute
BR	Bedroom
Brg.	Bearing
Brhe.	Bricklayer Helper
Bric.	Bricklayer
Brk.	Brick
Brng.	Bearing
Brs.	Brass
Brz.	Bronze
Bsn.	Basin
Btr.	Better
BTU	British Thermal Unit
BTUH	BTU per Hour
B.U.R.	Built-up Roofing
BX	Interlocked Armored Cable
c	Conductivity, Copper Sweat
C	Hundred; Centigrade
C/C	Center to Center, Cedar on Cedar

Cab.	Cabinet
Cair.	Air Tool Laborer
Calc	Calculated
Cap.	Capacity
Carp.	Carpenter
C.B.	Circuit Breaker
C.C.A.	Chromate Copper Arsenate
C.C.F.	Hundred Cubic Feet
cd	Candela
cd/sf	Candela per Square Foot
CD	Grade of Plywood Face & Back
CDX	Plywood, Grade C & D, exterior glue
Cefi.	Cement Finisher
Cem.	Cement
CF	Hundred Feet
C.F.	Cubic Feet
CFM	Cubic Feet per Minute
c.g.	Center of Gravity
CHW	Chilled Water; Commercial Hot Water
C.I.	Cast Iron
C.I.P.	Cast in Place
Circ.	Circuit
C.L.	Carload Lot
Clab.	Common Laborer
Clam	Common maintenance laborer
C.L.F.	Hundred Linear Feet
CLF	Current Limiting Fuse
CLP	Cross Linked Polyethylene
cm	Centimeter
CMP	Corr. Metal Pipe
C.M.U.	Concrete Masonry Unit
CN	Change Notice
Col.	Column
CO_2	Carbon Dioxide
Comb.	Combination
Compr.	Compressor
Conc.	Concrete
Cont.	Continuous; Continued
Corr.	Corrugated
Cos	Cosine
Cot	Cotangent
Cov.	Cover
C/P	Cedar on Paneling
CPA	Control Point Adjustment
Cplg.	Coupling
C.P.M.	Critical Path Method
CPVC	Chlorinated Polyvinyl Chloride
C.Pr.	Hundred Pair
CRC	Cold Rolled Channel
Creos.	Creosote
Crpt.	Carpet & Linoleum Layer
CRT	Cathode-ray Tube
CS	Carbon Steel, Constant Shear Bar Joist
Csc	Cosecant
C.S.F.	Hundred Square Feet
CSI	Construction Specifications Institute
C.T.	Current Transformer
CTS	Copper Tube Size
Cu	Copper, Cubic
Cu. Ft.	Cubic Foot
cw	Continuous Wave
C.W.	Cool White; Cold Water
Cwt.	100 Pounds
C.W.X.	Cool White Deluxe
C.Y.	Cubic Yard (27 cubic feet)
C.Y./Hr.	Cubic Yard per Hour
Cyl.	Cylinder
d	Penny (nail size)
D	Deep; Depth; Discharge
Dis.;Disch.	Discharge
Db.	Decibel
Dbl.	Double
DC	Direct Current
DDC	Direct Digital Control

Demob.	Demobilization
d.f.u.	Drainage Fixture Units
D.H.	Double Hung
DHW	Domestic Hot Water
Diag.	Diagonal
Diam.	Diameter
Distrib.	Distribution
Dk.	Deck
D.L.	Dead Load; Diesel
DLH	Deep Long Span Bar Joist
Do.	Ditto
Dp.	Depth
D.P.S.T.	Double Pole, Single Throw
Dr.	Driver
Drink.	Drinking
D.S.	Double Strength
D.S.A.	Double Strength A Grade
D.S.B.	Double Strength B Grade
Dty.	Duty
DWV	Drain Waste Vent
DX	Deluxe White, Direct Expansion
dyn	Dyne
e	Eccentricity
E	Equipment Only; East
Ea.	Each
E.B.	Encased Burial
Econ.	Economy
E.C.Y	Embankment Cubic Yards
EDP	Electronic Data Processing
EIFS	Exterior Insulation Finish System
E.D.R.	Equiv. Direct Radiation
Eq.	Equation
Elec.	Electrician; Electrical
Elev.	Elevator; Elevating
EMT	Electrical Metallic Conduit; Thin Wall Conduit
Eng.	Engine, Engineered
EPDM	Ethylene Propylene Diene Monomer
EPS	Expanded Polystyrene
Eqhv.	Equip. Oper., Heavy
Eqlt.	Equip. Oper., Light
Eqmd.	Equip. Oper., Medium
Eqmm.	Equip. Oper., Master Mechanic
Eqol.	Equip. Oper., Oilers
Equip.	Equipment
ERW	Electric Resistance Welded
E.S.	Energy Saver
Est.	Estimated
esu	Electrostatic Units
E.W.	Each Way
EWT	Entering Water Temperature
Excav.	Excavation
Exp.	Expansion, Exposure
Ext.	Exterior
Extru.	Extrusion
f.	Fiber stress
F	Fahrenheit; Female; Fill
Fab.	Fabricated
FBGS	Fiberglass
F.C.	Footcandles
f.c.c.	Face-centered Cubic
f'c.	Compressive Stress in Concrete; Extreme Compressive Stress
F.E.	Front End
FEP	Fluorinated Ethylene Propylene (Teflon)
F.G.	Flat Grain
F.H.A.	Federal Housing Administration
Fig.	Figure
Fin.	Finished
Fixt.	Fixture
Fl. Oz.	Fluid Ounces
Flr.	Floor
F.M.	Frequency Modulation; Factory Mutual
Fmg.	Framing
Fndtn.	Foundation

Abbreviations

Fori.	Foreman, Inside	I.W.	Indirect Waste	M.C.F.	Thousand Cubic Feet
Foro.	Foreman, Outside	J	Joule	M.C.F.M.	Thousand Cubic Feet per Minute
Fount.	Fountain	J.I.C.	Joint Industrial Council	M.C.M.	Thousand Circular Mils
FPM	Feet per Minute	K	Thousand;Thousand Pounds;	M.C.P.	Motor Circuit Protector
FPT	Female Pipe Thread		Heavy Wall Copper Tubing, Kelvin	MD	Medium Duty
Fr.	Frame	K.A.H.	Thousand Amp. Hours	M.D.O.	Medium Density Overlaid
F.R.	Fire Rating	KCMIL	Thousand Circular Mils	Med.	Medium
FRK	Foil Reinforced Kraft	KD	Knock Down	MF	Thousand Feet
FRP	Fiberglass Reinforced Plastic	K.D.A.T.	Kiln Dried After Treatment	M.F.B.M.	Thousand Feet Board Measure
FS	Forged Steel	kg	Kilogram	Mfg.	Manufacturing
FSC	Cast Body; Cast Switch Box	kG	Kilogauss	Mfrs.	Manufacturers
Ft.	Foot; Feet	kgf	Kilogram Force	mg	Milligram
Ftng.	Fitting	kHz	Kilohertz	MGD	Million Gallons per Day
Ftg.	Footing	Kip.	1000 Pounds	MGPH	Thousand Gallons per Hour
Ft. Lb.	Foot Pound	KJ	Kiljoule	MH, M.H.	Manhole; Metal Halide; Man-Hour
Furn.	Furniture	K.L.	Effective Length Factor	MHz	Megahertz
FVNR	Full Voltage Non-Reversing	K.L.F.	Kips per Linear Foot	Mi.	Mile
FXM	Female by Male	Km	Kilometer	MI	Malleable Iron; Mineral Insulated
Fy.	Minimum Yield Stress of Steel	K.S.F.	Kips per Square Foot	mm	Millimeter
g	Gram	K.S.I.	Kips per Square Inch	Mill.	Millwright
G	Gauss	kV	Kilovolt	Min., min.	Minimum, minute
Ga.	Gauge	kVA	Kilovolt Ampere	Misc.	Miscellaneous
Gal.	Gallon	K.V.A.R.	Kilovar (Reactance)	ml	Milliliter, Mainline
Gal./Min.	Gallon per Minute	KW	Kilowatt	M.L.F.	Thousand Linear Feet
Galv.	Galvanized	KWh	Kilowatt-hour	Mo.	Month
Gen.	General	L	Labor Only; Length; Long;	Mobil.	Mobilization
G.F.I.	Ground Fault Interrupter		Medium Wall Copper Tubing	Mog.	Mogul Base
Glaz.	Glazier	Lab.	Labor	MPH	Miles per Hour
GPD	Gallons per Day	lat	Latitude	MPT	Male Pipe Thread
GPH	Gallons per Hour	Lath.	Lather	MRT	Mile Round Trip
GPM	Gallons per Minute	Lav.	Lavatory	ms	Millisecond
GR	Grade	lb.; #	Pound	M.S.F.	Thousand Square Feet
Gran.	Granular	L.B.	Load Bearing; L Conduit Body	Mstz.	Mosaic & Terrazzo Worker
Grnd.	Ground	L. & E.	Labor & Equipment	M.S.Y.	Thousand Square Yards
H	High; High Strength Bar Joist;	lb./hr.	Pounds per Hour	Mtd.	Mounted
	Henry	lb./L.F.	Pounds per Linear Foot	Mthe.	Mosaic & Terrazzo Helper
H.C.	High Capacity	lbf/sq.in.	Pound-force per Square Inch	Mtng.	Mounting
H.D.	Heavy Duty; High Density	L.C.L.	Less than Carload Lot	Mult.	Multi; Multiply
H.D.O.	High Density Overlaid	L.C.Y.	Loose Cubic Yard	M.V.A.	Million Volt Amperes
Hdr.	Header	Ld.	Load	M.V.A.R.	Million Volt Amperes Reactance
Hdwe.	Hardware	LE	Lead Equivalent	MV	Megavolt
Help.	Helper Average	LED	Light Emitting Diode	MW	Megawatt
HEPA	High Efficiency Particulate Air	L.F.	Linear Foot	MXM	Male by Male
	Filter	Lg.	Long; Length; Large	MYD	Thousand Yards
Hg	Mercury	L & H	Light and Heat	N	Natural; North
HIC	High Interrupting Capacity	LH	Long Span Bar Joist	nA	Nanoampere
HM	Hollow Metal	L.H.	Labor Hours	NA	Not Available; Not Applicable
H.O.	High Output	L.L.	Live Load	N.B.C.	National Building Code
Horiz.	Horizontal	L.L.D.	Lamp Lumen Depreciation	NC	Normally Closed
H.P.	Horsepower; High Pressure	lm	Lumen	N.E.M.A.	National Electrical Manufacturers
H.P.F.	High Power Factor	lm/sf	Lumen per Square Foot		Assoc.
Hr.	Hour	lm/W	Lumen per Watt	NEHB	Bolted Circuit Breaker to 600V.
Hrs./Day	Hours per Day	L.O.A.	Length Over All	N.L.B.	Non-Load-Bearing
HSC	High Short Circuit	log	Logarithm	NM	Non-Metallic Cable
Ht.	Height	L-O-L	Lateralolet	nm	Nanometer
Htg.	Heating	L.P.	Liquefied Petroleum; Low Pressure	No.	Number
Htrs.	Heaters	L.P.F.	Low Power Factor	NO	Normally Open
HVAC	Heating, Ventilation & Air-	LR	Long Radius	N.O.C.	Not Otherwise Classified
	Conditioning	L.S.	Lump Sum	Nose.	Nosing
Hvy.	Heavy	Lt.	Light	N.P.T.	National Pipe Thread
HW	Hot Water	Lt. Ga.	Light Gauge	NQOD	Combination Plug-on/Bolt on
Hyd.;Hydr.	Hydraulic	L.T.L.	Less than Truckload Lot		Circuit Breaker to 240V.
Hz.	Hertz (cycles)	Lt. Wt.	Lightweight	N.R.C.	Noise Reduction Coefficient
I.	Moment of Inertia	L.V.	Low Voltage	N.R.S.	Non Rising Stem
I.C.	Interrupting Capacity	M	Thousand; Material; Male;	ns	Nanosecond
ID	Inside Diameter		Light Wall Copper Tubing	nW	Nanowatt
I.D.	Inside Dimension; Identification	M^2CA	Meters Squared Contact Area	OB	Opposing Blade
I.F.	Inside Frosted	m/hr; M.H.	Man-hour	OC	On Center
I.M.C.	Intermediate Metal Conduit	mA	Milliampere	OD	Outside Diameter
In.	Inch	Mach.	Machine	O.D.	Outside Dimension
Incan.	Incandescent	Mag. Str.	Magnetic Starter	ODS	Overhead Distribution System
Incl.	Included; Including	Maint.	Maintenance	O.G.	Ogee
Int.	Interior	Marb.	Marble Setter	O.H.	Overhead
Inst.	Installation	Mat; Mat'l.	Material	O&P	Overhead and Profit
Insul.	Insulation/Insulated	Max.	Maximum	Oper.	Operator
I.P.	Iron Pipe	MBF	Thousand Board Feet	Opng.	Opening
I.P.S.	Iron Pipe Size	MBH	Thousand BTU's per hr.	Orna.	Ornamental
I.P.T.	Iron Pipe Threaded	MC	Metal Clad Cable	OSB	Oriented Strand Board

Abbreviations

O.S.&Y.	Outside Screw and Yoke
Ovhd.	Overhead
OWG	Oil, Water or Gas
Oz.	Ounce
P.	Pole; Applied Load; Projection
p.	Page
Pape.	Paperhanger
P.A.P.R.	Powered Air Purifying Respirator
PAR	Parabolic Reflector
Pc., Pcs.	Piece, Pieces
P.C.	Portland Cement; Power Connector
P.C.F.	Pounds per Cubic Foot
P.C.M.	Phase Contrast Microscopy
P.E.	Professional Engineer; Porcelain Enamel; Polyethylene; Plain End
Perf.	Perforated
Ph.	Phase
P.I.	Pressure Injected
Pile.	Pile Driver
Pkg.	Package
Pl.	Plate
Plah.	Plasterer Helper
Plas.	Plasterer
Pluh.	Plumbers Helper
Plum.	Plumber
Ply.	Plywood
p.m.	Post Meridiem
Pntd.	Painted
Pord.	Painter, Ordinary
pp	Pages
PP; PPL	Polypropylene
P.P.M.	Parts per Million
Pr.	Pair
P.E.S.B.	Pre-engineered Steel Building
Prefab.	Prefabricated
Prefin.	Prefinished
Prop.	Propelled
PSF; psf	Pounds per Square Foot
PSI; psi	Pounds per Square Inch
PSIG	Pounds per Square Inch Gauge
PSP	Plastic Sewer Pipe
Pspr.	Painter, Spray
Psst.	Painter, Structural Steel
P.T.	Potential Transformer
P. & T.	Pressure & Temperature
Ptd.	Painted
Ptns.	Partitions
Pu	Ultimate Load
PVC	Polyvinyl Chloride
Pvmt.	Pavement
Pwr.	Power
Q	Quantity Heat Flow
Quan.; Qty.	Quantity
Q.C.	Quick Coupling
r	Radius of Gyration
R	Resistance
R.C.P.	Reinforced Concrete Pipe
Rect.	Rectangle
Reg.	Regular
Reinf.	Reinforced
Req'd.	Required
Res.	Resistant
Resi.	Residential
Rgh.	Rough
RGS	Rigid Galvanized Steel
R.H.W.	Rubber, Heat & Water Resistant; Residential Hot Water
rms	Root Mean Square
Rnd.	Round
Rodm.	Rodman
Rofc.	Roofer, Composition
Rofp.	Roofer, Precast
Rohe.	Roofer Helpers (Composition)
Rots.	Roofer, Tile & Slate
R.O.W.	Right of Way
RPM	Revolutions per Minute
R.S.	Rapid Start
Rsr	Riser
RT	Round Trip
S.	Suction; Single Entrance; South
SC	Screw Cover
SCFM	Standard Cubic Feet per Minute
Scaf.	Scaffold
Sch.; Sched.	Schedule
S.C.R.	Modular Brick
S.D.	Sound Deadening
S.D.R.	Standard Dimension Ratio
S.E.	Surfaced Edge
Sel.	Select
S.E.R.; S.E.U.	Service Entrance Cable
S.F.	Square Foot
S.F.C.A.	Square Foot Contact Area
S.F. Flr.	Square Foot of Floor
S.F.G.	Square Foot of Ground
S.F. Hor.	Square Foot Horizontal
S.F.R.	Square Feet of Radiation
S.F. Shlf.	Square Foot of Shelf
S4S	Surface 4 Sides
Shee.	Sheet Metal Worker
Sin.	Sine
Skwk.	Skilled Worker
SL	Saran Lined
S.L.	Slimline
Sldr.	Solder
SLH	Super Long Span Bar Joist
S.N.	Solid Neutral
S-O-L	Socketolet
sp	Standpipe
S.P.	Static Pressure; Single Pole; Self-Propelled
Spri.	Sprinkler Installer
spwg	Static Pressure Water Gauge
S.P.D.T.	Single Pole, Double Throw
SPF	Spruce Pine Fir
S.P.S.T.	Single Pole, Single Throw
SPT	Standard Pipe Thread
Sq.	Square; 100 Square Feet
Sq. Hd.	Square Head
Sq. In.	Square Inch
S.S.	Single Strength; Stainless Steel
S.S.B.	Single Strength B Grade
sst	Stainless Steel
Sswk.	Structural Steel Worker
Sswl.	Structural Steel Welder
St.; Stl.	Steel
S.T.C.	Sound Transmission Coefficient
Std.	Standard
STK	Select Tight Knot
STP	Standard Temperature & Pressure
Stpi.	Steamfitter, Pipefitter
Str.	Strength; Starter; Straight
Strd.	Stranded
Struct.	Structural
Sty.	Story
Subj.	Subject
Subs.	Subcontractors
Surf.	Surface
Sw.	Switch
Swbd.	Switchboard
S.Y.	Square Yard
Syn.	Synthetic
S.Y.P.	Southern Yellow Pine
Sys.	System
t.	Thickness
T	Temperature; Ton
Tan	Tangent
T.C.	Terra Cotta
T & C	Threaded and Coupled
T.D.	Temperature Difference
Tdd	Telecommunications Device for the Deaf
T.E.M.	Transmission Electron Microscopy
TFE	Tetrafluoroethylene (Teflon)
T. & G.	Tongue & Groove; Tar & Gravel
Th.; Thk.	Thick
Thn.	Thin
Thrded	Threaded
Tilf.	Tile Layer, Floor
Tilh.	Tile Layer, Helper
THHN	Nylon Jacketed Wire
THW.	Insulated Strand Wire
THWN;	Nylon Jacketed Wire
T.L.	Truckload
T.M.	Track Mounted
Tot.	Total
T-O-L	Threadolet
T.S.	Trigger Start
Tr.	Trade
Transf.	Transformer
Trhv.	Truck Driver, Heavy
Trlr	Trailer
Trlt.	Truck Driver, Light
TTY	Teletypewriter
TV	Television
T.W.	Thermoplastic Water Resistant Wire
UCI	Uniform Construction Index
UF	Underground Feeder
UGND	Underground Feeder
U.H.F.	Ultra High Frequency
U.L.	Underwriters Laboratory
Unfin.	Unfinished
URD	Underground Residential Distribution
US	United States
USP	United States Primed
UTP	Unshielded Twisted Pair
V	Volt
V.A.	Volt Amperes
V.C.T.	Vinyl Composition Tile
VAV	Variable Air Volume
VC	Veneer Core
Vent.	Ventilation
Vert.	Vertical
V.F.	Vinyl Faced
V.G.	Vertical Grain
V.H.F.	Very High Frequency
VHO	Very High Output
Vib.	Vibrating
V.L.F.	Vertical Linear Foot
Vol.	Volume
VRP	Vinyl Reinforced Polyester
W	Wire; Watt; Wide; West
w/	With
W.C.	Water Column; Water Closet
W.F.	Wide Flange
W.G.	Water Gauge
Wldg.	Welding
W. Mile	Wire Mile
W-O-L	Weldolet
W.R.	Water Resistant
Wrck.	Wrecker
W.S.P.	Water, Steam, Petroleum
WT., Wt.	Weight
WWF	Welded Wire Fabric
XFER	Transfer
XFMR	Transformer
XHD	Extra Heavy Duty
XHHW; XLPE	Cross-Linked Polyethylene Wire Insulation
XLP	Cross-linked Polyethylene
Y	Wye
yd	Yard
yr	Year
Δ	Delta
%	Percent
~	Approximately
Ø	Phase
@	At
#	Pound; Number
<	Less Than
>	Greater Than

Quantity Takeoff Form

This form lists lumber and other building materials; electrical, mechanical, and plumbing items; cabinetry and countertops; appliances; accessories; doors and windows; and specialties like pre-fab greenhouses, roof trusses, and spiral stairs. At the end of the list are rental equipment and a blank sheet for additional items. You can photocopy these sheets to use as a checklist and for quantity takeoff – or download them for computer use from http://www.rsmeans.com/supplement/67349.asp

Note: While this form lists a wide variety of materials, fixtures, and accessories, it's not possible to include every item that might be specified for a remodeling project. Use the form as a starting point, adding other items in the blank spaces as needed. Or modify the electronic version to focus on the items you use most frequently.

	Unit	Quantity	Price per Unit	Total	Dimensions	Source/Model #/ Specs
Fasteners						
nails						
drywall nails						
flooring and finishing nails						
galvanized nails						
framing nails						
roofing nails						
fascia nails						
joist hanger nails						
concrete nails						
lath nails						
siding nails						
screws						
sheet metal screws						
drywall screws						
brass screws						
wood screws						
bolts						
anchor bolts						
expansion bolts						
timber connectors						
welded studs						
pedestal sink wall brackets						
drywall clips						

	Unit	Quantity	Price per Unit	Total	Dimensions	Source/Model #/ Specs
Adhesives						
floor						
cabinet						
tile						
countertop						
wood						
Sealants						
caulking						
acoustical sealant						
epoxy						
waterproofing						
Hardware						
deadbolts						
exterior locksets						
hinges						
butt						
pivot						
spring						
latch sets						
cylinder locksets						
kickplates						
knockers						
levers						
passage set door knobs						
drawer and cabinet pulls						
keyed locksets for flush doors						
coat hooks						
Framing Lumber						
1 x 3 furring strips						
1 x 4						
2 x 3						
2 x 4						
2 x 6						
2 x 8						
2 x 10						
2 x 12						

	Unit	Quantity	Price per Unit	Total	Dimensions	Source/Model #/ Specs
4 x 4						
4 x 6						
11/16" x 3-1/2" pine casing trim						
pressure-treated lumber						
2 x 4						
2 x 6						
2 x 8						
2 x 10						
2 x 12						
4 x 4						
medium-density fiberboard						
composite lumber						
LVL lumber						
parallel strand lumber (psl) posts						
sheathing						
Plywood						
AC birch, 1/4"						
AC birch, 3/4"						
CDX, 5/8"						
CDX, 1/2"						
CDX, 3/4"						
hardboard underlay, 3/16"						
underlayment, 5/8"						
underlayment, self-adhering						
Decking Lumber						
mahogany						
composite						
pressure-treated pine						
redwood						
laminated						
Wallboard						
cement board						
gypsum board, 1/2"						
gypsum board, water-resistant, 1/2"						
gypsum board, 3/8"						

	Unit	Quantity	Price per Unit	Total	Dimensions	Source/Model #/ Specs
joint compound						
wallboard accessories						
Ceilings						
fiberglass						
mineral fiber						
wood fiber						
metal pan						
fire rated						
luminous panel						
drop pan						
eggcrate						
suspended						
T bar						
Z bar						
carrier channels						
tiles						
acoustic						
Insulation						
fiberglass batt, kraft-faced, 3-1/2"						
fiberglass batt, kraft-faced, 6"						
fiberglass batt, foil-faced, 6"						
fiberglass batt, unfaced, 6"						
sprayed foam						
cellulose						
cotton						
icynene						
mineral wool						
polyurethane						
extruded polystyrene (XPS)						
polyisocyanurate						
expanded polystyrene (EPS)						
Moisture Protection						
undereave vent						
siding						
wood clapboard						
wood shingles						

183

	Unit	Quantity	Price per Unit	Total	Dimensions	Source/Model #/ Specs
fiber cement shingles						
vinyl						
aluminum						
building paper						
asphalt						
housewrap						
rosin						
kraft						
foil-backed						
roof deck vapor barrier						
weather stripping						
roofing						
drip edge						
felt						
roof shingles						
asphalt						
clay tile						
fiber cement						
concrete tile						
slate						
wood						
mineral surface						
elastic sheet						
fluid applied						
roll						
rubber						
metal roofing						
aluminum						
copper						
lead						
steel						
terne						
zinc alloy						
fascia						
metal						
vinyl						
wood						
frieze board						

	Unit	Quantity	Price per Unit	Total	Dimensions	Source/Model #/ Specs
ice barrier						
soffit						
vented						
plywood						
open						
rafter breather vents						
ridge vent strip						
solar-powered roof vent						
flashing						
aluminum						
copper						
fabric						
lead						
lead-coated copper						
PVC						
rubber						
steel						
terne						
paper-backed						
mastic-backed						
fabric backed						
gutters, downspouts, & elbows						
aluminum						
copper						
lead-coated copper						
galvanized steel						
stainless steel						
vinyl						
wood						
HVAC & Electrical						
heating, cooling, & ventilation elements						
boiler						
pump						
thermostat						
gas supply system						
oil supply system						
baseboard radiation						

	Unit	Quantity	Price per Unit	Total	Dimensions	Source/Model #/ Specs
convection heat						
radiant floor heat						
toe-space heat						
central air conditioning system						
paddle fan						
ductwork						
exhaust fan						
exhaust fan ductwork						
baseboard radiation						
whole-house fan						
furnace						
lighting						
chandeliers						
fluorescent						
in-cabinet						
under-cabinet						
pendant						
recessed						
track strips and fixtures						
vanity						
shower						
wall sconces						
wall washers						
art/picture						
outdoor lanterns						
floodlights						
motion sensor						
landscape						
accessories and materials						
generator						
wire						
coaxial						
conduit						
power wire						
sound wire						
twisted pair wire						
type NM cable						
non-metallic sheathed cable						

	Unit	Quantity	Price per Unit	Total	Dimensions	Source/Model #/ Specs
smoke detectors						
radon detectors						
CO detectors						
computer receptacles						
switches						
dimmer						
standard						
cable receptacles						
durex receptacles						
telephone receptacles						
GFCI receptacles						
Internet receptacles						
speakers						
outlets						
intercoms						
doorbells						
alarm system						
Plumbing						
fixtures						
lavatories						
pedestal						
vanity						
china						
enameled steel						
laminate						
porcelain enamel						
solid surface						
stone						
kitchen sinks						
enameled steel						
porcelain						
solid surface						
stainless						
stone						
bar sinks						
vegetable sinks						
pot fillers						
laundry/utility sinks						

	Unit	Quantity	Price per Unit	Total	Dimensions	Source/Model #/ Specs
toilets						
elongated						
one-piece						
pressure-assisted						
two-piece						
vacuum flush						
bathtubs						
acrylic						
fiberglass						
enameled cast iron						
whirlpool tubs						
acrylic						
fiberglass						
shower stalls						
acrylic						
fiberglass						
glass						
solid surface						
tile						
shower pans						
special plumbing						
anti-scald device						
re-circulating hot water system						
bidet						
faucets/fittings/accessories						
kitchen sink faucet						
bar sink faucet						
hand-held sprayer						
instant hot water dispenser						
soap dispensers						
shower faucet sets						
lavatory faucet sets						
bathtub faucet sets						
shower heads/jets						
supply and waste piping						
traps						
valves						
water-filtration system						
hot water heater						

	Unit	Quantity	Price per Unit	Total	Dimensions	Source/Model #/ Specs
Wall Finishes						
gypsum wallboard finishes						
taped and finished						
thin coat plaster						
primer						
paint						
stain						
urethane						
varnish						
special treatments (glaze, faux finish)						
brushes/rollers						
tile						
wallpaper						
wallpaper paste/adhesive						
Flooring						
carpet						
carpet pad						
tackless strip						
laminate/floating floors						
resilient						
rubber						
vinyl						
cork						
linoleum						
wood						
block						
strip						
parquet						
laminate						
plank						
tile						
adhesives						
marble						
ceramic						
stone						
glass						

	Unit	Quantity	Price per Unit	Total	Dimensions	Source/Model #/ Specs
quarry						
grout						
sealer						
Cabinets						
base						
bookcase						
corner						
island						
desk						
pantry						
wall						
vanity						
cabinet doors						
flush						
recessed panel						
glass						
raised panel						
lazy susan						
appliance garage						
Countertops						
butcher block						
ceramic tile						
granite or other stone						
plastic laminate						
solid surface						
support framing						
corbel brackets						
trim						
Appliances						
convection oven						
cooktop						
dishwasher						
garbage disposal						
ice maker						
microwave						
range						

	Unit	Quantity	Price per Unit	Total	Dimensions	Source/Model #/ Specs
range hood						
refrigerator						
trash compactor						
wall oven						
warming oven						
wine refrigerator						
washing machine						
clothes dryer						
Accessories						
grab bars						
mirrors						
robe hooks						
shower curtain rods						
shower seat						
toilet tissue dispensers						
towel bars						
Molding, Trim, & Architectural Details						
quarter round molding						
beadboard						
baseboard trim						
mantels						
paneling						
chair rail						
wainscot						
crown molding						
cornice						
1-piece						
2-piece						
3-piece						
pine						
cedar						
ceiling medallions						
columns						
ornamental						
false						
wood						
square						
round						

	Unit	Quantity	Price per Unit	Total	Dimensions	Source/Model #/ Specs
solid						
built-up						
hollow						
tapered						
column base						
corner boards						
window trim						
cupola						
dentils						
cornice trim						
fascia trim						
rake trim						
soffit trim						
wood shutters						
exterior wood blinds						
Stairs & Accessories						
balusters						
handrails						
goosenecks						
oak						
wall-mounted						
lattice						
newel posts						
scotia molding						
skirt board						
treads						
risers						
winders						
Doors						
screen doors						
aluminum						
steel						
wood						
screen material						
paneled interior doors						
flush interior doors						
hollow-core						

	Unit	Quantity	Price per Unit	Total	Dimensions	Source/Model #/ Specs
bi-fold closet doors						
bi-pass closet doors						
pocket doors						
sauna doors						
shower doors						
accordion doors						
sliding glass doors						
French doors						
interior						
exterior						
French door jamb						
glazed doors						
patio doors						
Dutch doors						
bulkhead doors						
garage doors						
automatic garage door openers						
Windows						
casement						
double-hung						
single-hung						
palladian						
picture						
skylights						
fixed						
operable						
accent						
transom						
bay/bow						
Stone & Site Work						
grass seed						
retaining wall						
cement						
stucco						
steps						
brick						
common						

	Unit	Quantity	Price per Unit	Total	Dimensions	Source/Model #/ Specs
face						
brick veneer						
pavers						
grout						
mortar						
stone						
stone veneer						
Foundations						
footings						
pile caps						
spread footings						
continuous footings						
copings						
lintels						
piers						
rebar						
forms						
backfill						
gravel						
sand						
clay						
silt						
rock						
peat						
topsoil						
Prefabricated Items						
greenhouse						
sunroom						
sauna						
steam room						
fireplaces						
gas						
wood-burning						
roof trusses						
SIPs						
disappearing/pull-down stairs						
circular stairs						

	Unit	Quantity	Price per Unit	Total	Dimensions	Source/Model #/ Specs
Rental Equipment						
staging						
dumpster						
backhoe						
excavator						
bulldozer						
earth compactor						
concrete mixer						
front-end loader						
forklift						
trencher						
portable toilets						
space heater						
crane						
bobcat						

	Unit	Quantity	Price per Unit	Total	Dimensions	Source/Model #/ Specs

Safety Tips

Safety is an essential component of a successful contracting business. You need to know your legal responsibilities, make sure your employees are properly trained, and conduct each and every job safely. Often, your legal contract with the homeowner will hold you responsible for safety on the site. Making safety a priority has the added bonus of helping to control the cost of your insurance premiums.

The following are general safety guidelines for residential remodeling, and are not intended as complete coverage.

Protective Gear

Wear the proper clothing and gear to protect yourself while on the job – from equipment, foul weather conditions, and other possible hazards. Avoid loose or torn clothes, especially when working with power tools. Wear heavy shoes or work boots, safety glasses when working with power tools, a hardhat if materials or tools could fall on your head, and work gloves whenever possible, especially when handling hazardous chemicals or abrasive materials. Use hearing protection when operating loud machinery or when hammering in a small, enclosed space. Wear a dust mask to keep from inhaling sawdust, insulation fibers, or other airborne particles. When welding, be sure to wear approved eye protection, a welding shield, and gloves.

Job Site Safety

Keep the work area clean and organized. Eliminate tripping hazards, clutter, and stray materials and tools, especially in areas used for access. Take the time to clean up and reorganize as you go. This will not only make for a safer work area, but will help you be more productive over the long run, and, of course, increased productivity has a direct effect on the bottom line. Because you're working on the homeowner's property, be sure the site is clean at the end of the day, without wires, exposed nails, or other hazards. Remove or at least unplug power tools and properly stow any materials and equipment that could pose a safety hazard.

Working with Equipment, Tools, & Materials

Don't strain yourself: When lifting heavy equipment or materials, always let your leg muscles – not your back – do the work. Keep your back straight, both when lifting and when putting items down. When carrying heavy items, keep them close to your body, and avoid twisting motions. Plan what you need to move, when, and where, ahead of time. Seek assistance when moving heavy or awkward objects, and remember, if an object is on wheels, it is easier to push than to pull it.

Check equipment for safety: Make sure all electrical equipment and power tools are properly grounded, and that regular preventive maintenance is performed to ensure they function correctly.

Learn to use tools properly: Make sure workers are properly trained on all equipment. Keep in mind that you'll need special tools for some jobs. Study how to use them, and practice with them before undertaking a task.

Ladders, Staging, & Scaffolding

When working from a ladder, scaffold, or temporary platform, make sure it's stable and well-braced, and inspect it before *every* use. Inspect staging planks frequently for signs of wear. Double-check fall protection equipment and barricades before and after use. Replace defective equipment immediately. Stepladders should be locked (never leaned), and straight ladders should never be placed too steeply. The top of the ladder should extend three feet past the top of the structure it's leaning on, with the ladder top secured. Wood ladders should be used when near power lines instead of metal ones to reduce the risk of electrocution. The Occupational Safety and Health Administration (OSHA) in fact prohibits the use of portable metal ladders for electrical work, or wherever they may contact electrical conductors.

Hand Tools

Don't use any striking tool (such as a hammer or sledgehammer) that has dents or cracks, shows excessive wear, or has a damaged or loose handle. Also, do not strike a hammer with another hammer in an attempt to remove a stubborn nail, get at an awkward spot, etc. Don't strike hard objects (such as concrete or steel), which could chip the tool, causing personal injury. Don't use any tool for a purpose other than the one for which it was designed. In other words, don't use a screwdriver as a pry bar, pliers as a hammer, and so forth.

Power Tools

Keep children or bystanders away from the work area, and don't interrupt someone using a power tool or actively performing an operation. Never pin back or disable safety guards. Keep drill bits, blades, and cutters sharp; dull tools require extra force and can be dangerous. Always unplug tools when leaving them unattended or when servicing or changing blades.

Nail Guns

Nail guns are one of the most common, but also potentially dangerous, tools used for residential renovations and additions projects. Avoid injuries by safe handling. For instance, never squeeze the trigger unless you're ready to nail. Always keep hands far enough away from the nose of the gun so that if the nail hits an obstruction or knot, it won't bend and catch your finger. Disconnect the air hose prior to working on the gun. It's a good idea to use a gun hanger when working at heights, or secure your air hose so the gun doesn't fall or get dragged. When nailing off the roof or high floor sheathing, be sure to move in a forward direction to avoid slipping off the edge.

Circular Saw

Always follow manufacturer's guidelines on safe use of circular saws. Keep fingers away from the blade's path. Choose the correct cutting blade for the material. Never remove or pin back the saw's guard. Make sure the blades are sharp prior to each use. When cutting lumber, make sure there's enough space so that one end can fall freely, so that the blade doesn't bind and kick back. For more tips on saw use, consult OSHA (http://www.osha.gov) or the Canadian Centre for Occupational Health & Safety (CCOHS) (http://www.ccohs.ca)

Excavation

Excavation is one of the most dangerous of all construction operations, according to OSHA, which publishes strict safety guidelines. Excavation should be carefully monitored by a trained professional who is knowledgeable in soils analysis and the proper protective systems.

Utilities must be located and marked prior to excavation. Be sure that all workers are protected from loose rock or soil that could fall back into the site. Never work in an excavated area that contains running or standing water. Keep all materials and equipment at least two feet away from the excavated area.

A soils analysis should be performed in advance to determine the soil type in the excavation, and a separate analysis may be required for each change in soil conditions. Be sure proper methods are used for wall retention, piling, sloping, and shoring to maintain excavation walls. Consult OSHA's website for details on proper protection of the site: http://www.osha.gov/SLTC/trenchingexcavation/index.html

Roof Work

Working on roofs or framing for additions or dormers poses a great risk of lost footing, decreased stability, and objects slipping off. A full-body harness attached to a secure anchor is a good idea as a means of fall protection. Wherever possible, safety lines and nets should also be used, in addition to catch platforms.

When working on roof trusses/rafters, top plate scaffold brackets can be used to provide a walkway along the inside of the walls. These walkways can also be used for installing the first row of roof sheathing. When applying roof materials, always wear shoes that provide as much grip to the surface as possible. Roof work should be done only in decent weather; don't work on wet or icy roofs, or when winds are strong. Be sure to watch your step – make sure you're secure and stable when walking on roofs or other high platforms, joists, or trusses.

Working with Hazardous Materials

Take precautions when working with asbestos and around dust and fumes. Always wear the proper masks and protective gear. It's also a good idea to have a site control plan – setting up procedures to evaluate all materials as they come on the job to look for ways to eliminate exposure to hazards. Simple tasks like running tile and masonry saws wet, and wetting down (when appropriate) dusty materials, can help, as well as building temporary barriers to protect other parts of the owner's house.

Electrical Hazards

When working with electricity, be sure you know how to shut off the supply when needed. It may be wise to invest in a simple current-testing device to determine when electric current is present. If you don't already have one, purchase a fire extinguisher, learn how to use it, and keep it handy. Store materials away from power cords, power lines, and outlets. Use ladders made of wood or non-conducting material when working near power sources.

Fire Hazards

Supervise the use of flammable liquids, and make sure they're stored safely when not being used – away from any sources of heat. Prevent the accumulation of dust, sawdust, and other flammable materials by cleaning and sweeping daily. Keep an approved fire extinguisher on the site at all times. Make sure egress paths are always clear, and that workers refrain from smoking on the job. In winter when heaters may be used on the site, make sure they're never left unattended, and are inspected and tested by a qualified technician prior to first use. Never use them in areas where they may easily ignite combustible materials. If heaters are used to speed concrete hardening, care should be taken to prevent them from being knocked over.

Manufacturer's Recommendations

When working with adhesives, protective coatings, or other volatile products, be sure to follow their installation and ventilation guidelines. Pay particular attention to drying times, respiratory hazards, and fire hazards associated with the product. If possible, obtain from the supplier a Material Safety Data Sheet, which will clearly describe any associated hazards.

First Aid

Keep first aid supplies handy. To treat any injuries that may arise, be sure to keep a first aid kit on site at all times. Must-have first aid supplies include: bandages and adhesives tape; antiseptics and cleaners; disposable latex gloves; pain relievers; tweezers; pressure packs; iodine swabs; and eye care solutions/ointments. Also good to have are emergency blankets, scissors, and ice/heat packs. It's an excellent idea to keep up-to-date on your CPR certification, and to request that your crews and subs do the same.

Safe Communication

Make safety a priority. Equip yourself – and your crews and subs – with the necessary tools of communication: two-way radios, cell phones, pagers, and other devices for quick and easy access to one another. Minimize noise on the job to maximize verbal communication.

Make a habit of holding safety meetings to stay current on the status of the job site working conditions, hazardous materials, and safety procedures. Report and review accidents immediately, and discuss them with co-workers to determine what could be done differently next time. Recognize and reward safe job site practices.

Resources

The following list of product manufacturers is provided as a starting point for gathering project information. It is not intended to be all-inclusive or an endorsement of any particular products.

Products

Appliances

Asko
AM Appliance Group
P.O. Box 851805
Richardson, TX 75085
972-644-8595
www.askousa.com

Bosch
BSH Home Appliances Corporation
5551 McFadden Avenue
Huntington Beach, CA 92649
800-921-9622
www.boschappliances.com

Elmira Stove Works
232 Arthur Street, S.
Elmira, ON N3B 2P2
Canada
800-295-8498
www.elmirastoveworks.com

Gaggenau
BSH Home Appliances Corporation
5551 McFadden Avenue
Huntington Beach, CA 92649
800-828-9165
www.gaggenau.com

General Electric
800-626-2005
www.geappliances.com

Haier
877-337-3639
www.haieramerica.com

Insinkerator
800-558-5700
www.insinkerator.com

Jenn-Air
240 Edwards Street
Cleveland, TN 37311
800-688-1100
www.jennair.com

Kenmore
Sears
3333 Beverly Road
Hoffman Estates, IL 60179
800-349-4358
www.sears.com/kenmore

Kitchen-Aid
P.O. Box 218
St. Joseph, MI 49085
800-422-1230
www.kitchenaid.com

LG
1000 Sylvan Avenue
Englewood Cliffs, NJ 07632
800-243-0000
www.lgusa.com

Maytag
240 Edwards Street
Cleveland, TN 37311
800-688-9900
www.maytag.com

Miele
9 Independence Way
Princeton, NJ 08540
800-843-7231
www.miele.com

Sub-Zero
P.O. Box 44130
Madison, WI 53744
800-222-7820
www.subzero.com

Thermador
5551 McFadden Avenue
Huntington Beach, CA 92649
800-656-9226
www.thermador.com

Viking
111 Front Street
Greenwood, MS 38930
662-455-1200
www.vikingrange.com

Whirlpool Corporation
800-253-1301
www.whirlpool.com

Wolf Appliance Company, LLC
P.O. Box 44848
Madison, WI 53744
800-332-9513
www.wolfappliance.com

Bathroom & Kitchen Sinks, Fixtures, Fittings, & Accessories

American Standard
P.O. Box 6820
1 Centennial Plaza
Piscataway, NJ 08855
800-442-1902
www.americanstandard.com

Blanco America, Inc.
110 Mount Holly By-Pass
Lumberton, NJ 08048
www.blancoamerica.com

Delta Faucet Company
55 E. 111th Street
P.O. Box 40980
Indianapolis, IN 46280
800-345-3358
www.deltafaucet.com

Eljer
14801 Quorum Drive
Dallas, TX 75254
800-423-5537
www.eljer.com

Elkay
2222 Camden Court
Oak Brook, IL 60523
630-574-8484
www.elkayusa.com

Flushmate Toilets
800-533-3460
www.flushmate.com

Grohe America, Inc.
241 Covington Drive
Bloomingdale, IL 60108
800-444-7643
www.groheamerica.com

Jacuzzi Whirlpool Bath
14801 Quorum Drive
Suite 550
Dallas, TX 75254
800-288-4002
www.jacuzzi.com

Karran Plumbing Products
1422 E. Elkhorn Road
Vincennes, IN 47591
866-452-7726
www.karranproducts.com

Kohler
444 Highland Drive
Kohler, WI 53044
800-456-4537
www.kohler.com

Majestic Shower Company
1795 Yosemite Avenue
San Francisco, CA 94124
800-675-6225
www.majesticshower.com

Moen
800-289-6636
www.moen.com

MrSauna
43-20 34th Street
Long Island City, NY 11101
800-767-8326
www.mrsauna.com

MrSteam
43-20 34th Street
Long Island City, NY 11101
800-767-8326
www.mrsteam.com

Ondine Luxury Shower Systems
Interbath, Inc
665 N. Baldwin Park Boulevard
City of Industry, CA 91746
800-423-9485
www.interbath.com/ondine

Robern Bathroom Products
701 N. Wilson Avenue
Bristol, PA 19007
800-877-2376
www.robern.com

Saniflo Toilets
www.saniflow.com

Saunatec
575 E. Cokato Street
Cokato, MN 55321
888-780-4427
www.saunatec.com

Sterling Plumbing
888-783-7546
www.sterlingplumbing.com

Toto Toilets and Bidets
1155 Southern Road
Morrow, GA 30260
888-295-8134
www.totousa.com

Ultra Baths
956 Chemin Olivier
Saint-Nicolas, QC G7A 2N1
Canada
800-463-2187
www.ultrabaths.com

Waterworks
800-998-2284
www.waterworks.com

Cabinets

Crystal Cabinet Works, Inc.
100 Crystal Drive
Princeton, MN 55371
800-347-5045
www.ccworks.com

Fieldstone Cabinetry
600 E. 48th Street, N.
Sioux Falls, SD 57104
800-339-5369
www.fieldstonecabinetry.com

KraftMaid Cabinetry
P.O. Box 1055
Middlefield, OH 44062
440-632-5333
www.kraftmaid.com

Merillat Industries
800-575-8763
www.merillat.com

StarMark Cabinetry
600 E. 48th Street, N.
Sioux Falls, SD 57104
800-594-9444
www.starmarkcabinetry.com

Thomasville Cabinets
800-756-6497
www.thomasvillecabinetry.com

Wellborn Cabinet, Inc.
P.O. Box 1210
Ashland, AL 36251
800-336-8040
www.wellborn.com

Wood-Mode
570-374-2711
www.wood-mode.com

Ceiling Fans

Casablanca
761 Corporate Center Drive
Pomona, CA 91768
888-227-2178
www.casablancafanco.com

Hunter Fan Company
2500 Frisco Avenue
Memphis, TN 38114
888-830-1326
www.hunterfan.com

Closets

California Closets
1000 Fourth Street
Suite 800
San Rafael, CA 94901
415-256-8500
www.californiaclosets.com

Easy Closets
20 Stonehouse Road
Millington, NJ 07946
800-910-0129
www.easyclosets.com

Countertops

Cambria
866-226-2742
www.cambriausa.com

Chemetal
39 O'Neill Street
Easthampton, MA 01027
800-807-7341
www.chemetalco.com

Corian
DuPont Building
1007 Market Street
Wilmington, DE 19898
800-426-7426
www.corian.com

Formica Corporation
255 E. 5th Street
Suite 200
Cincinnati, OH 45202
800-367-6422
www.formica.com

LG Solid Source, LLC
8009 W. Olive
Peoria, AZ 85345
877-853-1805
www.lghi-macs.com

Silestone
Cosentino USA
13124 Trinity Drive
Stafford, TX 77477
800-291-1311
www.silestoneusa.com

Sonoma Cast Stone
P.O. Box 1721
Sonoma, CA 95476
888-807-4234
www.sonomastone.com

Volcanics
8009 W. Olive
Peoria, AZ 85345
877-853-1805
www.lgvolcanics.com

Wilsonart International
2400 Wilson Place
P.O. Box 6110
Temple, TX 76503
800-433-3222
www.wilsonart.com

Decking (Composite)

Carefree Decking
U.S. Plastic Lumber
2300 Glades Road
Suite 440W
Boca Raton, FL 33431
561-394-3511
www.usplasticlumber.com

ChoiceDek
Advanced Environmental Recycling
Technologies, Inc.
P.O. Box 116
Junction, TX 76849
800-951-5117
www.choicedek.com

Dream Deck
Thermal Industries
5450 Second Avenue
Pittsburgh, PA 15207
800-245-1540
www.thermalindustries.com

Epoch Composite Products, Inc.
P.O. Box 567
Lamar, MO 64759
800-405-0546
www.epoch.com

LockDry
2700 Alabama Highway 69, S.
Cullman, AL 35057
800-711-1785
www.lockdry.com

Perma-Poly
Renew Plastics
112 4th Street
Luxemburg, WI 54217
800-666-5207
www.renewplastics.com

TimberTech
894 Prairie Avenue
Wilmington, OH 45177
800-307-7780
www.timbertech.com

Trex Company, Inc.
160 Exeter Drive
Winchester, VA 22603
800-289-8739
www.trex.com

Energy-Efficient Building Products

Resource Conservation Technology
2633 N. Calvert Street
Baltimore, MD 21218
410-366-1146
www.conservationtechnology.com

Fireplaces

Napoleon Fireplaces
www.napoleonfireplaces.com

Regency Fireplace Products
www.regency-fire.com

Travis Industries
4800 Harbor Point Boulevard, S.W.
Mukilteo, WA 98275
800-654-1177
www.fireplacextrordinair.com

Flooring

Concrete, Stone, & Tile
Allied Tile Manufacturing Corp.
2840 Atlantic Avenue
Brooklyn, NY 11207
800-827-5457
www.alliedtile.com

American Olean Tile
www.aotile.com

Ann Sacks Tile & Stone
800-278-8453
www.annsacks.com

Artistic Tile
800-260-8646
www.artistictile.com

Dal-Tile
7834 C.F. Hawn Freeway
Dallas, TX 75217
214-398-1411
www.daltile.com

Diamond D Concrete
310 D Kennedy Drive
Capitola, CA 95010
831-464-7369
www.diamonddcompany.com

Florida Tile
P.O. Box 447
Lakeland, FL 33802
863-284-4156
www.floridatile.com

Limestone Concept, Inc.
P.O. Box 352026
Los Angeles, CA 90035
310-278-9829
www.limestoneconcept.com

The Stoneyard
2 Spectacle Pond Road
Littleton, MA 01460
800-231-2200
www.stoneyard.com

Summitville Tiles
330-223-1511
www.summitville.com

Laminate
Pergo Floors
3128 Highwoods Boulevard
Raleigh, NC 27604
800-337-3746
www.pergo.com

Witex
800-948-3987
www.witexusa.com

Resilient
The Amtico Studio
6480 Roswell Road
Atlanta, GA 30328
404-267-1900
www.amtico.com

Armstrong World Industries
P.O. Box 3001
Lancaster, PA 17604
800-233-3823
www.armstrong.com

Congoleum Corporation
Department C
P.O. Box 3127
Mercerville, NJ 08619
800-274-3266
www.congoleum.com

Domco Sheet Flooring
1001 Yamaska, E.
Farnham, QC J2N 1J7
Canada
800-367-8275
www.domco.com

Forbo Marmolean
P.O. Box 667
Hazleton, PA 18201
866-627-6653
www.themarmoleumstore.com

Mannington Resilient Floors
75 Mannington Mills Road
Salem, NJ 08079
856-935-3000
www.mannington.com

Metroflor Vinyl Flooring
15 Oakwood Avenue
Norwalk, CT 06850
203-299-3100
www.metroflorusa.com

Nova Linoleum
1710 E. Sepulveda Boulevard
Carson, CA 90745
866-576-2458
www.novafloorings.com

Wood and Cork
Bruce Hardwood
P.O. Box 3001
Lancaster, PA 17604
800-233-3823
www.bruce.com

Expanko Cork Flooring
3135 Lower Valley Road
Parkesburg, PA 19365
800-345-6202
www.expanko.com

Harris Tarkett Wood Floors
2225 Eddie Williams Road
Johnson City, TN 37601
423-979-3700
www.harris-tarkett.com

Lumber Liquidators
3000 John Deere Road
Toano, VA 23168
800-476-0007
www.lumberliquidators.com

Mirage/Boa-Franc, Inc.
1255 98e Rue
Saint-Georges, QC G5Y 8J5
Canada
800-463-1303
www.miragefloors.com

Mohawk Floors
www.mohawk-hardwoodflooring.com

Oshkosh Floor Designs
911 E. Main Street
Winneconne, WI 54986
877-582-9977
www.oshkoshfloors.com

Wide Plank International
Reclaimed Wood Flooring
427 E. 90th Street
New York, NY 10128
212-426-7505
www.wideplank.com

Garage Doors
Amarr Classica Collection
165 Carriage Court
Winston-Salem, NC 27105
800-503-3667
www.amarr.com

Artisan Custom Doorworks
975 Hemlock Road
Morgantown, PA 19543
888-913-9170
www.artisandoorworks.com

Fimbel
12 Coddington Road
Whitehouse Station, NJ 08889
908-534-4112
www.fimbeldoor.com

Garage Doors, Inc.
1001 South Fifth Street
San Jose, CA 95112
800-223-9795
www.garagedoorsinc.com

Real Carriage Door Co.
13417 82nd Avenue, N.W.
Gig Harbor, WA 98329
877-299-9492
www.realcarriagedoors.com

Summit Garage Doors
590 Brian Avenue
Silverthorne, CO 80498
877-513-8152
www.summitgaragedoors.com

Wayne-Dalton
1 Door Drive
P.O. Box 67
Mt. Hope, OH 44660
888-827-DOOR
www.wayne-dalton.com

Greenhouses

American Greenhouse Kit Company
877-718-2865
www.greenhousekit.com

American Natural Products Co.
2103 185th Street
Fairfield, IA 52556
800-221-7645, Ext. 105
www.americanatural.com

Gronhaus
1224 Fern Ridge Parkway
St. Louis, MO 63141
800-317-7225
www.gronhaus.com

International Greenhouse Company
806 N. Main Street
888-281-9337
Georgetown, IL 61846
www.igcusa.com

Historic Building Materials

The American Ceiling Co.
1825 60th Place, E.
Bradenton, FL 34203
888-231-7500
www.americantinceilings.com

Belisle Ancestral Doors and Windows
56 Gauvin est
St-Jean-de-Dieu, QC G0L 3M0
Canada
866-851-5113
www.belislewindows.com

Classic Gutter Systems, LLC
P.O. Box 2319
Kalamazoo, MI 49003
269-665-2700
www.classicgutters.com

Coppa Woodworking, Inc.
1231 Paraiso Avenue
San Pedro, CA 90731
310-548-5332

Historic Housefitters Co.
P.O. Box 26
Brewster, NY 10509
800-247-4111
www.historichousefitters.com

House of Antique Hardware
3439 N.E. Sandy Boulevard
PMB #106
Portland, OR 97232
888-223-2545
www.houseofantiquehardware.com

Hull Historical Millwork
201 Lipscomb Street
Fort Worth, TX 76104
817-332-1495
www.hullhistorical.com

The Renovator's Supply, Inc.
Renovator's Old Mill
Millers Falls, MA 01349
800-659-2211
www.rensup.com

Vintage Doors
66 S. Main Street
Hammond, NY 13646
800-787-2001
www.vintagedoors.com

Vixen Hill
69 E. Main Street
Elverson, PA 19520
800-423-2766
www.vixenhill.com

Insulation & Drywall

CertainTeed Corpooration
750 E. Swedesford Road
Valley Forge, PA 19482
800-233-8990
www.certainteed.com

Owens Corning
800-438-7465
www.owenscorning.com

USG Corporation
888.874.2450
www.usg.com

Lighting

Cooper Lighting
1121 Highway 74, S.
Peachtree City, GA 30269
770-486-4800
www.cooperlighting.com

ENERGY STAR
United States Environmental Protection
Agency Climate Protection Partnerships
Division ENERGY STAR Programs
Hotline & Distribution (MS-6202J)
1200 Pennsylvania Ave NW
Washington, DC 20460
888-STAR-YES
http://energystar.gov/index.
cfm?c=fixtures.pr_light_fixtures

Hudson Valley Lighting, Inc.
P.O. Box 7459
Newburgh, NY 12550
845-561-0300
www.hudsonvalleylighting.com

Lamps Plus
800-782-1967
http://lampsplus.com

Leviton
59-25 Little Neck Parkway
Little Neck, NY 11362
718-229-4040
www.leviton.com

Lightolier
631 Airport Road
Fall River, MA 02720
508-679-8131
www.lightolier.com

Lutron Electronics Company, Inc.
7200 Suter Road
Coopersburg, PA 18036
888-588-7661
www.lutron.com

Moldings & Architectural Products

Agee Woodworks Inc.
10997 Richardson Road, #2
Ashland, VA 23005
877-768-3678
www.ageewoodworks.com

Balmer Architectural Moldings
271 Yorkland Boulevard
Toronto, ON M2J 1S5
Canada
800-665-3454
www.balmer.com

Birger Juell Ltd.
150 Merchandise Mart Place
Chicago, IL 60654
312-464-9663
www.birgerjuell.com

Fypon Decorative Moldings
800-446-3040
www.fypon.com

Outwater, LLC
P.O. Box 500
Bogota, NJ 07603
800-631-8375
www.archpro.com

ResinArt Plastic Moldings
201 Old Airport Road
Fletcher, NC 28732
800-497-4376
www.flexmoulding.com

Paint

BEHR
3400 W. Segerstrom Avenue
Santa Ana, CA 92704
800-854-0133
www.behr.com

Benjamin Moore
51 Chestnut Ridge Road
Montvale, NJ 07645
800-344-0400
www.benjaminmoore.com

Sherwin Williams
www.sherwin-williams.com

Roofing

Carlisle SynTec Incorporated
1285 Ritner Highway
Carlisle, PA 17013
717-245-7000
www.carlisle-syntec.com

CertainTeed Corporation
750 E. Swedesford Road
Valley Forge, PA 19482
610-341-7000
www.certainteed.com

Dura-Loc
P.O. Box 220
Courtland, ON N0J 1E0
Canada
800-265-9357
www.duraloc.com

Follansbee Roofing
800-624-6906
www.follansbeeroofing.com

Ludowici Roof Tile
4757 Tile Plant Road
New Lexington, OH 43764
800-945-8453
www.ludowici.com

MBCI
NCI Building Systems
P.O. Box 692055
Houston, TX 77269
888-624-8678
www.mbci.com

TAMKO Roofing Products, Inc.
220 W. Fourth Street
Joplin, MO 64801
800-641-4691
www.tamko.com

Una-Clad
Copper Sales, Inc.
1001 Lund Boulevard
Anoka, MN 55303
800-426-7737
www.unaclad.com

Roof Trusses

Harmony Exchange Integrated Timberframes
2700 Big Hill Road
Boone, NC 28607
800-968-9663
www.harmonyexchange.com

TimberFab, Inc.
P.O. Box 399
Tarboro, NC 27886
800-968-8322
www.timberfab.net

Security Systems

ADT Security
866-746-7238
www.adt.com

Brinks Home Security
8880 Esters Boulevard
Irving, TX 75063
972-871-3500
www.brinkshomesecurity.com

Stairs

Mylen Stairs
650 Washington Street
Peekskill, NY 10566
914-739-8486
www.mylen.com

Salter Industries
105 GP Clement Drive
Collegeville, PA 19426
800-368-8280
www.salterspiralstair.com

The Iron Shop
800-523-7427
www.theironshop.com

Vapor Barrier

Green Guard
800-241-4402
www.green-guard.com

Typar
210 McLaren Gates Drive
Marietta, GA 30060
770-428-9430
www.typarhousewrap.com

Tyvek
Dupont
800-448-9835
www.tyvek.com

Ventilation & Heating/ Cooling Systems

Broan Ventilation
P.O. Box 140
Hartford, WI 53027
800-558-1711
www.broan.com

Carrier
1 Carrier Place
Farmington, CT 06034
800-227-7437
www.carrier.com

Kimball Design
200 Maddox Bend
Pencil Bluff, AR 71965
870-326-4236
www.kimballdesigns.com

Lennox Industries
P.O. Box 799900
Dallas, TX 75379
800-953-6669
www.lennox.com

NuTone
888-336-3948
www.nutone.com

Radiantec
P.O. Box 1111
Lyndonville, VT 05851
800-451-7593
www.radiantec.com

Trane
www.trane.com

Vent-A-Hood
P.O. Box 830426
Richardson, TX 75083
800-331-2493
www.ventahood.com

Zephyr Corporation
395 Mendell Street
San Francisco, CA 94124
888-880-8368
www.zephyronline.com

Windows, Doors, Skylights, & Solar Energy Systems

Ambiance Doors, Inc.
3208 Wellington Court
Suite 109
Raleigh, NC 27615
866-855-9220
www.ambiancedoors.com

Andersen Corporation
100 Fourth Avenue, N.
Bayport, MN 55003
651-264-5150
www.andersencorp.com

Bilco Company
P.O. Box 1203
New Haven, CT 06505
203-934-6363
www.bilco.com

Marvin Windows and Doors
P.O. Box 100
Warroad, MN 56763
888-537-7828
www.marvin.com

Peachtree Doors and Windows
888 Southview Drive
Mosinee, WI 54455
888-888-3814
www.peach99.com

Pella Windows and Doors
102 Main Street
Pella, IA 50219
www.pella.com

Screen Tight
1 Better Way
Georgetown, SC 29440
800-768-7325
www.screentight.com

Solatube International, Inc.
2210 Oak Ridge Way
Vista, CA 92081
800-966-7652
www.solatube.com

Sun Spot
P.O. Box 55
Delaware Water Gap, PA 18327
570-422-1292
www.sssolar.com

Velux
800-888-3589
www.velux.com

Weather Shield Windows
P.O. Box 309
Medford, WI 54451
800-447-6808
www.weathershield.com

Additional Information

American Bungalow Magazine
www.ambungalow.com

American National Standards Institute (ANSI)
1819 L Street, N.W.
6th Floor
Washington, DC 20036
202-293-8020
www.ansi.org

American Society of Heating, Refrigeration, & Air Conditioning Engineers (ASHRAE)
1791 Tullie Circle, N.E.
Atlanta, GA 30329
800-527-4723
www.ashrae.org

Americans with Disabilities Act (ADA)
U.S. Department of Justice
950 Pennsylvania Avenue, N.W.
Civil Rights Division
Disability Rights Section – NYAV
Washington, DC 20530
800-514-0301
www.ada.gov

Association of the Wall and Ceiling Industries (AWCI)
803 W. Broad Street
Suite 600
Falls Church, VA 22046
703-534-8300
www.awci.org

Ceramic Tile Institute of America
12061 Jefferson Boulevard
Culver City, CA 90230
800-356-9993
www.ctioa.org

ConcreteNetwork.com
Residential concrete information, products, and service providers.
www.concretenetwork.com

Early American Life Magazine
Firelands Media Group, LLC
P.O. Box 221228
Shaker Heights, OH 44122
www.ealonline.com

ENERGYSTAR®
United States Environmental
Protection Agency
Climate Protection Partnerships Division
1200 Pennsylvania Avenue, N.W.
Washington, DC 20460
888-782-7937
www.energystar.gov

Environmental Building News
122 Birge Street
Suite 30
Brattleboro, VT 05301
802-257-7300
www.buildinggreen.com

Equifax
800-685-1111
www.equifax.com

Experian
888-397-3742
www.experian.com

Forest Stewardship Council
1155 30th Street, N.W.
Suite 300
Washington, DC 20007
202-342-0413
www.fscus.org

Institute of Electrical and Electronic Engineers (IEEE)
1828 L Street, N.W.
Suite 1202
Washington, DC 20036
202-785-0017
www.ieee.org

International Association of Plumbing and Mechanical Officials (IAPMO)
5001 E. Philadelphia Street
Ontario, CA 91761
909-472-4100
www.iapmo.org

Kitchen Cabinet Manufacturers Association
1899 Preston White Drive
Reston, VA 20191
703-264-1690
www.kcma.org

International Code Council (ICC)
5203 Leesburg Pike
Suite 600
Falls Church, VA 22041
888-422-7233
www.iccsafe.org

Marble Institute of America
28901 Clemens Road
Suite 100
Westlake, OH 44145
440-250-9222
www.marble-institute.com

Masonry Institute of America
386 Beech Avenue, #4
Torrance, CA 90501
310-328-4400
www.masonryinstitute.org

National Association of Home Builders (NAHB)
1201 15th Street, N.W.
Washington, DC 20005
800-368-5242
www.nahb.org

National Association of the Remodeling Industry (NARI)
780 Lee Street
Suite 200
Des Plaines, IL 60016
800-611-6274
www.nari.org

National Electrical Contractors Association (NECA)
3 Bethesda Metro Center
Suite 1100
Bethesda, MD 20814
301-657-3110
www.necanet.org

National Kitchen & Bath Association (NKBA)
687 Willow Grove Street
Hackettstown, NJ 07840
800-843-6522
www.nkba.org

Occupational Safety and Health Administration (OSHA)
200 Constitution Avenue, N.W.
Washington, DC 20210
800-321-6742
www.osha.gov

Old House Journal
www.oldhousejournal.com

Old House Interiors Magazine
108 East Main Street
Gloucester, MA 01930
www.oldhouseinteriors.com

Painting & Decorating Contractors of America
11960 Westline Industrial Drive
Suite 201
St. Louis, MO 63146
800-332-7322
www.pdca.org

Professional Remodeler Magazine
www.housingzone.com/pr

RSMeans
63 Smiths Lane
Kingston, MA 02364
800-334-3509
www.rsmeans.com

Tile Council of America
100 Clemson Research Boulevard
Anderson, SC 29625
864-646-8453
www.tileusa.com

Traditional Home Magazine
800-374-8791
www.traditionalhome.com

TransUnion
800-888-4213
www.transunion.com

U.S. Green Building Council (USGBC)
1015 18th Street, N.W.
Suite 508
Washington, DC 20036
202-828-7422
www.usgbc.org

Victorian Homes Magazine
265 S. Anita Drive, Suite 120
Orange, CA 92868
800-999-9718
www.victorianhomesmag.com

Bibliography

Adding to a House: Planning, Design & Construction, by Philip S. Wenz, Taunton Press, 1995.

Additions Planner, Better Homes and Gardens, Meredith Publishing Group, 2005.

Advanced Framing Methods, by Scot Simpson, RSMeans 2002.

Basics: Home Renovation, by Ela Schwartz, Barnes & Noble, 2004.

Best Business Practices for Builders & Remodelers: An Easy-to-Use Checklist System, by Thomas Frisby, RSMeans, 2001

Exterior Home Improvement Cost Guide, 9th ed., RSMeans, 2004.

Framing & Rough Carpentry, 2nd ed., by Scot Simpson, RSMeans, 2001.

Interior Home Improvement Cost Guide, 9th ed., RSMeans, 2004.

Kitchen & Bath Project Costs, RSMeans, 2005.

Plans for Adding on and Remodeling, by Jerold L. Axelrod, McGraw-Hill, 2000.

Porch & Sunroom Planner, Better Homes and Gardens, Meredith Publishing Group, 2004.

Professional Remodeler Magazine, Reed Business Information. April 2005

Professional Remodeler Magazine, Reed Business Information, January 2005

Remodeler's Instant Answers, by R. Dodge Woodson, McGraw-Hill, 2004.

Repair & Remodeling Estimating Methods, 4th ed., by Edward Wetherill and RSMeans Engineering Staff, RS Means, 2002.

This Old House Complete Remodeling, This Old House Books, 2004.

Index